"It is a remarkable book that Bruce Morrissette has written on the novels of Alain Robbe-Grillet: remarkable as much by the choice of subject as by the method used and the conclusions reached. For, if it has happened that American writers were first discovered by French critics, it is much more extraordinary that an American professor should provide the first serious study of a French writer."

— **French Review***

The Novels of
Robbe-Grillet
Bruce Morrissette

A subtle and ingenious reading of a perplexing contemporary writer is offered in this exceptional book. It is an English-language version, prepared by the author, of a work that was enthusiastically received* when it was first published in France in 1963. Here revised and expanded, it includes a new chapter on Robbe-Grillet's most recent "cine-novel," **Glissements progressifs du plaisir.**

Bruce Morrissette uses Robbe-Grillet's criticism, his theories of the novel, and the novels themselves, one by one, to clarify Robbe-Grillet's fictional world. He analyzes, with verve and elegance, the structure, style, and content of **The Erasers, The Voyeur, Jealousy, In the Labyrinth, Last Year at Marienbad, La Maison de rendez-vous,** and **Project for a Revolution in New York.** Of major interest are his scrupulous summaries of the story lines in these novels and his bold evaluations of their literary importance. He shows that Robbe-

(continued on back flap)

works tui...

In **Symposium.**
of the French
Morrissette's
critical method
carefully reasone
It is the kind of bc
will eventually be
accomplishments,
see in their lifetime

BRUCE MORRISSI
and Chairman, Dep
Languages and Lite
University of Chica
the University of Ri
he holds the degree
l'Université, Unive
France, and a Ph.D
Hopkins Universi'
a member of the fa
University, St. Lo

THE NOVELS OF
ROBBE-GRILLET

THE NOVELS OF
ROBBE-GRILLET

by BRUCE MORRISSETTE

TRANSLATED FROM THE FRENCH, REVISED,
UPDATED, AND EXPANDED BY THE AUTHOR

with a Foreword by Roland Barthes

Cornell University Press | ITHACA AND LONDON

First published 1975 by Cornell University Press.
Published in the United Kingdom by Cornell University Press, Ltd., 2-4 Brook Street, London W1Y 1AA.

International Standard Book Number 0-8014-0852-0
Library of Congress Catalog Card Number 74-29089
Printed in the United States of America by York Composition Co., Inc.

To Dorothy

Contents

Foreword

> "Let us not give them a name. . . . They may have had
> so many other adventures."
>
> *Last Year at Marienbad*

The realistic intentions of our literature are strange. Has the
real become so lost that, to find it once more, we must repeatedly call upon an institution, a system of distribution, a
tradition, a technique, a talent, or even a genius? It would
seem that, in fact, the establishment of a certain distance
(based upon a certain function) is necessary for the modern
writer: he needs to believe (by reason of what necessity?) that
reality lies on one side, and on the other, language; that the
former precedes the latter, which has as its mission, so to speak,
to pursue the former until it catches up with it. Why does our
literature assume this analogical vocation? Probably because of
a certain disposition of the models themselves: the reality
which "is offered" to the writer can doubtless be a multiple
one—now psychological, now theological, social, political, historical, or even imaginary, each in its turn dethroning the
other. These realities have, however, one common property,
which explains their persistent projection: they all seem immediately charged with meaning; a passion, a tragic mistake, a
conflict, a dream, all refer inevitably to a certain transcendency, a soul, a divinity, a society, a supernatural teleology, so
that our realistic literature is not only analogical, but in addition infused with meaning.

9

Among these realities, psychological or social, the object, or thing, scarcely had any original place; for a long period, literature dealt only with a world of interhuman relationships (in Laclos's *Liaisons dangereuses*, if a harp is mentioned, it is because a love letter is concealed therein); and when things, tools, or substances began to appear with some frequency in our novels, it was as aesthetic or human indicators, to emphasize some soul state (the romantic landscape) or some social condition (the realistic detail). We know that the works of Alain Robbe-Grillet illustrate the problem of the literary object: are things indicators of meaning, or are they, on the contrary, opaque? Can, or should, a writer describe an object without assigning to it some human transcendency? Meaningful or meaningless, what is the function of objects in a novel? How does the manner in which they are described affect the meaning of the story, the consistency of the characters, or even the relationship of the work to the idea of literature? Now that Robbe-Grillet's work has matured and the cinema has given it new life and a second public, these questions may be raised in a new way. According to the answer, it will soon be seen that we are faced, abetted by Robbe-Grillet himself, with *two* Robbe-Grillets: on one hand the Robbe-Grillet of non-mediating things, the destroyer of meanings, as presented chiefly in the earliest criticism of his work, and on the other hand the Robbe-Grillet of mediate things, the creator of meanings, of whom Bruce Morrissette becomes, in these pages, the analyst.

The first Robbe-Grillet (it is not a question of temporal priority, but of classification) decides that things are meaningless, and they are not even absurd (as he justly remarks), since obviously the lack of meaning can become a meaning in itself. But, since these things are embedded in a quantity of different meanings, with which men of different sensibilities, poetic visions, and attitudes have suffused the name of each object, the work of the novelist becomes as it were cathartic: he purifies things of the meanings which men constantly assign to them. How? Obviously, by description. Robbe-Grillet therefore produces descriptions of objects sufficiently geometric to discourage any inductive derivation of poetic meaning residing in the thing, and sufficiently minute to break the fascination of the story. But in this very act, he encounters the problem of realism. Like the realists, he copies, or at least seems to copy, a model; in formalist terms, one could say that he proceeds as if his novel were only an event fulfilling a pre-existent structure. No matter whether this structure is true or not, and whether Robbe-Grillet's realism is objective or subjective; for what defines realism is not the source of the model, but its existence apart from the language that brings it into being. On the one hand, the realism of the first Robbe-Grillet remains classical because it is based on an analogical relationship (the quarter wedge of tomato described by Robbe-Grillet resembles its real counterpart); and on the other hand, his realism is new, because this analogy refers to no transcendency, but claims an existence based only on itself, content to designate necessarily and sufficiently the all-too-famous *être-là* (being-there, *Dasein*) of the thing (this tomato wedge is described in such a way that it is meant to provoke neither desire nor disgust, to have no referential meaning to the time of year, or the place, or even to the idea of food).

It is obvious that description alone cannot exhaust the texture of a novel, or satisfy the interest of the traditional reader; there is much more than description in Robbe-Grillet's novels. But it is also obvious that even a small number of descriptions that are both analogical and meaningless can, according to their placing in the story and the variants introduced by the author, completely change the overall meaning of the novel. Every novel is an intelligible organism of infinite sensibility; the slightest point of opacity, the slightest resistance (mute) to the desire which animates and motivates its reading, produces an astonishment which carries over into the whole of the work. The famous objects of Robbe-Grillet, therefore, are not bravura exercises for an anthology; they truly link the story itself and the characters that it brings together to a sort of "silence of meaning." This is why the conception of Robbe-Grillet the "chosiste" (the neutral describer of things) must be absolute, even totalitarian: there is a fatal bond between the meaninglessness of things and the meaninglessness of situations and characters. One may, in fact, read all of Robbe-Grillet's work (at least, up to *In the Labyrinth*) in an opaque or superficial manner; one needs only to stay at the surface of the text, with the understanding that such a surface reading can no longer be condemned in the name of old values of interior significance. Certainly one virtue of the first Robbe-Grillet (even if he is fictitious) is to demystify the so-called natural qualities of introspective literature (wherein depths are by right superior to what lies on the surface) in the interest of a textual being-there (not to be confused with the being-there of things themselves), and to refuse to allow his readers the enjoyment of a "rich," "deep," "secret," that is, meaningful, world.

Obviously, in the view of Robbe-Grillet No. 1, the neurotic or psychopathological state of his characters (one with an Oedipus complex, another sadistic, yet another obsessed) has no traditional value as content, as novelistic material of which the elements of the work are the more or less meaningful symbols offered to the reader or critic to decipher. Their state is only the purely formal term of a function: Robbe-Grillet seems to manipulate a certain content only because there is no literature without *signes*, and no signs without outside reference (*signifié*). But his whole art lies in destroying meaning in the very act of revealing it. To name this content, to speak of madness, of sadism, or even of jealousy, is then to go beyond what may be called the best perceptive level of the novel, the one at which it is immediately intelligible, just as looking very closely at a photographic reproduction is no doubt to penetrate its typographical secrets, but is also to lose all comprehension of the object it represents. Of course this denial of meaning, if it were authentic, could not be gratuitous: to produce meaning in order to bring meaning to a halt is nothing other than to extend an experiment which has its recent origin in surrealist activity, and involves the very essence of literature, that is, its anthropological function within the whole of historical society. Such is the picture of a Robbe-Grillet No. 1 that can be drawn from some of his theoretical writings and his novels, as well as from the earliest criticism of his work.

From these same writings and novels (but not, of course, from these same commentaries), one can draw the picture of a Robbe-Grillet No. 2, not "chosiste," not a devotee of material things, but "humaniste," since his objects—without, however, again becoming symbols—acquire once more a mediating function in relationship to "something else." This second picture Bruce Morrissette, in the study that follows, constructs in minute detail. His method is both descriptive and comparative; on one hand, he recounts the novels of Robbe-Grillet, and this procedure permits him to reconstruct the often very distorted organization of the episodes, that is, the structure of the novels, which no one before him had undertaken to do; and, on the other hand, extensive knowledge permits him to connect these episodes (scenes or descriptions of objects) to models, archetypes, sources, echoes, and thus to re-establish the cultural continuity which unites a so-called "opaque" body of novels to a whole literary, and thus human, context. Bruce Morrissette's method yields indeed an "integrated" picture of Robbe-Grillet, one "reconciled" with the traditional aims of the novel. It no doubt reduces the revolutionary aspect of his work, but it establishes, on the other hand, the excellent reasons that the public has in discovering Robbe-Grillet (and the critical acclaim of *In the Labyrinth*, as well as the wide reception of *Last Year at Marienbad*, seems to prove the correctness of this view). This Robbe-Grillet No. 2 does not say with the poet André Chénier, "Sur des pensers nouveaux, faisons des vers antiques" ("On new thoughts, let us write old-style poems") but, rather, "Sur des pensers anciens, faisons des romans nouveaux" ("On old themes, let us write new novels").

What does this reconciliation involve? First, it obviously involves the famous "objects" whose neutral, meaningless nature was originally asserted. Bruce Morrissette recognizes the originality of Robbe-Grillet's visions of things, but he does not think that in this universe the object is cut off from all reference or that it ceases radically to constitute a sign; he has no difficulty in detecting among Robbe-Grillet's collections of objects those that are obsessive, or at least repeated often enough to imply a meaning (since what is repeated is considered to have meaning). The gum eraser (in *The Erasers*), the cord (of *The Voyeur*), the centipede (of *Jealousy*), these objects, reintroduced with variations throughout a given novel, all imply an act, criminal or sexual, and, beyond this act, an interiority. Morrissette refuses, however, to call these objects symbols; with more restraint (but perhaps a bit speciously?), he prefers to define them as supports (or objective correlatives) for sensations, emotions, memories. In this manner, the object becomes a contrapuntal element of the work, becoming part of the story to the same extent as a given turn of events. Surely one of the greatest contributions made by Morrissette to Robbe-Grillet criticism is to discover a story line in each of the novels; thanks to detailed, scrupulously exact résumés, Morrissette shows clearly that the Robbegrilletian novel is a "story," and that this story has a meaning: Oedipal, sadistic, obsessive, or purely literary—if *In the Labyrinth* is, as he believes, the story of the novel's own writing. These "stories" are not, of course, composed in a traditional manner, and Morrissette, aware of the modernity of the techniques used, brings out clearly the variations and complexities of narrative viewpoint, the distortions that Robbe-Grillet makes of chronology, and the author's rejection of psychological analysis (but not of psychology). The result is that, provided with a story, a psychology (pathological), and a subject that are if not symbolic at least referential, the Robbegrilletian novel is no longer the "flat" design of the early criticism; it is a thing not only full but full of secrets. Therefore, criticism must begin to search out what lies behind and around this object: criticism becomes an act of deciphering, of hermeneutics; it seeks for "keys" (and usually finds them). This is what Bruce Morrissette has done for the novels of Robbe-Grillet; we must salute the courage of a critic who dares apply to a young, contemporary writer the method of textual analysis that it took critics more than half a century to apply to authors like Nerval and Rimbaud.

Between the two Robbe-Grillets, the Robbe-Grillet No. 1, the "chosiste," and the Robbe-Grillet No. 2, the "humaniste," between the writer as seen in the earliest criticism and the one presented by Bruce Morrissette, must a choice be made? Robbe-Grillet himself will be of no help here; like all authors, and in spite of his theoretical declarations, he remains, concerning his own work, by nature ambiguous; moreover, his work changes, and he has the right to be ambiguous. In the final analysis, it is this ambiguity which counts, which concerns us, which bears the historic meaning of a work that appears to reject in peremptory fashion all subject, or story. What is this meaning? It is the very opposite of meaning; it is a question. What do things mean, what does the universe mean? All of literature is this question; but we must immediately add, for this is what constitutes its special role, literature is this question without the answer. No literature has ever answered the question that it raised, and this very suspense has made it literature—that fragile language men have interposed between the violence of the question and the silence of the answer. Religious and critical in its interrogation, it is irreligious and conservative in its failure to reply. Literature is a question that the centuries constantly interrogate; it is never an answer. What god, wrote Valéry, would dare take as his motto, "I deceive"? Literature is this god; perhaps it will be possible some day to describe all literature as the art of deceit. The history of literature would then become, not the history of the contradictory answers that writers give to the question of meaning, but, on the contrary, the history of the questioning itself.

For it is self-evident that literature cannot directly formulate the question that alone constitutes literature; it has never extended, and could never extend, its meaning into rational discourse, without passing through techniques such as critical commentary; and if literary history is, in sum, the history of literary techniques, it is not because literature is only a technique (as was ostensibly claimed during the art-for-art's-sake period), but because technique is the only power capable of suspending the meaning of the universe and of keeping open the imperative question addressed to it. It is not answering that is difficult, it is questioning; it is speaking while questioning and remaining silent while answering. From this point of view, the "technique" of Robbe-Grillet was, at one time, radical—when the author believed that it was possible, directly, to "kill" meaning, so that the work would allow only its basic effect of astonishment to filter through (for to write is not to state, but to express astonishment). The originality of this attempt arose from the fact that the question was provided with no false reply, while at the same time it was not given the form of a question. The (theoretical) error of Robbe-Grillet was only to believe that there is a being-there of things, antecedent to and outside of language, which literature must, as he thought, discover once again in a last spurt of realism. In fact, anthropologically speaking, things always "mean," and rightfully so; it is indeed because meaning is their more or less natural characteristic that, by depriving them merely of their meaning, literature can affirm itself as an admirable artifice: if "nature" is meaningful, a certain high point of "culture" can occur through ridding it of its meaning. Whence, as a logical result, come these opaque descriptions of objects, these events "superficially" related, these characters with no interior, which make up according to one way of reading the text the style, or if you prefer, the choice, of Robbe-Grillet.

Yet these empty forms irresistibly attract a content, and we see gradually, in criticism and in the work of this author, the temptation of emotion, the return to archetypes, the use of symbolic fragments: in short, everything associated with the realm of the adjective slips into the superb being-there of things. In this sense, there is an evolution in Robbe-Grillet's work, due paradoxically at the same time to the author, to criticism, and to the public: we are all part of Robbe-Grillet, to the extent that we engage in reinvesting things with meaning, once the chance is given. Considered in its development and its future (which cannot be stipulated), the work of Robbe-Grillet then becomes the test of meaning experienced by a certain society, and the history of this work will be in its own way the history of this society. Already, meaning floods back in: expelled from the famous tomato wedge of *The Erasers* (but already doubtless present in the eraser itself, as Bruce Morrissette shows), meaning fills *Marienbad*, its gardens, its paneled walls, its feathery dresses. Except that, while ceasing to be nonexistent, meaning is still in this case a matter of conjecture: everyone has explained *Marienbad*, but each explanation was a meaning immediately denied by a neighboring meaning; if meaning is no longer abolished, it nevertheless remains in suspense. And if it is true that each novel by Robbe-Grillet contains in its center ("en abyme") its own symbol, there can be no doubt that the final allegory of *Marienbad* is the statue of Charles III and his wife—an admirable symbol, moreover, not only because the statue itself leads to many meanings, all uncertain, and yet identified (it is you, it is I, it represents the Greek gods, Helen, Agamemnon, et cetera), but even more because the prince and his wife are pointing with certitude toward some uncertain object (located in myth, in the garden, in the theater?): this, they say. But what is *this?* All literature lies perhaps in this fragile anaphora which at the same time speaks and remains silent.

ROLAND BARTHES

Paris

THE NOVELS OF
ROBBE-GRILLET

I shall consider the actions and passions of men as if they were matters of lines, surfaces, and volumes.

SPINOZA

1 A New Art of the Novel: The Theoretical Writings

A novelistic technique always implies a metaphysics.

SARTRE, *Situations 1*

Robbe-Grillet's position as the leader of the *Nouveau Roman* or French New Novel—a literary phenomenon now some twenty years old—is due almost as much to his essays and theoretical writings as to his novels, each of which, from *The Erasers* (1953) to *Project for a Revolution in New York* (1970), has marked an important if not decisive stage in the evolution of the genre. The purpose of this book is not to make a systematic, detailed analysis of his theories, or to attempt to situate them within the framework of contemporary literary philosophy. Instead, the frequent references to these ideas made in the following chapters are always related to some particular characteristic of a given work; the aim of each *rapprochement* is to throw light on one or another aspect of each work, and not to argue the theoretical merits of the doctrine or idea in question.

It is appropriate, however, to retrace briefly the development of these theories, which have provoked much comment, and to point out some of the problems raised by the apparent divergence that a number of critics (including Roland Barthes in his Foreword to this study) have detected between the theoretical positions of Robbe-Grillet and his novelistic practice. Here, then, is a short ideography of his doctrines.

21

Robbe-Grillet's earliest ideas on fictional content, form, and technique appeared in book reviews and critical essays written for the *Nouvelle Revue Française* and *Critique* in 1953 and 1954, following the publication of *The Erasers*. At that time, Robbe-Grillet displayed a singular interest in novels and stories with plots containing paradoxical reversals that rebounded against their protagonists. An example is Jean Duvignaud's *The Trap* (*Le Piège*), a story Robbe-Grillet summarizes as follows: "A beggar pursued for a crime that he has not committed, but has only *invented*, and so convincingly that it will lead him to murder and death." In another review, Robbe-Grillet relates with obvious pleasure the story of an Italian resistance fighter who pretends to have executed a Fascist leader, who decides to make a film based on his false account, and who discovers while shooting the movie that "reality requires a real corpse. . . . It will be his own!" The main point in these reviews is almost always the ingenious structure of the plot, the surprising twist of the story, and the role of imagination and of lies in the outcome. The persistent emphasis on story line seems to run counter to later declarations by Robbe-Grillet (eagerly seized upon by critics and interpreters not only of Robbe-Grillet, but of the whole alleged "school" of the *nouveau roman*, the *école du regard*, *nouveau réalisme*, *anti-roman*, and *alittérature*) to the effect that in modern fiction the plot becomes unimportant, assumes forms of pure convention, or disappears altogether. One has only to read Robbe-Grillet's description of *Jealousy* as a novel "in which nothing happens" or his remarks on the "convention of a plot" that he claims to have used in *The Erasers* and which, he says, "had no importance for me, aiming neither at plausibility nor at authenticity."[1]

1. *Prétexte I*, Jan. 1958, p. 100. Except in one instance (see note 1 of Chapter 4), all quotations from Robbe-Grillet have been translated by the present author, with the kind permission of the owners of the rights to Robbe-Grillet in English, Grove Press, Inc., of New York,

To put these announced views in perspective, we must see that they hinge upon a definition of plot in the most conventional, "conditioned" sense (social themes, political "commitment," and the like). In recent years, Robbe-Grillet has admitted that he has "always written *stories*." From the outset, as the first critical writings show, he was fascinated by "structured" plots, fictional puzzles, and complicated actions, both in the novels of others (like Graham Greene's *Brighton Rock* and James M. Cain's *The Postman Always Rings Twice*, two of his early favorites) and in his own, from the baroque plot developments of *The Erasers* to the latest "impossible" incidents of his recent work, with its multiple plot lines, its ambiguities, and its "open" contradictions.

Insistence on the narrative values of plot is also revealed in the various notices called "*prières d'insérer*," undoubtedly the work of the author himself, which are printed on the back covers of many of Robbe-Grillet's novels. The compact résumés always trace the outline of a definite story, guiding the prospective reader as he prepares to penetrate into a fictional universe where he will find suspense, shock, surprise, ambiguity, and—often—murder. Even the least complicated of the novels, *Jealousy*, carried on the back of the first edition a sort of summary of the action, without which some critics, such as Edouard Lop and André Sauvage, admitted they would not have known that the text was "narrated" by a jealous husband.[2] At times critics, determined to outdo Robbe-Grillet himself in the avoidance of plot, tried to set aside these cover descriptions as the work of interfering editors: thus

---

and Calder & Boyars, Ltd., of London. English translations of other materials in a foreign language are also by the present author. Omissions from quoted materials are indicated by spaced dots within brackets: [. . .]. Dots without brackets are as found in the text of the author quoted.

2. Lop and Sauvage, "Essai sur le Nouveau Roman," *Nouvelle Critique*, April 1961.

Maurice Blanchot, in *Le Livre à venir* (1959), said that *Jealousy* had not only no story but no narrator, only a "pure anonymous presence." Robbe-Grillet replied (in a note which Blanchot reproduces) that the story was indeed narrated (seen, heard, felt, etc.) by the husband, a point to which he returns in his later essay, "Nature, Humanism, Tragedy." If any doubt remains that Robbe-Grillet does write stories, it is dispelled by his *prières d'insérer* and, as in *Last Year at Marienbad* and *L'Immortelle*, his prefaces.

Two essays of 1953 show that Robbe-Grillet was already, at that date, developing principles of fiction and ideas about the future path of the novel. His study of *Waiting for Godot* in *Critique* praises Beckett for his attack on the literature of ideas, lauds his regression to a point "beyond nothingness," and extols not only his negation of meaning in general but also his rejection, through the use of amorphous protagonists and other devices, of the idea of "personality" and identity. In a later piece, "Samuel Beckett, or Presence on the Stage," written in 1957 but not published until 1963, Robbe-Grillet returned to these themes as illustrated in *Endgame*.[3] In an essay on "Joë Bosquet the Dreamer," Robbe-Grillet identifies specific surrealist influences on that author and points out doctrines and techniques capable, by modification and extension, of furthering the purposes of a new generation of writers. Since Robbe-Grillet has often, in interviews and lectures, referred to surrealism as one of the main sources (along with Kafka, Raymond Roussel, Joyce, and Faulkner) of the New Novel, his single written treatment of the subject deserves attention.

3. The study of *En attendant Godot* appeared in *Critique*, Feb. 1953; that of *Fin de partie* (*Endgame*) in *Critique*, Oct. 1963. Cf. my article, "Robbe-Grillet as a Critic of Samuel Beckett," in *Beckett Now*, edited by Melvin Friedman (Chicago: University Press, 1970), pp. 59–71. The essay "Joë Bosquet le rêveur" appeared in *Critique*, Oct. 1953.

Robbe-Grillet foresees the emergence, from what he terms the "false dream sleep" of the surrealists, of techniques of description more or less in accord with the "objectal style" that Roland Barthes soon was to identify with Robbe-Grillet's own hyper-real renditions of things, in a new literary movement that Barthes was to call "chosisme." Despite the "phantasmagorias and poetic charlatanism" of some surrealist efforts, Robbe-Grillet writes, André Breton's poetics at least had the merit of bringing out hidden aspects of objects, expressing "the abnormal *sharpness* with which the simplest objects, a chair, a pebble, a hand, appear in dreams, or the fall of some piece of *débris* [. . .] as if the fragment were *eternalized in the act of falling.*" (Later, Robbe-Grillet was to attribute this same "realism of presence" to objects shown in films.) Another idea advanced in the Bosquet article, and prophetic of fictional structures in Robbe-Grillet's future novels, is that gratuitous objects and the play of "objective chance" (as the surrealists insisted) illuminate "the enigmatic connections which bind everyday life to art." Fascination with things described in the style of surrealist "magic realism" (Magritte, Roy), preoccupation with "stopped movement" (as in the "frozen scenes" of his novels), discovery in the outside world of a system of object-signs (which will become the objective correlatives of our affective life or our mental states), all these are present in the Bosquet article. One passage on the role of things is especially noteworthy: "Finally, we must be on guard against allegorical constructions and symbolism.[. . .] Each object, each event, each form, is in fact its own symbol. [. . .] Bosquet's universe—which is ours—is a world of signs. Everything is a sign; and not a sign of something else, something more perfect and situated beyond our reach, but a sign of itself, of an essence which asks only to be revealed."[4]

The evolution of Robbe-Grillet's thought from this view to

4. *Critique*, Oct. 1953, p. 828.

that expressed five years later in "Nature, Humanism, Tragedy" takes him from the theory of neutral "chosisme" to the doctrine that things or objects may also serve as "supports" or objective correlatives of human emotions, from the existentialist "*être-là des choses*" to the highly charged, structured objects such as the figure-of-eight series of *The Voyeur* or the obsessive correlative of erotic resentment represented by the centipede of *Jealousy*.

Following the controversy over *The Voyeur*, a number of important French critics made serious attempts to analyze and evaluate Robbe-Grillet's possibly revolutionary theories and procedures.[5] Among others, Roland Barthes, Bernard Dort, Maurice Blanchot, Jean-Michel Royer, Jacques Brenner, Luc Estang, Bernard Pingaud, and Gerda Zeltner sought to state the implications in terms applicable to a new school of novelists, thus laying the foundations for the category of what shortly became known as the *nouveau roman*.[6] Robbe-Grillet joined the discussions by publishing in *L'Express* during the winter of 1955–1956 a series of nine pieces called "Literature Today." These were succinct, forceful expressions of simple, yet basic, views. Making point after point in a disarmingly declarative fashion, Robbe-Grillet set about undermining with the rhetoric of Cartesian logic many beliefs and assumptions on which the conventional novel rested. Speaking now in the name of a "new realism," he put before the public a number of propositions skillfully presented as if they were self-evident truths. Here, condensed and paraphrased, are the most important:

The novel must evolve, for reasons both inherent (or purely literary) and external (or sociological).

5. See "La Querelle du *Voyeur*," a pamphlet published by Editions de Minuit in 1955 that included a large sampling of critical opinion on the novel.

6. See especially the special issue of *Esprit*, July–Aug. 1958, entitled "Le Nouveau Roman."

Repetition of past forms means the death of the novel, as well as the death of all art.

The idea of "involuntary" or unconsciously produced masterpieces is invalid, since it implies a metaphysical "beyond."

The contemporary novelists must be "intelligent," must recognize that the old Balzacian realism was an art of social and psychological meanings outmoded today, and must write novels in accordance with modern thought, paying particular attention to the relations which exist between objects, gestures, and situations apart from any psychological or ideological "commentary" on the behavior of characters.

The cinema reflects the modern, phenomenological view of the reality of objects, and may influence the future novel.

"The French read too much." The fact that so many (too many) people "read" makes it difficult for the new author to find a public that is not already conditioned by outmoded or obsolescent conceptions of the novel.

Commitment or *engagement* for the writer cannot be political; his only possible commitment is literary, or artistic. For the "committed" writer, literature is the most important enterprise in the world, its own justification and end.

The "new realism" must scrape away the "crust" of interpretations and hidden meanings. The damage done by those who seek allegories and symbols everywhere is illustrated by what happened to Kafka, whose admirers have discredited him with their metaphysical interpretations. Kafka's stairways may *lead* elsewhere, but, in the text, they are only *there*.

In literature, there is no place for an *au-delà*, or beyond, for humanity. Any explanation or interpretation can only be *de trop* or gratuitous, when confronted by the thereness or reality of situations, gestures, and things.

Many of these ideas, with revisions, additions, and changes in terminology, were incorporated into Robbe-Grillet's first real manifesto, the celebrated article "A Future for the Novel," which established him as the foremost theoretician of the *Nouveau Roman*. Long passages on the realism and "presence" of objects in films, the avoidance of a false *au-delà* behind things and gestures, and the rejection of "interpretations" of characters in the novel were retained almost unchanged. They were supported now, however, by two terms destined to become permanently associated with Robbe-Grillet's doctrines: "*surfaces et profondeurs*," surfaces and depths.

In the new article, Robbe-Grillet reasserted the need for a radical, *tabula rasa* operation, resulting in the scraping away of the "crust" of old forms, preconceived aims, and conditioned responses to fiction. Psychological habits acquired chiefly from the reading of literature have, he writes, constructed a mental and emotional grill filtering all our reactions, preventing us from seeing things and our situation among them "with free eyes." Conditioned man insists on incorporating everything into this pseudo understanding; and anything which seems to him nonrecuperable he manages to appropriate anyway by cataloguing it as "absurd." We—since we all suffer from this conditioning—project psychology, sociology, morals, religion, politics, and all other kinds of "meaning" into everything. And yet, if existentialism and phenomenology have taught us anything, it is that "the world is neither meaningful nor absurd. It *is*, and nothing more. [. . .] Opening our eyes suddenly, we have experienced [. . .] the shock of this stubborn reality." Robbe-Grillet adds that "around us, [. . .] things are *there*. Their surface is clean and smooth, *intact*. [. . .] All our literature has not yet succeeded in penetrating the smallest corner of it, or in altering its slightest contour."[7]

The principal task for the writer of fiction is the destruction of the old "*mythe de la profondeur*," the myth of hidden depths of meaning lurking beneath the surfaces of the world we inhabit. Modern thought has partly accomplished this

7. "Une Voie pour le roman futur," *Nouvelle Revue Française*, July 1956.

revolution; now, in the wake of its achievements, novelists must cease depicting the fictional world as man's private property, created to fit human needs and purposes. "We no longer believe," writes Robbe-Grillet confidently, "in these *depths*."

By failing to reiterate the positive aspects of the program outlined earlier in the *Express* series, as reflected there by his remarks on constructional principles, and by increasing his emphasis on the negative attempt to divest fiction of its untenable bonds with the past, Robbe-Grillet furthered in many quarters the view that he was, in truth, a proponent of the *anti-roman*, the "anti-novel." The effects of Sartre's use of Sorel's seventeenth-century term *anti-roman* in his preface to Nathalie Sarraute's *Portrait of a Man Unknown* (1948) had already led to Claude Mauriac's doctrine of "*alittérature*" and to largely fruitless polemics over the *anti-roman* by Jean Bloch-Michel, Pierre-Henri Simon, and others.[8] Though Robbe-Grillet attacked in the new manifesto, not psychology itself, but "sacrosanct psychological analysis," the general tone of his essay suggested a rejection of all interiority, including psychological states and reactions. The ambiguity of Robbe-Grillet's position with respect to psychology has always constituted a difficult point of his doctrine, and his somewhat inconsistent treatment of the matter over the years has failed to clarify the issue. A careful reading of the 1956 text "A Future for the Novel" proves, however, that he is asking only that the novelist refrain from injecting into the novel any commentary or explanation relating to possible psychological interpretations of his characters, and is not attempting to deny in any way the existence of psychic life itself.

Further evidence for the charge that Robbe-Grillet wished to abolish psychology per se from the novel was found by

8. See especially, Jean Bloch-Michel, "Nouveau Roman et culture des masses," *Preuves*, March 1961, pp. 17–28, and the same author's book-length critique, *Le Présent de l'indicatif: essai sur le Nouveau Roman* (Paris: Gallimard, 1963).

critics in his article on Nathalie Sarraute's important theoretical treatise on fiction, *The Age of Suspicion* (1956). After endorsing Sarraute's strictures on the outmoded formalism of the conventional novel, her argument that the day had passed when the novelist's task was to invent "unforgettable characters" in the Balzacian tradition, and her reservations concerning the attempts of so-called behaviorists to eliminate outworn psychological or moral attitudes only to leave them present by implication (as in Camus' *The Stranger*, a work Robbe-Grillet later identified as a historically important failure in the development of a deconditioned fiction), Robbe-Grillet proceeded to oppose Sarraute's own search for new depths of psychology, or infrapsychology. By her insistence upon interior monologues mixed with "subconversations" and surrounded by inexpressible surges of psychic magma called "tropisms," in her attempts to erase the boundaries separating the vocal from the subvocal, Sarraute was in turn reverting to the doctrines of interiority and inner depths that have plagued the novel. Robbe-Grillet's defense of the clear-cut presentation and identification of spoken dialogue (in reply to Sarraute's attack on typographical conventions, phrases such as "said he" and the like), is especially worth noting: "There is in the spoken phrase a solid *presence*, monstrous, definitive, which separates it radically from all thought, especially from the rapid thoughts to which Nathalie Sarraute wishes most to direct our attention, drowned in their movements and perpetual agitations. Nothing must be neglected, then, in order to isolate these *words*, to render their surfaces and sharp outlines."[9] The case of Nathalie Sarraute, Robbe-Grillet concludes, is striking proof that the "old myths of hidden depths" are far from dead.

Inevitably, critics found discrepancies between Robbe-Grillet's theory and his practice. Nothing in his doctrine

9. *Critique*, Aug.–Sept. 1956, p. 701.

seemed to explain, for example, either the distorted visions and "false scenes" involving Mathias in *The Voyeur*, or the apparent proliferation of "symbols" in that work. Was the novel a study in psychopathology or not, and if so, did it not repose on interior psychology? How could one speak of a "realism," new or otherwise, in connection with manifestly imaginary scenes, pseudo memories, and erotic fantasies? If Robbe-Grillet's objects indeed existed without reference to man (as Roland Barthes claimed),[10] why all these arrangements of figures of eight, tangent circles of coiled rope, curling cigarette smoke, eyeglass forms on door panels, and the like? As for the novel *Jealousy*, was it not either (as some maintained) a dehumanizing of fiction, through a reducing of emotion to "camera eye" visual descriptions, or (as others protested) a betrayal of the author's own principles because it sank deep into implied psychology and covert symbolism, if not (viewing the centipede as standing for Sexuality, for example) into allegory?

Robbe-Grillet, concerned over the need of further clarifying his position with respect to the apparent symbolism in his work, wrote to me at this time: "You have saved me from symbolism by inventing the objective correlative." I had not, of course, invented the term which T. S. Eliot popularized, but I had, in conversations with Robbe-Grillet and in print, proposed this conception, and term, as a more accurate one than symbol, both for the objects of *The Voyeur* and for the highly charged centipede image of *Jealousy*.[11] Meanwhile, Robbe-Grillet had made a new effort to define his views on inner form, design, and "intentional" relationships in the novel, publishing the results in a series that appeared in the autumn of 1957 in *France-Observateur*.[12] His next major

10. "Littérature objective," *Critique*, July–Aug. 1954.
11. "Surfaces et structures dans les romans de Robbe-Grillet," *French Review*, April 1958.
12. Oct.–Dec. 1957, *passim*.

statement, and still one of his most important contributions to fictional theory, appeared the following year, entitled "Nature, Humanism, Tragedy."

Here Robbe-Grillet set out to free the novel as he saw it from an apparent impasse of nonsignificance. Some important questions needed answers. If the novel must divest itself of the "so-called riches" of psychology, sociology, politics, and the rest, limiting itself to the exclusive depiction of a phenomenological universe of "surfaces," how could it avoid becoming a sterile game, a true *anti*-novel? If even such a "cleansed" or "emptied" work as *The Stranger* was "betrayed" by an ending that restored moral significance to a no longer "absurd" hero, what kind of novel could now be written, and what purpose could it serve? Furthermore, since it was evident that a work like *Jealousy* was more than an interplay of surface designs, was not the author (as Robbe-Grillet himself asks) in fact proposing one kind of novel while writing another?

The essentials of Robbe-Grillet's tightly conceived answer to these attacks may be summarized as follows. At the bottom of most objections to his doctrines lies a false humanism, a humanism that is in reality a transcendental metaphysics by which man is linked to nature through mystical correspondences, anthropocentric images and metaphors, symbols, and the like. Even when man is envisaged as "separated" from oneness with nature, it is only because those who see him thus wish to exploit this division in the name of tragedy. Tragedy, along with humanism, implies the possibility of man's "recuperation" into a divine or quasi-divine scheme of potential oneness. But modern man, says Robbe-Grillet, must say "No" to tragedy, must accept existence in an *objectively meaningless* universe before he can turn his attention to his own humanity in a "true" humanism untainted by emotional and ideological projection or by the belief in a metaphysical "beyond."

Without naming the work, Robbe-Grillet proceeds to defend *Jealousy* against the charge of "dehumanization." How can a novel be inhuman, when it follows, scene by scene, a man's every step, describing exactly "what he does, what he sees, or what he imagines"? (The term *deshumanización*, made popular by Ortega y Gasset, was never in Ortega's view one of depreciation, but something like the equivalent of Brecht's *Verfremdugseffekt* or aesthetic endistancing; whereas Robbe-Grillet's critics had used dehumanization as a synonym for coldness, detachment from human values, use of purely objective descriptions, and the like). That Robbe-Grillet includes what the protagonist "imagines" among the actions and objects "seen" at their "surfaces" only is a clear indication that his doctrine may be applied to interiority in the form of imaginary scenes, as had already been done in both *The Voyeur* and *Jealousy*. Discussing specifically the role of *things*, Robbe-Grillet explains how, though they are in themselves unrelated to man, indifferent to his emotions, unaffected by his glance, totally unsymbolic, they may nevertheless acquire the psychic "charge" that they obviously carry in many crucial passages of the author's novels, becoming, in a word, objective correlatives:

[Man] refuses to set up with them [that is, with *things*] any dubious understanding, any connivance; he asks nothing of them; he experiences toward them neither agreement nor disagreement of any sort. He can, as the occasion arises, make of them supports for his emotions, or for his glance. [. . . But] his passion [. . .] remains on their surface, making no attempt to penetrate within, since there is nothing inside.[13]

In allowing objects to function as the support of passions, as their correlatives, Robbe-Grillet made a necessary concession, if not an actual reversal, since he had declared in "A Future for the Novel" that *things* "will no longer be a vague reflection of the hero's soul, the image of his torment, or the sup-

13. "Nature, humanisme, tragédie," *Nouvelle Revue Française*, Oct. 1958, p. 583.

port of his desires." By adopting now the doctrine of the *objet-support*, Robbe-Grillet cleared the way for the novel to express or rather contain significances, within a formal system of relationships between object-signs, structured situations, and optically or sensorially depicted surfaces.

It is a system that accommodates a wide range of novelistic purposes, from that of objectified psychological reactions and motivations (*Jealousy*, for example) to the "un-novelistic" or pure novel projected in a subsequent work, *In the Labyrinth*, which almost fulfills Flaubert's ideal of "a book about nothing [. . .] with no external connections," and in which interferences, displacements, reinforcements, in an elaborate interplay of objects, movements, signs, positive and negative images, and repetitive or contradictory situations create the aesthetic tensions and resolutions that serve to validate a nominal, if not, from the psychological viewpoint, virtually "empty" plot.

In a later essay, "New Novel, New Man," Robbe-Grillet reiterates various points of his doctrine in the guise of a reply to false views of the New Novel, as widely circulated by its detractors.[14] Some critics, among them Jean-René Huguenin of *Arts*, claimed that this new manifesto represented a "softening" of Robbe-Grillet's views, and a retreat from earlier positions;[15] but such is hardly the case. It is easy to show that Robbe-Grillet's description of the popular image of the New Novel is by no means exaggerated. A typical outline of the new doctrines is given by André Frossard in *Candide*, under the title "The Nothing Technique." Here is the familiar litany of grievances:

It is obvious that what is important in the contemporary French novel is not the subject,
is not the plot;

14. "Nouveau Roman, Homme Nouveau," *La Revue de Paris*, Sept. 1961.
15. *Arts*, Sept. 27–Oct. 3, 1961.

is not love;
is not life;
is not death;
is not the characters;
nor the situations;
nor things;
but the Technique of the novelist.[16]

There is nothing concessive in the counterstatements Robbe-Grillet makes to these accusations, in "New Novel, New Man." The New Novel, he asserts, is not a "school," but only a convenient label to group certain writers who share the same general convictions: that the novel is a form of "research," which never tries in any way to impose fixed rules or patterns; that the New Novel does *not* wish to "wipe away the past," but to evolve beyond the best of what the past offers; it does not "turn aside" from man, but seeks to adapt itself to man's situation in the present-day world; it does not practice an "impartial" objectivity, but is governed to the contrary by a basic *subjectivity*, in that it often expresses the mental content of a character caught up in some passionate experience; its "dechronology" and other apparent deformations are closer to our real psychic life than the false "psychology" inherited from the works of the past; its refusal of predetermined meaning is only a reflection, in the literary field, of ideas first put forth by modern science and philosophy; and finally, the only commitment possible to the writer of novels is the commitment to literature itself. The one word with a new ring in this article is "subjectivity": "The New Novel aims only at total subjectivity." But this idea, if newly stated in incontrovertible terms, was already fully implicit in Robbe-Grillet's fictional system, constituting, as we have tried to show, one of its most basic tenets.

Further evidence of the concept of "objectified subjectiv-

16. "Technique du rien," *Candide*, July 13–20, 1961.

ity" underlying all of Robbe-Grillet's fictional creation is given in the preface to *Last Year at Marienbad*. This *ciné-roman* is a multivalent, polysemantic work of chronologically and spatially displaced images and dialogues, at once "mental" and "real" (or ostensibly so). The author calls it "the story of a persuasion, [. . .] a reality that the hero creates by his own vision." In Robbe-Grillet's ontology, as expressed in the *Marienbad* preface, thoughts and emotions *are* the mental images of their "subject" or "content." Dialogue is not so much the uttering of words as, literally, an "exchange of views," a confrontation between mental images of those involved in the "conversation." Moreover, the cinema, Robbe-Grillet claims, is especially well adapted to such a projection of images, real or false: memories, anticipations, or imaginations. In the flexibility of its transitions and nonchronological sequences (Robbe-Grillet almost seems to imply that he has accomplished these effects only in films), the cinema can closely parallel or embody psychic life or the mental content that makes up life as it actually *is*. In this regard, Robbe-Grillet's ideas rejoin those of such theorists of the film as Edgar Morin[17] and Jacques-Bernard Brunius. Brunius writes: "The cinema appears to be an unhoped-for instrument for the objectification of the mental *aqua-micans*. [. . .] The lighted screen is the middle surface or interface between the objective and the subjective. [. . .] The order of images on the screen *in time* is absolutely analogous to the ordering that thought imposes. [. . .] Neither chronological order nor the relative values of duration are real. [. . .] It is impossible to imagine a more faithful mirror of *mental representation*."[18] That *Last Year at Marienbad* not only should exhibit a Pirandellian ambiguity of situation and personal identities but also should bear a noncommensurable relationship to the "logical" order of

17. *Le Cinéma ou l'homme imaginaire* (Paris: Minuit, 1956).
18. "En marge du cinéma français," 1954; reproduced in Pierre Lherminier, ed., *L'Art du cinéma* (Paris: Seghers, 1960), p. 330.

conventional films and novels, that it should be irreducible to a linear "story line," is then inevitable, desirable, and artistically correct. Since mental content is "never chronological," it would be absurd to confine the literary or cinematic work to a linear progression of time from past to future, just as it is absurd to limit the space of thought to the space in which we are located at a given moment.

In 1963, Robbe-Grillet published most of the texts discussed above, with modifications and additions, in *For a New Novel*.[19] But only by studying his fictional works can we see the true evolution and refinement of his creative doctrines, and test the applicability of his theories to specific problems of textual production and organization. However interesting Robbe-Grillet's doctrines may be, they would lose much of their interest and importance if his novels and films did not exist to support, or rather to incarnate, these ideas. If we set aside the novels themselves, Robbe-Grillet's doctrinal "message" can be summed up in a few very simple and precise points: an evolving art form, like the novel, must not be understood or judged by past criteria; the New Novel, like the New Film, must break with sterile imitation of the past; the reader or spectator must "decondition" himself, become free to see things with a fresh vision; the novelist, and the scenarist as well, must cultivate a *creative formalism* based on the principle that both novel and film exist as art. The values of art are never ideological, sociological, or political; they reside only in forms and structures. But this creative formalism does not mean that the values of art are detached from man, or that they are "inhuman." Nor is it a question of an ivory tower doctrine of art for art's sake; since man is by nature an aesthetic animal, it is instead a question of art for man's sake.

19. Alain Robbe-Grillet, *Pour un nouveau roman* (Paris: Minuit, 1963); English version, *For a New Novel: Essays on Fiction*, translated by Richard Howard (New York: Grove Press, 1965).

2 Oedipus or the Closed Circle: *The Erasers* (1953)

> Through any single manifestation of the myth, therefore, there opens up the perspective of a serialistic pattern endlessly repeating itself, what Mann calls "time-coulisses."
>
> A. MENDILOW, *Time and the Novel*

Viewed in retrospect, Alain Robbe-Grillet's first published novel, *The Erasers* (*Les Gommes*, 1953), now appears remarkably prophetic of his later works. Far from being an uncertain, tentative experiment in a mixed genre (detective story *cum* "objectal" or *chosiste* descriptions), *The Erasers* established an archetype for the Robbegrilletian novel, in which an isolated protagonist completes a Vicoesque cycle that returns him virtually to the point of departure, where, although appearing identical, his destiny has been irreversibly altered. The fabled Gnostic serpent Ouroboros bites his own tail, and the variegated, aberrant, yet interlocked scales of his curled body form a cryptic series of elements each stubbornly existent in its objectal *thereness*.[1]

1. Robbe-Grillet described to me his first project for a novel, conceived and then abandoned before the writing of *Un Régicide* (of which only a single chapter has been printed to date, in *Médiations*, Summer 1962, pp. 5–16). It was to consist of a plot utilizing 108 "elements" (or narremes?), corresponding to the 108 scales on the body of the serpent Ouroboros, the occult snake that sometimes symbolizes the universe (in the *Hieroglyphics* of Horapollo), sometimes the endless cycle of metamorphoses (in the Gnostic doctrine of the Ophite sect), and, finally, time (in Ficino's gloss of Plotinus). In one

Although *The Erasers* received praise from reviewers (Jean Blanzat called it "a book with surprising authority," and Jean Cayrol saw it as "a novel of high quality, a great book"), the work had little immediate public success and remained unstudied until Roland Barthes, the first important exegete of Robbe-Grillet, put forth in two articles ("Objective Literature" and "Literal Literature," both published in *Critique*) certain ideas that became guiding principles for Robbe-Grillet criticism. Barthes sharply dichotomized *The Erasers* by deliberately excluding any discussion of the plot of the novel, and by directing his attention almost solely to what he termed the "Einsteinian dimension of the *object*" in Robbe-Grillet's descriptions of *things*, seen as existing or moving in "a new mixture of space and time," as having surfaces but no depths, as possessing "neither function nor substance." Brilliantly delineating the originality of Robbe-Grillet's object descriptions,

---

hermetic version the scales of the Ouroboros are numbered so that the sum of two adjacent numbers gives the number of the following scale, in a manner analogous to, but not identical to, the famous Fibonacci series. The entire sequence forms a unique numerical possibility, impossible with any number other than 108, a number Mircea Eliade has discussed in connection with Hindu doctrines. Robbe-Grillet considered distorting plot chronology by taking up the 108 story elements in this staggered order, creating a fixed series or "row" as in serial or duodecaphonic music. In discarding this artificial and baroque idea, Robbe-Grillet nevertheless retained both the notion of circular plot structure and the conception of serial images and their mutations, two fundamental features of his fictional technique. In *The Voyeur*, Mathias, after his doubly circular itinerary around the island, departs, as he arrived, in a state of highly dubious "innocence." The husband-narrator of *Jealousy* is no further advanced toward a "solution" of his problem when, as the novel ends, he is still returning in his mind to events of the story's beginning. The narrator of *In the Labyrinth* begins with an "I" which is left in suspense until the final sequence closes with a "me" which brings the story full cycle back to its point of departure. Circularity in the later novels will be made abundantly clear in subsequent chapters.

Barthes at the same time, through the *parti-pris* of his limited angle of interest, contributed to the development of the myth of a Robbe-Grillet indifferent to plot and human emotions, a "chosiste" preoccupied with things and intent on filling his novels with minutely described but "gratuitous" objects. This misconception persists today among many critics.[2]

Roland Barthes properly underlined in *The Erasers* what he

2. This interpretation of Robbe-Grillet is current not only in France (where his writings have been called "descriptions of land deeds," "extracts from machinery catalogues," etc.), but also elsewhere. *Time* has stated on several occasions that Robbe-Grillet takes a derisive view of characters and plot, as well as of human emotions, suggesting that he would end up writing "a novel about a room full of furniture," featuring "the affair between the armchair and the ottoman" (*Time*, Oct. 13, 1958; cf. also *Time*'s review of *Jealousy*, Dec. 14, 1959). A number of serious students of his novels have tended to view them exclusively from the *chosiste* angle: J. Robert Loy writes that "things come to life under his detached eye and seem to possess the only real existence in the work" ("'Things' in Recent French Literature," *PMLA*, March 1956). José-María Castellet expresses similar ideas in "De la objetividad al objeto," *Papeles de Son Armadans*, June 1957. One of the most perceptive critics of Robbe-Grillet, Renato Barilli, continues to regard *The Erasers* as interesting mainly because of its objectal "texture," and affirms that the plot is irrelevant, "absurd," and chosen as if "by lot" ("La narrativa di Alain Robbe-Grillet," *Il Verri*, Jan., 1959). In recent years, Robbe-Grillet has himself contributed to this viewpoint, in lectures and comments, by minimizing the significance of the story in *The Erasers*. In *Prétexte* (Jan. 1958, p. 100) he calls it "a plot of pure convention [. . .] which was to me of no importance." Such declarations must, however, be taken with reservations. The analysis here presented does, I believe, show the importance of the plot of *The Erasers* for the Robbe-Grillet of 1953, and its place in the evolution of the author's ideas of what constitutes plot structure. A further exploration of the problem of changing views on Robbe-Grillet is made by the present author in "Points de repère: Robbe-Grillet No. 1, 2 . . . X," *Nouveau Roman: hier, aujourd'hui*, II, 119–133 (Paris: Editions 10/18 [Union Général d'Editions], 1972).

termed an effort to "look at the world [. . .] with no other authority except that of one's eyes." If, as we must, we interpret "eyes" here as the eyes of a perceiving consciousness, we find Robbe-Grillet directly connected to the branch of existentialist thought represented in France by Jean-Paul Sartre (especially in his treatise *Being and Nothingness* and his early novel, *Nausea*) and by such phenomenologists as Maurice Merleau-Ponty, who writes, in his *Phenomenology of Perception*, "Nothing is more difficult than to know exactly *what we see*."[3] Robbe-Grillet's attack on "depth" and "meaning" is an extension of the existentialist attack on object-subject duality, as well as on introspective thought, previously denounced by the American behaviorists. The influence of behaviorist ideas on the French novel is well established; in the wake of Camus' *The Stranger*, behaviorism furnishes an additional rationale for emphasizing descriptions of actions, gestures, and outward conduct, as perceived in a phenomenological context.[4]

A detailed scrutiny of *The Erasers*—and only such an examination can do justice to this complicated novel—may well begin with the *prière d'insérer* that Robbe-Grillet composed for the back cover of the first edition. This compact *résumé* stresses not objects, but plot:

The subject is a definite, concrete, essential event: a man's death. It is a detective story event—that is, there is a murderer, a detective, a victim. In one sense, their roles are conventional: the murderer shoots the victim, the detective *solves* the problem, the victim dies. But the ties which bind them only appear clearly once the last chapter ends. For the book is nothing more than the account of the twenty-four hours that ensue between the pistol shot

3. *Phénoménologie de la perception* (Paris: Gallimard, 1945), p. 71.
4. See Claude-Edmonde Magny's pioneering study of the "behaviorist" novel, *L'Age du roman américain* (Paris: Seuil, 1948), *passim*.

and the death, the time the bullet takes to travel three or four yards—twenty-four hours "in excess."[5]

The tone of this account emphasizes the value placed on ingenious, puzzlelike elements composing a plot of twists with a surprising ending. Most early reviewers followed this lead, as did foreign translators, who for the most part dropped the French title (with its rather obscure hidden association between *gomme*, gum eraser, and the slang term for a policeman or "gum shoe") and replaced it with such titles as the Spanish *La doble muerte del profesor Dupont* (The Double Death of Professor Dupont) and the German *Ein Tag zuviel* (One Day in Excess), which reflect the aspect of paradoxical plot as described in the *résumé*.

What are these twenty-four hours "in excess"? There are, in fact, two "circles" of twenty-four hours in *The Erasers*, each of which could be considered a classical unity of time. The prologue begins at 6:00 A.M. and the epilogue ends at 6:00 A.M. the following morning with an—almost—identical scene. But the action of the main plot has begun with a first pistol shot at 7:30 P.M. of the evening before the morning of the prologue, and is concluded with a second (and fatal) shot fired at 7:30 P.M. of the evening before the morning of the epilogue. Thus two circular time spans overlap, and interlock; "classical" unity of time is split, syncopated, and doubled in

5. Further evidence of the author's attention to both ambiguities of plot and mythic implications in *The Erasers* is found in the now exceedingly rare pamphlet *Les Gommes*, issued by the Editions de Minuit under Robbe-Grillet's supervision in 1953. Robbe-Grillet's cover notices, stressing the *story* and providing a guide to the interpretation of the novels, played an essential role for many reviewers, at least one of whom, Emile Henriot, admitted that he would never have recognized the presence of a mute narrator in *Jealousy* without the clues provided by the *"prière d'insérer."*

Other evidence of the evolution of the cover notice as an adjunct of the accompanying fiction is given in later chapters.

a structural displacement that is, as it will become apparent, reflected or reinforced throughout the novel by other displacements and mutations affecting objects, gestures, itineraries (or *parcours*), and events.

By simplifying, through synthesis, the multiple modes of narration employed in *The Erasers* (mode of the omniscient observer, stream of consciousness and interior monologues, free indirect discourse, rearranged or reversed chronology, flashbacks and pseudo flashbacks, "false" scenes presented literally), we may schematize for purposes of critical study a plot whose general movement, despite its involutions and its "return to the beginning," is conveyed in a relentless forward direction—in contrast, say, to the plot of *Jealousy* or *Last Year at Marienbad*, with their profusion of radical *retours en arrière* and their chronological echolalia.

Sartre, aware or not of the theories of Henry James and other predecessors, had made French authors and critics aware of the ideological and aesthetic shortcomings of the omniscientauthor formula. In his famous attack on François Mauriac, in *Situations I*, Sartre argued that an existentialist writer must limit the contents of his novel to what actually "exists," that is, to what the characters perceive through their own consciousness, within the fictional framework of their individual situations. Robbe-Grillet in *The Erasers* follows this principle by presenting both action and background almost exclusively through the use of rotating points of view in which he constructs objectively the mental content of a dozen or more characters: a café proprietor, the failed professional assassin Garinati, Doctor Juard, the merchant Marchat, police chief Laurent, the maid Anna Smite, the terrorist leader Bona, the witness Mme Bax, the riddle-propounding drunkard, the former postal employee Mme Jean, the victim Daniel Dupont, and, of course, the "special agent" and protagonist, Wallas. A few passages belong to the mode of the omniscient author;

they emanate, as we shall see, from a kind of hidden chorus that constitutes a special "observing conscience" related to the structural parallel between the novel and its model in Greek tragedy.

The prologue opens at 6:00 A.M. of Tuesday, October 27, in the Café des Alliés on the Rue des Arpenteurs (note the theme of measurement and *parcours*, with its echo of Kafka's surveyor or *arpenteur* in *The Castle*), just outside the Boulevard Circulaire which, paralleled by a canal over two quarter-sectors of its route, runs around a city of Flemish atmosphere, a labyrinth of perpendicular and oblique streets cut across by canals, both lined with severe, identical façades (prophetic of the *décor* of *In the Labyrinth*). Drawbridges, squares, fountains, and statues all have a conventional yet disquieting appearance.

As he wipes a blood-colored area of a table top, the proprietor recalls events of the previous evening: someone had tried to shoot Daniel Dupont, the professor of economics whose house stands nearby; Dupont's maid Anna had phoned for medical aid from the café, since the professor's phone was mysteriously out of order. A stranger named Wallas had arrived in the night to take the café's one room for rent. Now another stranger arrives to ask for Wallas, who is no longer in his room. Two habitués enter the bistro; one, Antoine, has read that "Albert" Dupont was murdered last night; the other, a drunkard, tries to ask a riddle, but no one listens.

The enquiring stranger, standing at a drawbridge looking down at the oily canal water, is identified: he is Garinati, a hired killer who the night before in an attempt on Dupont's life succeeded only in wounding Dupont in the arm. An almost imperceptible shift to past tenses indicates a flashback in Garinati's mind: following detailed plans given him by his boss Bona (as, we later learn, part of a program of political assassinations, each scheduled for 7:30 P.M.), Garinati enters Dupont's house, goes up to the professor's study, and there, as Dupont appears at the door, fires at his intended victim, who turns and flees.

Seeking medical attention and refuge at Doctor Juard's clinic, Dupont, in a scene which, though it occurred the night before, is written in the present tense, reveals his plan to escape the plot on his life. He will issue the news that he is, in fact, dead. Juard will sign the death certificate, and government officials at the capital will pretend to take possession of his "corpse," so that the local police will not discover the ruse (they may, it is implied, be linked to the terrorist mob). Dupont needs certain papers from his study; his friend, the merchant Marchat, agrees to return to Dupont's house next evening to pick them up. Dupont's divorced wife will be informed by letter of her ex-husband's "death."

As the prologue ends, Garinati goes to report to his chief. In his thoughts, he visualizes a return to the scene of his unsuccessful crime, in order to make a second attempt on Dupont's life.

The drama begins. Wallas, standing at a bridge early this Tuesday morning, glances at his watch: it stopped last night at exactly 7:30 P.M. and refuses to run. Arriving by train from the capital around midnight in this city which he vaguely remembers visiting as a child, Wallas has found lodging at the café near the scene of the crime he has been sent by the Bureau des Enquêtes to investigate. Wallas begins walking through the maze of streets, noting the cold brick façades, the curious motifs embroidered on the window curtains, an odd statue in the square. He loses his way and becomes entangled in a confused conversation with a woman concerning the location of the "center" of the city. His destination is the office of police chief Laurent, but before arriving there he stops in a stationery store to ask for a *gomme*, a gum eraser of special texture and quality, only to discover, as always happens to him, that there is none in stock. Wallas eyes the attractive girl clerk with evident erotic interest.

At the commissariat, Wallas discusses the case with Laurent. The police chief expresses skepticism concerning the manner of Dupont's death, which he believes may have been a suicide. The victim may even be, since no one has seen the corpse, Albert Dupont, as reported by one newspaper. Wallas produces a pistol; it is a 7.65 mm. identical to the murder weapon (Doctor Juard has reported the caliber of the bullet removed from the "dying" Dupont). Since one bullet is missing from the magazine, Laurent points out that Wallas himself could be a suspect. Visiting Dupont's house, Wallas has a difficult conversation with the nearly deaf Anna (who believes her master is dead) and carries off Dupont's own pistol, also a 7.65 mm. with one cartridge missing.

Alone in a bare room, Bona (Jean Bonaventure) waits for Garinati to arrive and make his report. Garinati, expecting to be reprimanded for his failure, is surprised to discover that Bona has accepted the newspaper account of Dupont's death. Can he, Garinati, be wrong? Is Dupont dead?

Wallas learns from a witness living across the street, Mme Bax, that a man in a raincoat had appeared in front of Dupont's house an hour before the crime, and had tampered with the lock of the garden gate, despite interference from a passing drunkard. Returning to the café, Wallas is "recognized" by the drunkard, who relates the same scene, claiming that it was Wallas he accosted. Wallas in turn recreates this scene in his imagination, projecting himself into it as the man in the raincoat. The proprietor decides to report Wallas to the police; Wallas, wishing to establish his identity, takes out his *carte d'identité*, but he notices that the photo thereon, taken some time ago when he wore a moustache, resembles him so little that he hastily puts the document back in his pocket.

On a streetcar going into the city, Wallas overhears two

women discussing what seems to be an important story or event, but in terms so fragmentary and confusing that its significance escapes him. Leaving the tram, he finds another stationery store. Its window display consists of a dummy dressed as a painter standing before an easel on which may be seen a fine line drawing of the ruins of a Greek temple. Yet the "subject" in front of the painter, to Wallas' amazement, is a large photo-mural of Dupont's house, the scene of the crime. Wallas enters and again asks for the special eraser; he even manages to recall one syllable of its name. But again he must content himself with an inferior substitute. Again he looks with erotic interest at the woman clerk. Evasive childhood memories tantalize him. He sets out toward the clinic to question Doctor Juard.

A literal (yet false) scene of Dupont's "suicide" fades into complicated speculations by Laurent, tending always nearer to the correct conclusion (that Dupont is alive). Here, in mid-novel, one becomes increasingly aware that the full knowledge given to the reader of Dupont's true situation hides some developing mystery, and that the reader, instead of watching a group of characters uselessly struggling to discover what has already been revealed to him, is instead witnessing the preparation for an unsuspected *dénouement*.

Laurent receives a visit from Marchat, who fears he will be killed if he returns to get Dupont's papers. Marchat visualizes climbing the stairs to meet his death in Dupont's study. Frightened at his vision and at the questions Laurent puts to him, the merchant decides to leave town without carrying out his mission to the house in the Rue des Arpenteurs.

Eating lunch in a self-service restaurant, Wallas overhears an ambiguous conversation among three railway employees; their remarks seem related to the Dupont case. Sensing defeat in his investigation, Wallas broods. He recalls the bizarre requirements of his job as special agent: Chief Fabius (parodied from Simenon if not from Fantômas) had insisted, according to his rule, that the area of Wallas' forehead measure at least fifty square centimeters; when calculations showed that it fell short by less than one square centimeter, Wallas had been accepted on probation only.

Informed that a man in a raincoat resembling the person seen by Mme Bax had been observed entering the post office, Wallas hastens there. To his surprise he is "recognized" and handed a letter. Opening it in Laurent's presence, Wallas reads, without understanding its contents, Bona's communication to a new hired killer, "André VS" ("VS" pronounced in French suggests "Wallas"). André VS is to replace Garinati tonight for the tenth political murder (as the reader remembers from an earlier scene with Bona). Laurent dismisses the letter as unimportant, and resumes his speculations.

Wallas stops in a third *papeterie* in search of his unobtainable *gomme*. In an associative flashback whose values are reversed somewhat in the manner of a solarized print, he sees a painter standing among classical ruins painting a picture that is metamorphosed, as the description develops, into a sharp photograph of the house of the crime. Suddenly Wallas realizes that the woman owner of the stationery store with the photo-mural must be Dupont's ex-wife.

Interviewing Evelyne Dupont (for it is she) in the back room of her shop, Wallas intently studies photographs on the desk showing a middle-aged man and a woman accompanied by a small boy. Someone enters the shop; Evelyne goes to serve him. On her return she reveals that the customer has purchased a picture postcard of the Dupont house. Wallas hastens after the man, but loses him. A series of interviews with postal employees at Laurent's office leads nowhere, except to involve Wallas further in conflicting testimony identifying him as the man who has received incriminating letters.

One of Laurent's inspectors presents in writing a new theory of the crime: Dupont has an illegitimate son who is probably the guilty party. A young man has been seen prowling near Dupont's house in company with a tough-looking friend. A literal (yet false) scene follows in which Dupont is murdered by his son's friend, but this version also fails to convince Laurent, who imagines it. Doctor Juard awaits Wallas at the railway station, where he had made an appointment (to avoid letting Wallas into the clinic where Dupont is still hiding). Their interview fails to enlighten Wallas, though Juard has let slip words that could have betrayed his secret. On his return to the clinic, Juard learns that Marchat will probably not return for the papers at Dupont's house.

In his room, Garinati rearranges certain statuettes and objects on the mantelpiece before the mirror. Descending to the street, he imagines Bona visiting Dupont's house to verify the professor's death. When he draws from his pocket the postcard bought at Evelyne's store, the reader's suspicions are confirmed that it was Garinati who entered during Wallas' visit. The time of this section of the novel undergoes a curious compression when Garinati now contemplates a tug passing a drawbridge, in a passage virtually identical to the one which, forty pages earlier, had preceded the entire chapter.

As night falls, Wallas recalls events of the day, mixing, distorting, altering them. Then he revisits Mme Bax. Later, at the café, the drunkard engages him in an argument over the meaning of the word "oblique," and propounds his earlier riddle in several contradictory variants.

Laurent receives a letter containing a photo of the Dupont house (which he does not recognize), on which is written "Rendez-vous ce soir à sept heures et demie." He shows the card to Wallas, who, without saying so, does recognize the house. Returning toward it, Wallas fights obscure memories. He sees himself standing on the steps of a ruined temple, playing some dim role in an elusive scene. Suddenly he remembers that the person his mother had brought him to see in this city, long ago, was his father. He stops in another stationery store in search of the *gomme*; again, failure. Abruptly, he decides to return to Dupont's study, convinced that the murderer will for some reason return to keep the appointment referred to on the postcard. There Wallas will capture the criminal and solve the case.

Wallas' entry into the house of the crime, his climbing the stairs, his ingress into the study, all duplicate, with variations, those of Garinati at the beginning of the story. Wallas waits.

In his office, Laurent at last deduces the correct "solution": Dupont is not dead. He tries to reach Wallas by phone at the café. The action begins to accelerate. At the clinic, Dupont decides he must fetch his papers himself; his entry into the house, despite his usual courage, is accompanied by a certain fear. It is nearly 7:30. Dupont, taking from a drawer the pistol that Wallas had replaced there only a few moments earlier, opens the door to his study. Wallas is there. Each man, at the sight of the other, fires, but the professor's pistol is jammed, and Dupont falls dead from Wallas' bullet. The special agent's wristwatch, stopped for twenty-four hours, starts ticking again. The phone, lately out of order, rings. The call is from Laurent, who, guessing that Wallas may have returned to Dupont's study, is eager to announce that he has deduced the truth—Dupont is not dead!

As the epilogue opens, it is again early morning in the café. Garinati again asks for Wallas, whose surveillance is now his task. During the night, Garinati has visited the hospitals and clinics of the city, and has *seen* Daniel Dupont's body—so he had succeeded in his assassination after all! Wallas, sitting with swollen feet (how many kilometers has he walked in twenty-four hours?) on the edge of his bed, ponders his failure: he, the detective, has killed the victim. In the mirror he notices that fatigue and sleeplessness have restored much of the lost resemblance to the photo on his identity card. He will return to the capital and await Fabius' decision on his future.

Antoine, who had claimed the day before that Albert and not Daniel Dupont had been murdered, triumphantly enters the café with a newspaper proving that Albert Dupont has indeed been assassinated (the night before, Albert Dupont had become the tenth of Bona's victims). Wallas vainly tries to get the drunkard to repeat his riddle, but the one the man now propounds is quite different. In an incoherent interior monologue, the café proprietor mulls over his telephone conversation with police chief Laurent: something about whether a son of Dupont might have frequented his bistro.

A whirling, lyrical passage takes the reader from the proprietor standing before his aquariumlike bar mirror into a distant, watery realm of "petits bateaux perdus sur la mer [. . .] les vieux tonneaux, les poissons morts, les poulies et les cordages, les bouées, le pain rassis, les couteaux et les hommes." The circle of time has closed around Wallas, and the novel is ended.

At a superficial level, *The Erasers* may be read as an ingenious detective story with a surprise ending: something in the style of *Trent's Last Case*, or *The Murder of Roger Ackroyd*, in which the detective or protagonist is revealed in the end as the guilty party. (The same may be said, to some degree, of *The Voyeur*, in which Mathias' guilt is gradually brought to light.) In the hastiest perusal, however, it must become obvious that innumerable elements in the dense pages of *The Erasers* must constitute, if they are not merely gratuitous hidden riches, cunning traps for the reader, ambiguous allusions to "something else," reflections, displacements, doublings. A seemingly innocent passage taken from an early scene of Wallas' peregrinations epitomizes this aspect of the novel:

There are three yellow posters [. . .] with a large headline at the top: Attention Citizens! Attention Citizens! Attention Citizens! [. . .] The kind of literature that no one ever reads, except, from time to time, an old gentleman who pauses, puts on his glasses, and painstakingly deciphers the whole text [. . .], steps back slightly to view the whole display, shaking his head [. . .], then, perplexed, goes his way, wondering if he has not missed the essential message. Among the usual words there stands out here and there like a beacon some suspect term, and the sentence that it illuminates so slyly seems for an instant to conceal many things, or nothing at all. [Pp. 52–53][6]

To the multivalent phrases, allusions, and images of the text must be added the varying aspects or facets presented in *The Erasers* by *time* itself. In destroying the linear advance of classical chronology as it is found in the traditional novel, modern authors have, as is well known, sought many objectives: to "recapture" the past (as in Proust); to create a multiple duration related to various personalities (as in Gide, Dos Passos, Virginia Woolf, and Sartre); to destroy the fixity of time through ambiguity (as in Faulkner); to mix past and present through interpenetrations (as in Graham Greene and Aldous Huxley); to expand a short span of a time—a day, a night—into a universal life cycle (as in the Joyce of *Finnegans Wake*). Robbe-Grillet's attempt in *The Erasers*, related in some degree to many of these efforts, is to replace linear or clock time with what he has called *le temps humain*, the time that in our own ceaseless duration we produce about ourselves like a cocoon, full of retreats into the past, repetitions, imaginings, and revisions, causing the same event to take on as many different aspects as there are moments in the lives of different observers. As in Einstein's theory of relativity, the moment of time and space, the frame of reference, varies with the observer and his point of view. Such a "human time" may properly be called existential time, since it exists only as a *creation of the observer in his situation*. Viewed from the standpoint of existentialist time, any of the "solutions" projected by the various characters of *The Erasers* is, at the moment of its projection, possible if not true. A consequence is

6. Page references to *The Erasers* are to the 1961 printing of *Les Gommes* (Paris: Minuit).

that external reality, like external time, becomes shifting, uncertain, hypothetical. This theme is sounded in the prologue:

> Soon, unfortunately, time will no longer be the master. Sur-
> rounded by their circle of error and doubt, the incidents of this
> day, however insignificant, will shortly begin their task, progres-
> sively disrupting the ideal order, introducing here and there, in-
> sidiously, an inversion, a displacement, a confusion, a distortion,
> in order to gradually accomplish their work: a day, at the begin-
> ning of winter, lacking plan and direction, incomprehensible and
> monstrous. [P. 11]

Even events that appear objectively false (for example, Antoine's belief that "Albert" Dupont has been murdered;
Laurent's assistant's theory that the murderer of Dupont is
his illegitimate son) may find external verification *après coup*,
just as correct deductions (Laurent's belated conclusion that
Dupont is still alive) may be contradicted by outcomes that
revert (with subtle differences) to an earlier status quo. In a
sense, the entire twenty-four hours of the main action is "outside of time" ("vingt-quatre heures 'en trop' "), as objectified
or reinforced by the stopping of Wallas' watch from the moment of Garinati's shot to the instant of Dupont's death when
Wallas fires, returning the situation substantially to that which
seemed to prevail the night before.

Yet, though he accomplishes an act already presumed to belong to the "past," Wallas is not an aberrant, gratuitous intruder into a plot lacking in dynamic development. He is, in
the truest sense, and although he never entirely realizes it himself, the protagonist in a drama of profound, if parodied,
tragic irony.

The story of Wallas in *The Erasers* is a modern version of
the tragedy of Oedipus. From its epigraph taken from Sophocles' *Oedipus Rex* (which Robbe-Grillet slightly rewords to
read, "Time, which watches over everything, has brought
about the solution in spite of you"), through its prologue, five

acts, and epilogue crowded with more or less hidden references to the Greek legend, its use of authorial "choruses," to the foredoomed outcome in which the man who has sworn to uncover a murderer finds that he himself is the criminal, *The Erasers* owes its form and content in large measure to this powerful ancient story.

Not only is there the ironic surface parody of one whose role is to solve problems (the *Petit Larousse* states that "the name of Oedipus has passed into the language to designate those who can solve enigmas and obscure questions") but who "solves" it only through executing the victim whose murderer he seeks to detect. There is a much deeper image of man's condition, in which the ancient origins of Oedipus as a solar myth of day and night combine with the Freudian doctrine of the Oedipus complex to enable the novel to produce in the reader that singular and "profound shakeup" of which Jean Cayrol wrote in his review of *The Erasers*. No less a writer than Gaston Bachelard has flatly declared that "a work of art can hardly derive its unity from anything other than a *complex*," adding that if the complex is missing, the work, cut off from its roots, can no longer communicate with the unconscious. *The Erasers*, like Robbe-Grillet's subsequent novels, follows this principle in its appeal to subconscious as well as conscious psychological demands.

The example of James Joyce's *Ulysses*, which manipulates (as T. S. Eliot wrote in "*Ulysses*, Order and Myth") a continuous correspondence "between contemporaneity and antiquity" through its parallel use of the *Odyssey* and events in the lives of Bloom-Ulysses and Stephen-Telemachus, may have influenced Robbe-Grillet in his choice of a classic legend with mythic or archetypal overtones. The circular nature of the action chosen in *The Erasers*, as well as the deep unconscious significance of the Oedipal situation, may in turn be related to the cyclic and mythic structure of *Finnegans Wake*. At any rate, Joyce is one of few modern authors (with Faulkner, Kafka, Raymond Roussel and one or two others) to whom Robbe-Grillet is admittedly indebted.

Support for the inherent relevance of such a theme as that of Oedipus to the plot function of a novel like *The Erasers* may also be found in the ideas expressed by W. H. Auden in his article "The Guilty Vicarage." Defending the serious underlying aesthetic and psychological bases of the detective novel, Auden identified its common properties with Greek tragedy: concealment, peripetia or reversal, manifestation or recognition, and catharsis. Auden points out that "in Greek tragedy the audience knows the truth; the actors do not, but discover or bring to pass the inevitable"; such a statement might serve as a motto for *The Erasers*. Normally, in the detective story, the audience is left ignorant of the truth to the end; in *The Erasers*, the audience is at once aware of the truth (Dupont is alive) and ignorant of it (Wallas will kill him). The protagonist knows neither the true present nor the true future, but brings to pass what is inevitable.

Allusions to Oedipus and to Sophocles' *Oedipus Rex* in *The Erasers* form too extensive a network to be discussed exhaustively; only the most important will be studied. One of these is an elaborate development of the riddle of the Sphinx. After an initial but fragmentary statement in the prologue, this *devinette*, propounded by the drunkard ("l'ivrogne-Sphinx," who also suggests Tiresias), returns in an expansion of ambiguous variations:

"What is the animal that is parricidal in the morning, incestuous at noon, and blind at evening?" [. . .]

"Well," the drunkard insists, "can't you guess? It's not so difficult: parricidal in the morning, blind at noon. . . . No. . . . Blind in the morning, incestuous at noon, and parricidal at evening. Eh? What animal is it? [. . .] Hey, pal! Deaf at noon and blind at evening?" [P. 234]

It is the version "blind in the morning, incestuous at noon, and parricidal in the evening" that best fits Wallas' case, since he is blind to the truth as he starts his investigation, covets his stepmother (and perhaps, sister) Evelyne at midday, and slays his "father" Dupont as night falls. The Egyptian Sphinx itself appears briefly in the shifting configuration of pieces of floating débris on the surface of a canal; corks and pieces of wood form "a mythical animal: with its head, neck, breast and forefeet, a lion's body with its great tail, and eagle's wings" (p. 37).

The abandonment of Oedipus in childhood (Wallas evidently suffered a similar fate) appears in the motifs embroidered on the curtains of the windows Wallas passes: "beneath a tree two shepherds in ancient costumes are holding a little naked child to suckle an ewe" (p. 40). Wallas even muses upon the "unsanitary" aspects of the early feeding of his unrecognized mythic prototype (p. 98). The theme of the abandoned or bastard child is gradually linked with the emerging memory of Wallas' childhood visit to this city (cf. pp. 36, 49, 126–127, and 231), to see a "relative." Paralleling this is the alternative "bastard son" theory of Dupont's murder advanced by Laurent's assistant.

The chariot in which Oedipus' father Laius was slain on the road to Corinth (cf. the "rue de Corinthe"), allegedly by a band of thieves (Bona's "bande" of terrorist assassins), stands on the Place de la Préfecture, unrecognized by Wallas:

In the middle of the square, on a low base protected by an iron fence, stands a group sculptured in bronze representing a Greek chariot pulled by two horses. In the chariot a number of persons, probably symbolic, are installed. Their unnatural pose hardly corresponds to the ostensible speed of the vehicle's movement. [P. 62]

Passing the statue later, Wallas notes the inscription: "Le Char de l'Etat—V. Daulis, sculpteur" (p. 75), a name containing an anagram of Laius. In a streetcar, Wallas overhears two women discussing an event in the manner in which "common people like to comment on the glorious episodes in the lives of important criminals and kings"; their remarks contain hidden references to Laius' chariot, to the prophecy of the oracle at Delphi that led to Oedipus' flight from Corinth, and to the danger of his unwitting encounter with his father (pp. 119–120). Apollo, as the patron of oracle and prophecy, fits into a number of references. There is, on the mantelpiece in front of Garinati's mirror (Garinati himself is a *sosie* or mirror image of Wallas), a statuette of "a handsome wrestler about to crush a lizard" (a theme of classic Apollo statuary), whose position relative to that of another statuette of an "old blind man led by a child" (Oedipus led by Antigone after his blinding) is subject to rearrangement and mirrored doubling (p. 209). When the drunkard engages in a lengthy argument over the meaning of the word "oblique" (pp. 224–226), the references to oblique and straight lines are related both to Garinati's "ligne droite" preoccupations as he mounts the steps to kill Dupont (pp. 13–15) and to the term *oblique* applied in classical references to Apollo (*loxias*), because of the "obliqueness" of his oracles.

Oracles, prophecy, and fortune telling are found in many allusions ignored by the protagonist and perhaps also by the reader. A newspaper headline, among others, reads "The fortune teller deceived her clients" (p. 54); the main post office becomes a sort of temple of messages, a site of "multiple rituals, mostly incomprehensible," and "sibylline writings" (p. 184). The railway station is transformed into the abode of an undecipherable and terrifying oracle (p. 200). Nor is the oracular theme limited to classic parallels. The name of Jean *Bonaventure* (in French "la bonne aventure" refers to prediction of the future) suggests cards, and is thus related to perhaps the most hidden of all references in *The Erasers*, those to the tarot pack. The tarot, whose images go back to medieval and earlier allegories, some uninterpretable (and whose "hanged man" card furnished a well-known passage in Eliot's

Waste Land), includes twenty-two trumps or major arcana, twenty-one of which are numbered and one, the Fool, not numbered (the Fool is dressed as a king's jester, with cap and bells). We read, as Garinati ascends the stairs to Dupont's study:

> The stairway consists of twenty-one wooden treads, plus, at the bottom, one step of white stone, noticeably wider than the others, and whose rounded extension supports a copper column bearing complicated ornamentations, surmounted by a rounded top in the form of a jester's head with its three-belled cap. [. . .]
>
> Above the sixteenth step, a small picture hangs on the wall, at eye level. It is a landscape in romantic style depicting a stormy night: lightning illuminates the ruins of a tower, at the foot of which may be distinguished two men lying down, despite the fury of the storm; or have they been struck by lightning? Perhaps they have fallen from the tower. [. . .] The image has the look of great antiquity. [P. 24]

If the twenty-one wooden steps and the single stone step might appear coincidental, the figure of the Fool removes all doubt as to the intended parallel. The description of the picture over the sixteenth step, corresponding to the sixteenth trump card called *La Maison Dieu*, is equally conclusive. Moreover, far from representing a gratuitous insertion, the tarot themes are carefully integrated into the novel. That the Fool trump (normally considered as number twenty-two) is, so to speak, at the bottom of the row (since its counterpart, the white step, is at the foot of the stairs), means that this card must be interpreted, in fortune-telling parlance, as being "renversée." Here is the interpretation given by a current tarot manual: "The Fool [. . .] *Upside down:* Since the Fool is a character normally shown in the act of walking, this means that he has fallen or been stopped in the act."[7] Now, precisely as Garinati

---

7. Passages on the tarot are taken from an anonymous work, *L'Ancien Tarot de Marseilles* (Paris: Grimaud, n.d.), pp. 55 and 40.

steps toward the blank stone step that represents the Fool reversed, there occurs the first example of the "frozen scene" or
stopped action to be found in Robbe-Grillet's works.[8] Garinati, the "character in the act of walking," is suddenly immobilized during a miniature instant of eternity:

The stairway of this house consists of twenty-one steps, the
shortest path from one point to another. [. . .]
Suddenly [. . .] against this background determined by law,
without an inch of ground to the right or to the left, without one
second's delay, without pause, without a backward glance, the
actor suddenly stops, in the middle of a sentence. [. . .] He
knows by heart the role he plays each evening, but tonight he refuses to continue.
All around him the other characters freeze, with lifted arm or
half-bent knee. The measure started by the musicians is eternally
prolonged. [. . .] Something would have to be done now; words
should be uttered, words not found in any script. [. . .] But, as
happens every evening, the sentence that had been begun is completed, in its foreordained form, the arm falls back, the knee completes its movement. In the pit, the orchestra plays on with its
usual vigor.
The stairway consists of twenty-one steps [. . .] plus [. . .]
one step of white stone. [Pp. 23–24]

Similarly, the conventional meaning of trump card number
sixteen, *La Maison Dieu*, fits the author's designs through its
general relevance to the Oedipus story. The tarot manual
states: "La Maison Dieu [. . .] *Abstract meaning:* Fictional
constructions of man's desires, which he thinks he is building
soundly and which the very flame of his desire devours, thus

The tarot cards are described in detail in many works; cf. Kurt Selig-
mann's *History of Magic* (New York: Pantheon, 1948), pp. 226 ff.
8. Robbe-Grillet's obsession with stopped action was pointed out in
his early critical essays (see Chapter 1), and will be amply illustrated
throughout this study. Cf. also Wylie Sypher's comments in *Rococo
to Cubism in Art and Literature* (New York: Random House, 1960).

bringing about his downfall. *Practical meaning:* Project brutally brought to a halt. Always means *coup de théâtre,* unexpected shock" (p. 40). When Wallas later sees the picture over the sixteenth step (as he ascends to play Garinati's role), one of the two men depicted takes on a definite aspect of royalty (Laius the king): "One is wearing royal garb, and his golden crown shines in the grass beside him" (p. 235).

Among the Oedipus images and correspondences in *Les Gommes,* the temples and ruins of Thebes play a crucial part. Glimpsed first as the sketch in the stationery store window, Thebes, the "lost city" in which the drama we are witnessing originally unfolded, has, as it were, emerged from the streets and canals of the Nordic city that is its counterpart:

A store dummy [. . .] is shown busily working at his easel. [. . .] He is putting the last touches on a charcoal landscape sketch of great finesse—which in reality must be a copy of some masterwork. It is a hillside on which, in the middle of cypress trees, stand the ruins of a Greek temple; [. . .] in the distance, down in the valley, appears an entire city with its triumphal arches and its palaces—executed, despite the distance and the mass of buildings, with a rare concern for detail. But in front of the man, instead of the Hellenic countryside, there is set up as background an enormous photographic print of a street intersection in a twentieth-century city. [. . .] Suddenly, Wallas recognizes the spot: [. . .] it is a private house on the corner of the Rue des Arpenteurs. [P. 131]

Wallas in a flashback later reverses this scene, inverting the relation of original to copy. The dummy painter now stands before the ruins of Thebes, and his drawing or picture undergoes a remarkable metamorphosis into a photograph:

The ruins of Thebes.
On a hillside overlooking the city, a Sunday painter has set up his easel, in the shade of the cypresses, among the scattered stumps of broken columns. He is painting carefully, looking constantly at his model; with a very fine brush he reproduces many details al-

most imperceptible to the naked eye, but which take on, when transfered to the picture, a surprising intensity. He must have singularly keen vision. One could count the stones that form the edge of the quay, the bricks of the gables, even the slates of the roof. At the corner of the iron fence, the leaves of the spindle tree shine in the sun, which outlines their form. Behind, a bush extends above the hedge, a leafless bush each of whose small branches is marked by a brilliant line on the sunny side and a black line on the shadow side. The photograph was taken in winter, on an exceptionally clear day. What reason could the young woman have had to photograph this house? [. . .]

She cannot have been its occupant before Dupont. [. . .] His wife? [. . .] At least fifteen years younger than her husband [. . .], a brunette with black eyes. [. . .] That is who she is! [. . .]

He [Wallas] again follows the arrow pointing in the direction of the "Victor Hugo" stationery store. [Pp. 177–178]

An effort at mental deduction on the part of Wallas, related to the hidden problem of the protagonist's identity and his relation to the woman who may be his stepmother and sister, is here objectified; out of his solarized fantasy on the reciprocal relations between Thebes and the modern city, Wallas emerges aware at least that Evelyne must be Dupont's ex-wife.

Finally, as Wallas approaches the act which will climax his Oedipal destiny, the protagonist senses dimly that he is, or has been, an actor in some ancient drama (the theme of the actor had already been stated in one of the Garinati passages cited earlier). A new effort at self-recognition, again objectified in terms of a Theban background, leads to another partial discovery: Wallas realizes now that the "relative" his mother had brought him to this city to visit was in fact his father:

The scene takes place [. . .] in a rectangular square in back of which is a temple (or a theatre, or something of that kind). [. . .] Wallas cannot remember the source of this picture. He is speaking [. . .] with various characters. [. . .] He himself is playing a specific part, probably one of great importance [. . .]. The memory suddenly becomes very sharp: for a fraction of a second, the whole scene takes on an extraordinary density. But what scene? He has just caught himself saying:

"And did all that happen a long time ago? [. . .]"

Wallas and his mother had at last reached this canal. [. . .] It was not a female relative they were looking for: it was a male relative, one that he had not known. [. . .] It was his father. How could he have forgotten that? [Pp. 238–239]

Each of the three visions of Thebes leads in the direction of discovery. At the first, in Evelyne's shop, Wallas almost recalls the name of the *gomme* he seeks (cf. p. 63, below); at the second, he realizes Evelyne's identity (at least, in part); and at the third, he correctly identifies as his father the "relative" living in this city. Where an author using traditional techniques of psychological analysis might have described tortuous mental processes, Robbe-Grillet presents the mental content of his protagonist in visual, mythic objective correlatives that are at once (since they speak to our unconscious) beautiful and profoundly moving.

At several points, the name of Oedipus itself almost breaks through to the surface of the text, or of Wallas' consciousness. Just as the name "Laius" was hidden in "Daulis," so the name *Oedipe* would seem to be the "mot illisible" in the letter to André VS "mistakenly" handed to Wallas at the post office— the word he deciphers variously as "ellipse," "éclipse," "échope," or even "idem" (p. 160), all words suggestive of indirect destiny, death, "picturalization," and identity. The literal meaning of the name Oedipus ("swollen foot") is hinted at when Wallas' legs begin to swell from too much walking (p. 217), and is mentioned openly when, after he has murdered Dupont, Wallas observes that "his feet are swollen" (p. 253).

But it is the *gomme* that Wallas constantly seeks which has the most interesting rapport with the name Oedipus, for the

name imprinted on this soft rubber cube cannot be other than
"Oedipe." Since this *gomme* has come to represent among
many critics the isolated or detached Robbegrilletian "thing"
par excellence, the exemplar of the objectal, concrete objects
whose meticulous geometrical description is one of the author's main specialties, it becomes important to know why the
gum eraser should have this name of Oedipus, and what the
function of such an object is within the analogical matrix of
the Oedipus myth in the novel.

If there is a dichotomy in *The Erasers*, then just as Descartes
in his metaphysics of duality (thought and matter) found it
necessary to establish a point of contact between the spiritual
and the material at the pineal gland of the human brain, so
Robbe-Grillet may be said to connect his two worlds (that
of Oedipus plot structure on one hand, and of existentialist,
chosiste background or texture, on the other) at the point
represented by Wallas' *gomme*.

"I would like a gum eraser," says Wallas.
"Yes, what kind?"
But that is the whole problem. Wallas again tries to describe
what he is looking for: a soft, light, friable gum eraser, which
rubbing does not make misshapen but merely reduces to powder;
a gum eraser which breaks easily and whose broken surfaces are
smooth and shiny, like the inside of a pearly shell. He saw one
[. . .] at a friend's house. [. . .] It was a yellowish cube, about
an inch on each side, with its edges slightly rounded—perhaps
through use. The maker's name was printed on one side, but was
too rubbed off to be still legible: only the two middle letters "di"
were decipherable; there must have been at least two letters before and two after. [P. 132]

Oe-di-pe, of course.[9] But apart from its name, in its irreducible,

9. Léon Roudiez' essay "The Embattled Myths," in *Heriditas*
(Austin: University of Texas Press, 1964), pp. 75–94, contains an alternative explanation of the possible name of Wallas' eraser. In studying the differences between the use of myth in Butor's *Time Passing*

stubborn, concrete mass of *thereness* this *gomme*, to an even greater extent than such objects as the door handle or chestnut tree root of Sartre's *Nausea*, exists neutrally, apart from man, in the nonhuman world of things that hear no appeal from man and make no signs back to him. The *gomme* contains no mystic correspondences *à la* Baudelaire; it is not a symbol.

Yet man, in Robbe-Grillet's system, makes of such objects the *supports* of his passions and thoughts; they become, not metaphoric talismans, but living embodiments of his emotions. Thus each attempt made by Wallas to find such a *gomme* is accompanied by passage of an erotic nature, directed at the woman in the shop; these become intensified in the case of Evelyne and constitute an objective correlative for the important incest motif. (Even Roland Barthes, who refuses to concede that Robbe-Grillet's objects have a "function," admits that the *gomme* is a "psychiatric object.")

The gum eraser has two further modes of existence in the novel. First, through a kind of functional analogy, the *gomme* represents the self-defeating quality inherent in Wallas-Oedipus: a cube of matter that contains the principle of its own

---

(*L'Emploi du temps*) and in Robbe-Grillet's *The Erasers*, Roudiez sees the latter novel as a demonstration of the uselessness, if not the impossibility, of modern man's nourishing himself on archetypes or myths inherited from the past; Wallas' gum eraser thus becomes a symbolic tool for erasing the continuity linking man to his humanistic past. For Roudiez, the syllable "di" could equally well be part of a commonplace trade name, such as "Di-di-er," thus turning to derision any reference to a mythic heritage. Roudiez takes, however, an unsympathetic view of the attitude he attributes to Robbe-Grillet, which he calls "erroneous [. . .] because it denies the idea of a meaningful permanence of myth in the contemporary world," preferring instead the views of Butor, who tries to show that modern man can learn to recognize that he can, like Jacques Revel in *Time Passing*, relive the myth of Theseus, for example, since "the labyrinth is in him [. . .] and the monster he kills, is his soul." Roudiez does not, moreover, offer any "commonplace" alternatives for the myriad other unmistakable allusions to Oedipus in *The Erasers*.

negation or annihilation in the idea of erasure.[10] As it performs its function, it destroys itself. Both tangibly (eroticism of the soft substance) and ideologically (parallelism with destructive destiny) the *gomme* becomes charged with projected feelings.

Finally, the *gomme* fits into the system of mutations, metamorphoses, doublings, and *décalages* of objects which Robbe-Grillet in all his novels has ceaselessly depicted. Although the *gomme* is not part of such an extensive image series as that formed by the figure-of-eight objects in *The Voyeur* (in which perhaps twenty different "things" are correlated among themselves and with the plot of the novel through their relation to the figure 8), the cube of gum rubber is placed in functional juxtaposition with another cube, the hard stone cube (a paperweight) that rests on Dupont's desk. It is Garinati, Wallas' "double," who first sees this cube: "A kind of cube, but slightly deformed, a shiny block of grey lava, with its surfaces polished as if by wear, with its edges blunted, compact, seemingly hard, as heavy as gold, about as big as a fist" (p. 26). Unmistakable similarities in phraseology prove the author's intention to equate these two materially opposite cubes (one "with its edges slightly rounded—perhaps through use," the other "slightly deformed [. . .] as if by wear, with its edges blunted"). The cube of Dupont (the father) is large, hard, nonfriable, suitable for protecting papers and their contents; that of Wallas (the son with the tragic flaw) is soft, flexible, suitable only for the erasure of writings or drawings,

10. On the metal *store* protecting the window of a left-bank *papeterie* in Paris, I saw the following advertisement: TOUT S'EFFACE DEVANT "LES GOMMES" MALLAT ("Everything is erased by 'The Erasers' made by Mallat"). Obviously, the quotation marks would normally be either omitted or placed around the brand name "Mallat." The literal appearance of "THE ERASERS" perfectly enclosed in quotation marks is an example, no doubt, of what the surrealists call "le hasard objectif," or objective chance. At any rate, Robbe-Grillet was fascinated when I showed him a snapshot of the sign.

and achieving its own destruction. When Wallas approaches Dupont's desk the hard cube undergoes a metamorphosis as it becomes a correlative or support for the deed Wallas is about to accomplish; it is seen now as a "cube of vitreous stone, with *sharp* edges, with *murderous* corners" (p. 236; italics mine). Moments later, Wallas kills his "father."

If, as Robbe-Grillet has stated, there are influences and exchanges, even—in a nonmystical sense—correspondences between matter, space, and time, then objects, in all their heaviness, surface, and geometry, in their existence as phenomena, may be at the same time reassuring and equivocal. They impose themselves at once on our perceptions, but only in order soon to become veiled in a halo, to become double, asymmetrically superimposed, subtly transformed. As they become the supports of man's passions, objects—like actions, gestures, words, and events—acquire multiple meanings.

The multivalent *gomme* illustrates how we may pass from the Oedipus fictional structure of the novel (which may itself be variously regarded as intellectual "intertextual" parody, mythic parallel, or psychiatric unifying principle) to its material texture of objects (aberrant, neutral, unstable, doubled, yet always linked by formal relationships into rows, pairs, or series).[11]

11. Only Samuel Beckett, according to Robbe-Grillet, noticed at once that *The Erasers* made extensive use of the Oedipus myth and of Sophocles' play *Oedipus Rex*. When the pamphlet *Les Gommes,* cited in note 5 above, appeared some time later, other critics mentioned Oedipus in connection with the novel. Most of the allusions brought out here were not noticed. Curiously, Roland Barthes, who does not mention Oedipus in writing of *The Erasers,* relates the belated discovery of Mathias' guilt in *The Voyeur,* through what Barthes terms the protagonist's "reconstructing consciousness," to the theme of Oedipus ("Littérature littérale," *Critique,* Sept.–Oct. 1955). No mention had been made prior to the appearance of the present study to the tarot references in *The Erasers.* For an examination of ways in which the tarot and the Oedipus allusions are brought together to

In the material universe of *The Erasers* we again discover Robbe-Grillet's debt to existentialism, and his extension of certain of its principles. In his world of objects, Robbe-Grillet is a neoexistentialist. Readers will recall those passages in Sartre's *Nausea* in which the hero Roquentin becomes acutely aware (to the point of nausea) of the *thing* quality of the stone on the beach, the ink bottle carton (a "parallélépipède"), the door handle, and the black chestnut tree root; they will also remember the "neutral" or "cleansed" objects of Camus' *The Stranger* (including the mother's coffin). Certainly such passages strongly influenced Robbe-Grillet, especially those of Sartre, with their geometric terminology and use of a phrase that has become almost a motto for Robbe-Grillet, the *"être-là"* of objects. But as Robbe-Grillet has pointed out, in his assessment of his relationship and debt to these authors included in the article "Nature, Humanism, Tragedy," the objects of Sartre and Camus are not completely existential or phenomenological, for they repose constantly on anthropomorphic metaphor—if not on moral self-projection—and imply a Nature linked to man to form a "tragi-fied" universe. Instead of freeing man, as existentialism is supposed to do, such a view actually binds him to the old trammels of humanism: the recuperation of human misery, oneness with Nature, even salvation through separation and tragic division.

Unlike the objects of Sartre and Camus, those of Robbe-Grillet, despite their role as correlatives and their formal interrelationships, never express an inherent or metaphysical bond between Nature and man. Nor are they, like the objects of Francis Ponge, conceived of as having "personalities" that the writer cunningly expresses. While critics have admitted that *things* in Robbe-Grillet are not, like Baudelaire's perfumes,

---

reinforce each other in the novel, see the letters sent me by the surrealist film maker and critic Jacques Brunius, quoted and discussed in my article "Games and Game Structures in Robbe-Grillet," *Yale French Studies*, No. 41, 1968, pp. 159–167.

mystically tied to man in secret correspondences, these critics have often failed to grasp that Robbe-Grillet's objects are not artificially invented symbols, either. In a conventional literary symbol (Mallarmé's cigar smoke as man's soul, for example), the process of symbolization involves recognition of an intellectual analogy of form and function. For Robbe-Grillet, an object may convey passions or other aspects of man's existence for the sole reason that man can only exist through his *perception of objects*. Without images and objects to support his thoughts and feelings, man in Robbe-Grillet's view could not think, feel, or even exist, at all.

The specific techniques of object descriptions in *The Erasers* warrant discussion. One is struck first by the accumulation of spatial, formal, and geometric terms, and by the precision of the localization of objects ("the chair at a distance of 30 centimeters"). The terms employed in *The Erasers* include "straight line," "obtuse angle," "square," "cubical," "transversal," "rectilinear," "acute angle," "segment," "bevelled," "spiral," "a ninety-degree bend," "ruled in squares," and others, most of which will be found again in later novels, with many additions. It is obvious that this "Robbe-Grillet style" corresponds not only to the author's predilection for objective, precise language but also to certain ontological principles he has expressed. The "visual" geometric vocabulary serves effectively to "decondition" the objects described, to remove them from the affective network of terms usually employed to depict them, to render them "accessible." At times this semantic device is closely linked to the implied psychology of the protagonist, as we shall see in the case of *Jealousy*.

The minute descriptions of Robbe-Grillet sometimes suggest *trompe-l'oeil* painting, "magic realism," or photography. Each of these analogies, however, would falsify or ignore the generic differences that always separate visual or pictorial representations from verbal descriptions. It is not the visual image that the mind may form in reading such passages as the following, but the verbal reality, the pattern of words and phrases, that is important. (One proof of this essential distinction between a mental picture and a piece of writing is that no one, confronted with a pictorialization of the following— even by such a master "magic realist" as Roy—could possibly recreate from the picture, independently, the actual phrases used by Robbe-Grillet—or he would be Robbe-Grillet himself!) We are in the automatic restaurant, where Wallas finds on his plate:

A quarter portion of tomato truly without defect, cut by machine from a perfectly symmetrical fruit.

The flesh around the periphery, compact and uniform, of a fine chemical redness, is of constant thickness, between a band of shiny skin and the cell wherein the seeds lies in a row, yellow, equally sized, held in place by a thin layer of yellowish jelly, beside a swelling of the center. This latter, of a slightly granulous faded pink, originates, alongside a lower depression, in a network of white veins, one of which extends towards the seeds—in, perhaps, a somewhat uncertain pattern.

At the very top, a scarcely visible accident has occurred: one corner of skin, separated from the flesh for a millimeter or two, projects into space imperceptibly. [P. 161]

Such a virtuoso passage is not, however, a mere still life; it is more than an "objectal" exercise in literary materialization. For the author makes his object function to support the mental and emotional life of his character. A theme of uncertainty runs through all this precision; not only is Wallas' perplexity embodied therein, but his protagonist's defect, his tragic flaw, the fatal error he makes (all reflected elsewhere in such incidental phrases as "a little space for error," "the slightest fault," "a tragic error") are evoked, as well as his absurd lack of "one single centimeter" of forehead area: "the only lack was this ridiculous space."

By such devices as syncopation and doubling, Robbe-Grillet not only links objects and their arrangements with the mental content of his characters, but also relates objects to each other. Consider the modes of relationship used to reinforce the theme of *reflections* (a principle so important to Robbe-Grillet that he has written a set of "Three Reflected Visions"). Formally paralleling the novel structure as a reflection of myth or tragic plot, reflections appear first in several mirror passages. As the café proprietor stands before the aquariumlike mirror of his bar, we read:

Above the bar, the long mirror with its sickly reflection, the proprietor [. . .] liverish and greasy in his aquarium. [. . .] In the mirror, already almost decomposed, the reflection of this phantom trembles; and beyond, more and more uncertainly, the indefinite litany of shadowy images: the proprietor, the proprietor, the proprietor. [Pp. 11–12]

This "reflected vision," obviously a correlative of the character's musing over lost memories, is paralleled by Garinati's shifting of an object series before his mirror, as he seeks to sort out his own uncertainties (p. 209). But Robbe-Grillet does not limit reduplication, superposition, and *décalage* to a "litany" of mirror reflections. As police chief Laurent toils mentally to disentangle the confused threads of the case, his fingers in their motion, exceeding the speed at which the eye can stop action, create a virtual volume expressive of an entropic chaos of analytical dizziness:

Eight fat, short fingers rub delicately up and down against each other, the backs of the right hand fingers against the inside surfaces of the four left hand ones.
The left thumb caresses the thumb nail of the right one, gently at first, then pressing harder and harder. The other fingers change position, the backs of the left hand ones rubbing the inside of the four right hand fingers, vigorously. They interlock, become entangled, twisting and turning; the motion accelerates, grows more complicated, becomes gradually irregular and confused to the point that nothing can any longer be distinguished in the swarming movement of fingers and palms. [P. 235]

When Doctor Juard fearfully awaits Wallas at the train station, visual reflections and displacements are transmuted into their auditory counterpart of *reverberations*. These are progressively syncopated as they embody the increasing tensions of the character who perceives them:

An enormous voice fills the hall. Falling from invisible loud speakers, it collides in every direction against the walls covered with notices and advertising signs, which amplify it further, cause it to ricochet, multiply it, adorn it with a cortege of resonances and echoes, more or less out of phase, in which the original message is lost—transformed into a gigantic oracle, magnificent, undecipherable, and terrifying. [P. 208]

Finally, words and phrases begin, in moments of anxiety, to come apart, to rearrange themselves radically. The telephone conversation between Laurent and the café owner (reported quite "normally" earlier) is recalled by the latter, who senses in it danger and persecution. The verbal disintegration and recombination convey a sort of paranoid seizure:

. . . And why did that man from the police department want to speak to him, last evening?
"I am the proprietor."
"Oh, so it's you! You are the one who told an inspector that stupid story about a so-called son of Professor Dupont?"
"I didn't tell any story . . ."

. . . . .

"Are you the one who told that stupid story, or is it the proprietor?"
"I am the proprietor."
"So it's you, young man stupid story, professor behind the counter?"
"I am the proprietor."
"Very well. I would like abundantly son, a long time ago, young woman alleged to have died mysteriously . . ."
"I am the proprietor. I am the proprietor. It's me. It's me. I am the proprietor . . . the proprietor . . . the proprietor . . ." [Pp. 263–264]

Thus verbal patterns become verbal echoes, rebounding, re-combining, transmuted into distorted reciprocity, until an identical phrase ("the proprietor . . . the proprietor . . . the proprietor") repeats and *reflects* a visual mirror image of 250 pages earlier, at the start of the work.

Above all, its formalized universe of objects, related through specific "serial" analogies and functioning as supports for characters' thoughts and emotions, is what distinguishes *The Erasers* from an ingenious parody of the detective novel in the style of Simenon or Graham Greene. The atmosphere is often, in fact, very Simenonesque: the aquarium metaphor of the bar mirror occurs, for example, in a typical Simenon passage (from *Maigret and the Headless Corpse*), in which similar mirrors are described in the same way: "In the bars, a greenish light made them [the mirrors] look like aquariums." Another seedy bar, with a similarly bizarre clientele, appears in Graham Greene's *Brighton Rock*, along with numerous other elements reminiscent of *The Erasers:* a weak individual who arrives in a city on a mission that subjects him to unforeseen but pre-determined movements; ambiguous and confused characters' names; an enigmatic, prophetic, or riddlelike formula, re-peated at significant moments in the plot; a gang leader with an Italian name; a professional man in the role of a terrified false witness (a lawyer in Greene's novel, a doctor in Robbe-Grillet's); unexplained, sinister references to the earlier death of a young woman (Molly, Pauline "the sweet"); posters and advertising signs (absurd and ridiculous in *Brighton Rock*, formally interesting and brought into the novel's structure in *The Erasers*); and even, in Greene's work, an "object" that is not only a tacit objective correlative (like the gum eraser or the paperweight of *The Erasers*) but also perhaps a murder weapon—the stick of rock candy called "Brighton Rock," which when broken always shows the same letters and is ex-plicitly identified by one of the characters in the novel as a symbol of human nature (an idea that is, of course, alien to Robbe-Grillet's thinking).

What did Robbe-Grillet learn from the writing of *The Erasers?* He appears to have discovered in composing his first novel that the mode of rotating or multiple viewpoints, involving the successive presentation of the contents of many characters' minds, had serious drawbacks. Such a technique corresponded, it is true, to ideas expressed at the time by Robbe-Grillet concerning the profusion of private viewpoints that make up the real or fictional world, itself a composite of limited, relativistic time and space frameworks. But the structure of *The Erasers* became, as a result, excessively diversified, and the unity of its conception seemed at times to become lost. Moreover, the apparently "omniscient" passages seemed to violate the relativistic principle of fictional perspective which Robbe-Grillet inherited from Sartre, even though the author saw them as formally justified by their correspondence to the choruses of Sophocles' play. From *The Voyeur* on, therefore, Robbe-Grillet brings fictional viewpoint increasingly closer to that of one protagonist, until the procedure, reaching its climax in *Jealousy*, undergoes new modifications by way of the innovative expansions of first-person narration in such novels as *La Maison de rendez-vous* and *Project for a Revolution in New York*. After *The Erasers*, Robbe-Grillet presents mental content almost exclusively through objectification, abandoning the conventional commentaries and Joycean interior monologues of his first work. The objective correlatives of the later novels are increasingly linked and organized in serial style. As for plot, it becomes for a time less complicated, less baroque, before branching out into the new plot forms of the most recent novels. In any case, Robbe-Grillet does not base another work entirely on a myth or specific model, as Sophocles' *Oedipus Rex*.

On the other hand, Robbe-Grillet retains and develops further a great number of techniques of structure and style already present in *The Erasers*. He continues to exploit circularity of plot, in which the return to an illusory point of departure will play an important role. He develops and strengthens techniques used in *The Erasers* to make novel time correspond to "human time," freed from clock time and unfolding in his own characteristic modes: repetitions, imaginary scenes, superimposed scenes, dissolves, interferences, displacements, false memories, objectified emotions, flashbacks, and—as Bernard Pingaud aptly dubbed them in writing of *Last Year at Marienbad*—"flash-forwards." Despite his antipsychological posture, Robbe-Grillet continues to use themes deeply rooted in personal obsessions and complexes: crime, passion, eroticism, sadism, jealousy, alienation, morbid suggestibility, murder, anguish. All these themes and motifs find expression in the fictional world through manipulation of ostensibly neutral objects. But objects, according to the existentialist phenomenology that guided, and still guides to a large extent, the authors of the "new novel" such as Robbe-Grillet, are the only means by which man may accede to consciousness, thought, emotion, and—even—action.

3 Mathias or the Double Eye: The Voyeur (1955)

Authentic shots of "real" reality are the most subjective of all. Everything that the protagonist sees through his "camera eye" expresses his own personality.

BELA BALAZS, *Theory of the Film*

If a number of avant-garde critics hailed the publication of *The Erasers* in 1953 as the beginning of a new "objective literature," it was not until *The Voyeur* appeared two years later that a veritable deluge of theoretical speculations poured forth on the evolution of the contemporary novel, giving rise to a multiplicity of terms, such as the novel of presence, the novel of refusal, the anti-novel, the objective novel, the phenomenological novel, the novel of *being-there* (*être-là*, or *Dasein*), the novel of "New Realism," and finally, the *Nouveau Roman* or New Novel.

The critics' insistence on such groupings into schools or movements, under the banner of some aesthetic principle (symbolism, cubism, new novel, or whatever), often leads to the creation of a "school" which does not exist, causing confusion by substituting for the analytical reading of works the search for abstract doctrines or theories. In truth, only disparate works and individual conceptions exist, and no doubt the golden rule of literary criticism is to "bien lire," as Etiemble says, to read them correctly. Otherwise one may become lost in the maze of a word game of doctrinal abstractions.

What is attempted here is, then, to examine closely the text of *The Voyeur* in order to arrive at a general view of the work that will avoid, as far as possible, the errors of previous criticism. In addition, a clarification of the intentions of the author, both avowed and unavowed, will be proposed.

Every artist, every writer—according to André Malraux—begins by imitating another, before "wresting" from this preliminary, borrowed style the elements corresponding to his own genius and adaptable to his personal style. Without going back to the possible origins of Robbe-Grillet's earliest style (in Kafka, Raymond Roussel, Greene, even Simenon), it is obvious that the majority of the techniques of *The Voyeur* are an extension of procedures already used, or adumbrated, in *The Erasers*. If the tone and atmosphere of *The Voyeur* seem new and different, the explanation lies in the special background—an island bathed in light—and in the highly original use of viewpoint, which, instead of being multiple (as in *The Erasers*), is "dual," and to the incorporation of an implicit unifying psychological principle, as will be seen later.

Such an analysis requires a summary of the novel. Despite the many difficulties caused by an ambiguous narrative mode, by flashbacks, anticipations, and "false scenes" (without reference as yet to the objective correlatives and the figure-of-eight structures of the novel), it is possible to restate, omitting only minor details, the events of the plot. Here, schematically, is how the story goes:

Mathias, a traveling salesman who, after several failures in other enterprises, has started selling wristwatches, arrives by boat on an island located some three hours' voyage from the continent. There are indications that he was born there, though he has not been back since childhood (a situation similar to that of Wallas in *The Erasers*).

During the landing, which is described both impersonally and from a viewpoint that sometimes merges with that of

Mathias himself, various significant elements are introduced: a piece of rope twisted into the shape of an eight, a young girl leaning against a pillar on the boat as if she were tied to it, a blue cigarette pack floating in the water, the eight-shaped mark left by an iron ring on the side of the wharf, seagulls with "inexpressive" eyes wheeling in the sky, Mathias' fingernails, which are excessively long. Meanwhile, Mathias, the hero, goes through mental calculations: he has six hours, if he leaves by the evening boat, to sell ninety wristwatches. He tries to work out the average time he can allow for each sale, the quickest way to approach his clients. Hypothetical scenes of unsuccessful attempts to sell his wares (which will later appear, with variations, as real scenes) are incorporated into a text that remains ostensibly in the third person, creating the first hallucinatory perspectives opening into Mathias' mind—visions in whose center the reader places himself, first as a disoriented *observer,* and later, despite the persistence of a certain "aesthetic distance," as a *participant.*

Arriving at the town's central square, whose façades and stone statue have the obsessional aspect of a Chirico painting, Mathias walks by a movie poster showing a scene of violence—a man strangling a young girl who is kneeling near a doll that has been torn apart. Mathias had already, on the boat, remembered seeing a similar scene through a window, in a deserted street, before the dawn departure of the boat.

Mathias rents a bicycle from an enigmatic tradesman. Before setting out around the island, he tries in vain to sell his watches to the drinkers in the café near the port and in several nearby houses. Losing his way in a dark corridor, he comes upon an empty bedroom whose contents seem curiously disturbing: a bed in disorder, a picture representing a young girl kneeling, a black and white tile floor.

Taking his bicycle, Mathias rides to the edge of a cliff and dismounts to look at the sea. A large wave "slaps" the rocks, and the sound evokes in Mathias a series of violent images: a young girl stretched out on a bed in disorder, followed by the details of a crime as related in a newspaper clipping that he carries in his wallet. As he reconstructs the crime, Mathias elaborates on the bedroom scene that he saw in the early morning—an attempt by a large, burly man to rape a young girl.

Recovering from his erotic-sadistic revery, Mathias hastily sets forth on his bicycle. His first stop is an isolated house located outside of town, beside a road that leads to the large lighthouse, at the far end of the island. There, the imaginary scene of attempting to sell a watch, that he had envisioned during the disembarkment, is repeated in reality; but he had not foreseen the main feature—a photograph, on the mantelpiece, of a young girl leaning against a tree. Mathias' latent erotic sadism manifests itself when, in talking with the mother, he transforms the daughter's name, Jacqueline, into Violette (possibly the name of the victim in the clipping?) and when he suddenly *sees* the girl tied to the tree in the midst of flaming shrubs. The woman says that her daughter is out watching some sheep at the edge of a cliff, in a secluded spot. Mathias replies that he will not see her, since he intends to continue on to the lighthouse, unless of course he leaves the road at the next crossing to make a detour to the farm belonging to the Mareks, whom he has known since childhood. But when he reaches the spot where the roads cross, he turns his bicycle into the path leading to the cliff, and lets it roll down toward the sea.

When the text resumes, after a blank page separating the first and second parts, Mathias is back at the crossroads, leaning down to examine the body of a crushed toad. Madame Marek suddenly appears, returning from the settlement near the lighthouse. Mathias immediately begins to invent an account (whose "reality" the reader cannot yet judge) of actions calculated to fill in the "blank" hour between his first arrival at the crossroads and his return to the same spot. In a sort of indirect discourse that the text treats at the level of "reality," a continuous and plausible sequence of events is developed. Guided in part by Madame Marek's replies to his assertions, Mathias relates in detail a visit to her farm, where, he says, he saw no one. The episode becomes more and more suspicious and confused as Mathias enlarges his account, and the reader begins to feel that the protagonist is obeying an imperious need to hide an unnamed guilt. Finally disentangling himself from his recital of events (whose falsity the reader can only as yet vaguely suspect), Mathias sells Madame Marek a watch and goes on his way. He manages to sell two others at houses down the road, thanks to his now practised sales technique, treated in a nightmare style of obsessive repetitions.

Arriving at the café of the village near the lighthouse, Mathias is stunned to find that the proprietress already knows his name. He is told that Jacqueline's sister had come ahead of him (how could their paths have crossed without her seeing him?) to report Jacqueline's disappearance. Mathias gives an incoherent account of his itinerary from Jacqueline's house, skirting outright contradictions in his report. The reader's uneasiness begins to assume more definite form; it must have to do with some action involving Jacqueline, one that Mathias tries desperately to suppress. But what action?

An unknown sailor comes up to Mathias in the café-restaurant and greets him as an old friend. His name is either Pierre or Jean Robin. But "Jean Robin" is the very name Mathias had invented as an island acquaintance while trying to make one of his sales in town; now this man whom he thought to be imaginary appears before him, even insisting on taking him along for lunch in his cabin. The woman living with him seems as terrified as the one glimpsed earlier in the mysterious bedroom with crimson curtains. "Jean Robin" speaks at great length of Jacqueline. Here the text becomes extremely complicated—a mixture of transposed memories, objectified lies, evasions, and anticipations—in a mood of growing panic that overcomes Mathias and, with him, the reader.

Managing at last to take leave of "Jean Robin," Mathias returns to the port. But not without difficulties: the chain comes loose on his bicycle; time grows short; the boat whistle sounds. The tradesman is away and he cannot turn in the bicycle. When he reaches the quay, the boat is pulling out. Mathias cannot leave the island. His hand feels for the cord in the pocket. Are there, he asks himself, any police on the island?

The movie poster by the garage has now changed: a different film is posted, "Monsieur X on the Double Track." The traveler rents a room for the three days that he must wait until the next boat leaves. The room merges with memories of his childhood bedroom, and Mathias looks in one of the bureau drawers for the box in which he used to keep his collection of strings and cords.

Next morning, the news of Jacqueline's death spreads. Her body has been found at the foot of the cliff: did she fall, or was she pushed? Snatches of talk among the sailors hint at murder. The smoke from Mathias' cigarette curls up in the form of an eight; he recalls throwing away three cigarette butts at the cliff. He goes to find them. As he is searching through the grass, the young woman from "Pierre" or "Jean" Robin's cabin appears. She claims that "Pierre" is the assassin; her proof is the cigarette butt she holds in her hand, of the same brand that "Pierre" (and, the reader knows, Mathias) smokes. Mathias seizes the "proof" from her, and she flees in terror. Mathias finds the second cigarette end, but not the third. Returning to the town café, Mathias again recounts his pretended visit to the Marek farm; it is now clear to the reader that he is inventing an alibi.

In order to change this "*contre-vérité*" or lie into mere anticipation, Mathias now visits the Marek farm. He enters noiselessly; in the hallway, he overhears a family argument: the

Mareks are accusing their stepson Julien of having killed Jacqueline. When Mathias steps into the room, the conversation stops. Once more, Mathias repeats his story: he had come to the farm yesterday before meeting Madame Marek at the crossroads. Unexpectedly, Julien, who has been staring at him steadily, confirms this imaginary visit, adding all sorts of confirming details which he claims he saw from a window while Mathias was in the courtyard. Confronted with this unforeseen and bold corroboration, Mathias succumbs to a violent migraine, excuses himself and leaves. On the road, he tries further to arrange the events of the day before in such a way as to fill in the "hole" in time, just at the hour when Jacqueline disappeared.

A new search at the cliff brings no further results: both the missing cigarette butt and the candy wrappers he remembers leaving there remain lost. But he does see, over the edge of the cliff, Jacqueline's sweater caught on a projecting rock; climbing down, he pulls it loose and throws it into the sea. When he gets back to the top, he sees Julien watching him curiously. In the ensuing conversation, it becomes obvious that Julien has "seen everything." The boy holds out a piece of rope identical to the one Mathias has lost. In a paroxysm of fear and anguish, Mathias stammers incoherently.

As if in a nightmare, he returns to the café by the lighthouse. There a peasant tells an island legend: each year, in the old days, a young girl was sacrificed to make the sea calm for travelers. Mathias, leaning on the counter, has a fainting spell: he sees himself as two persons, and two men walk between "Mathias and the traveler." He loses consciousness; when he comes to his senses, he is seated outside, in front of the café. He sets forth on foot.

In the darkness he again comes upon Jean Robin's house. Through the window he watches a mute scene in which his "friend" threatens the young woman. Is this an effect of his imagination? In any case, the lamp becomes the lamp in his rented bedroom, where he is now busy setting down in a notebook his false schedule of events for the preceding noon. He falls asleep, and dreams of that scene which has so often been told to him—his drawing the profile of a sea gull, on a rainy day, when he was a small child here on the island. In the morning, he takes out the newspaper clipping of the crime and destroys it by burning it slowly with his lighted cigarette, first making two burning holes like the loops of a figure of eight.

As his departure time approaches, Mathias tries frantically to suppress his anxiety. A scene of "frozen" or shifted actions objectifies his impatience to leave. Suddenly, the sight of the girl waitress—a timid and fearful girl, like all those who figure in Mathias' thoughts—provokes a "recapitulation" of what must have happened on the cliff: the torture, rape, and, no doubt, murder of Jacqueline, thrown by Mathias into the sea. The piece of stout cord had served to tie her first to stakes placed in the ground.

Finally, in a last scene involving the sale of a watch, which repeats mechanically the visual elements of similar preceding scenes, Mathias busies himself with his sample case, his wrist-watches, his notebook. With his long, pointed fingernail (Mathias, throughout the book, worries about his nails, promising himself that he will soon cut them), he indicates the time on the dial. Immediately the scene shifts to the quay, where the next boat is getting ready to leave. While waiting for it to set forth, Mathias recalls in great detail a complicated geometrical buoy lying outside the harbor. Its sides are covered with long threads of algae, forming vague, changing designs. Mathias thinks of the fact that in three hours, he will be on the mainland.

The Voyeur, like most of Robbe-Grillet's narratives, requires such a working summary as a point of departure in much the same way that a hermetic poem (one of Mallarmé's, for example) needs at least a tentative statement of its rational line or pattern before more detailed problems of structure or meaning can be dealt with. The fact that Robbe-Grillet has so often been accused of practising an exaggerated or even "baroque" formalism, producing works that are unintelligible or difficult to "understand," is another reason for schematizing the novel. Finally, the curious unwillingness of many critics to recognize or admit the presence in *The Voyeur* (as well as in most of Robbe-Grillet's works) of a well-defined story, involving a coherent psychological system (usually implicit, not expressed), makes it necessary to demonstrate that the formal aspects of the novel are attached to, and serve as supports for, a quite analyzable "plot."

The first important structural problem raised by *The Voyeur* is that of its narrative mode; how, exactly, may it be described? The absence of the pronoun "I," or of any other autoreference in the first person, would seem to imply that the mode is one of traditional third-person authorial "omniscience." But at once, as we read many scenes, it is obvious that the point of view—visual as well as psychological—is directly related to Mathias, and that the narrative third person functions here only as a more "objective" way of presenting his sensations and his interior world. Must one then conclude that even the apparently "real" passages, those in which we find no visions, emotions, or deformed perspectives, are also composed from Mathias' viewpoint? It might be tempting to believe, indeed, that the text represents, in its oscillations between the real and the imaginary, between the "true" and the "false," the double personality of a protagonist who goes back and forth from a normal state to an abnormal one, and there is reason to think that such a conception may have figured in the author's intentions. Nevertheless, two technical objections arise. First, the "optics" of the scenes are not always Mathias'; and, furthermore, the universe of the novel is described in stylized forms that emanate less from Mathias' presumed "personality" than from the author's coherent and systematic vision, revealed by such traits as vocabulary, sentence structure, verbal mannerisms, and other features of the author's style. That the deformations which this novelistic field undergoes occur as a function of the viewpoint of the protagonist cannot be denied; but the background against which he acts is always the author's world, not Mathias'.

The problem of viewpoint in *The Voyeur* has bothered many critics, especially those preoccupied with finding a satisfactory interpretation of the word *voyeur* (we will return to this question) as applied to Mathias. Most of them argued that the visual perspective of the novel is that of a *voyeur*-protagonist possessing exceptionally sharp vision, a retina on which "objects take on an extraordinary relief and intensity" (Emile Henriot). For these critics, Mathias is not only the *voyeur* of the title, but even a "*voyant*" (or "seer," a term usually applied to Arthur Rimbaud), as Pierre Gascar called him. One writer, André Dalmas, saw in the undifferentiated sight or glance of Mathias as *voyeur* the reason why the novel had no coherence, consisting only of disparate objects: "a rag falling to the ground, a streak on a floor tile, a gray pebble, the eye of a gull." In these theories, there would be no "objective" world in *The Voyeur* which Mathias could confront; on the contrary, everything in the novel would be rigorously reduced to an expression of his "*contenu mental*."

Let us look at several samples of the text. The action starts between two bursts of the boat's siren: "It was as if no one had heard anything." The first sound, an absent sound which imperceptibly states the motif of the "hole" in time, lies both outside the text and inside, in a classical first-word ("*It was*") use of the principle of beginning *in medias res*. Next comes a description of the passengers waiting rigidly, with fixed stares, their heads cocked in identical postures. Is this description made from Mathias' viewpoint? Hardly, since the reader not only *sees* Mathias before him, but also watches the scene at which Mathias is *not looking*, since he is depicted as standing motionless to one side looking down at the deck of the boat:

Slightly off to one side [. . .], a traveler remained *remote* from this scene. The siren had no more disturbed his *abstraction* than it had altered his neighbors' impatience to land. Standing straight like them, his body and limbs rigid, he *kept his eyes fixed on the deck*. [P. 9, italics supplied.][1]

The viewpoint here could scarcely be that of Mathias. In like fashion, throughout the text, the way in which the outside world is presented, when it is not being altered by the protagonist's distorting vision, corresponds little if at all to what we would expect from Mathias. It is rather the author's world which serves as point of departure for the protagonist, who is less the creator than the inhabitant of the novelistic universe. Let us examine another passage:

In an equal cadence despite slight variations in amplitude and rhythm—perceptible to the eye, but scarcely exceeding ten centimeters and two or three seconds—the sea rose and fell, in the far angle of the slip. [. . .] From time to time, at no doubt regular intervals, though of complex periodicity, a stronger surge would disrupt this swaying: two masses of liquid, one meeting the other, would collide with the sound of a slap, and drops of spume would splash a little higher against the side. [P. 15]

Except for the single word, "slap" (which is to play an important part in later passages), this whole scene materializes, outside Mathias, the novelistic field in which the protagonist is placed; it is not to be interpreted, as Bernard Dort would have us interpret the entire text of the novel, as a result of the "veritable *passion* of the glance" with which the main character is supposedly possessed. Passages like the above create the world in which Mathias attempts to orient himself, as various

1. Page references are to the 1955 edition of *Le Voyeur* (Paris; Minuit).

objects—all creations of the author—present themselves to his view:

Mathias tried to locate a reference point. In the angle of the slip, the water rose and fell. [. . .] Against the far vertical side wall, Mathias finally let his gaze come to rest on a mark shaped like a figure eight, outlined with sufficient precision to allow it to serve as a fixed reference. [Pp. 15–16]

It is Mathias who "chooses" (within the fictitious framework) the two tangential circles in the form of an eight that Robbe-Grillet, at quite a different level, has conceived and invented. This is, in my opinion, the only logical explanation of viewpoint in *The Voyeur*, consistent with all the details of the text. Elsewhere, in *Jealousy* for example, Robbe-Grillet transforms his protagonist into the creator, or rather the *only witness*, of the novelistic field; but in *The Voyeur*, the author —absent, impersonal, but possessing a special "vision" of the universe he creates—imposes his order on the world of the novel and its objects, only then turning it over to his central character. The latter, in turn, struggles with this "reality," projecting his emotive troubles upon it, changing it or attempting to bring about its destruction.[2]

2. The question of narrative mode in *The Voyeur* is typical of the difficulties raised in the modern novel by the presence of a more or less clear difference between the world in which the protagonist moves, and the vision which he, as direct or indirect narrator, has of this world. A film like *Doctor Caligari's Cabinet* provides a good illustration of the problem. It is known that the original intentions of the scenarists Janowitz and Mayer were radically altered by the director Robert Wiene, and that the film as made presents the outside world in such a way—using expressionistic sets with deformed and exaggerated perspectives—that only one interpretation was deemed possible: namely, that the world was that seen by a madman, the hero. Yet in the scenes devised by Wiene to "frame" the story and to situate it in the mind of Francis (who was quite a "normal" young man in the original scenario), the hero is placed "objectively" in an insane

In creating transitions between the "external," or authorial, world of *The Voyeur* and that of Mathias' subjective visions, Robbe-Grillet uses a variety of procedures. In the simplest cases, indirect free discourse permits a traditonal, if momentary, shift from outside to inside: "Mathias looked at his watch. The crossing had lasted exactly three hours." At times this indirect style is carried much further:

An uneasy thought crossed his mind: most of the individual pieces stored in the box had been put there without having been kept in his pocket, or at least after being tried out there for only a few hours. What faith, then, could be had in them? Obviously, less than in the others. To make up for that, they should have been subjected to a more thorough examination. Mathias was seized by a desire to take out from his coat pocket the piece of cord rolled in a figure eight, in order to study anew its trustworthiness. [P. 30]

First, the authorial phrase, "An uneasy thought crossed his mind." Then, after a phrase in indirect discourse, directly ex-

---

asylum, before and after the flashback which forms his own narration of the story. Not only the events of the flashback, but also those of the epilogue in which Francis is presumably seen "from the outside" occur against a background of expressionistic deformations (leaning chimneys, slanting corridors, bizarre façades); if these constitute Francis' view of the world, who is looking at Francis? If we disregard the "framing" incidents, the film is to some extent analogous to *The Voyeur* in its narrative mode: the protagonist already exists in a world that is expressionistic (for the film) or "Robbe-Grilletian" (for the novel), and which from time to time he further distorts by projections of his passions and fears. If we try to make the special visual universe of the film or novel correspond to a "rational" schema, by arguing that everything is seen through the eyes of the protagonist only, we fail to account for numerous aspects of either work. (It is also probable that Robert Wiene was motivated by social and political cautions when he modified the anti-totalitarian scenario originally provided by Janowitz and Mayer; see Siegfried Kracauer, *From Caligari to Hitler* [London: Dennis Dobson, 1947]).

pressed "thoughts," such as, "What faith, then, could be had in them?" Finally, emergence from the protagonist's subjectivity, with third-person commentary: "Mathias was seized by a desire. . . ." The same alternation between direct and indirect statement is found in the various scenes relating to Mathias' remaining at home on a rainy day during his childhood, sketching a sea gull (see p. 16, for example).

The first real shock experienced by the reader occurs a bit further on: the point of view, located outside of or alongside Mathias, intrudes into his mind through an indirect phrase; then, the third-person perspective returns, or seems to, in a scene that could only be a part of Mathias' memory, related to the sketching episode:

Mathias looked around for the discarded cigarette package—incapable of fixing the exact spot where it should come to the surface. He is sitting, looking out the window, at the huge table situated in the window well. [. . .] He is drawing a large sea gull, white and gray. [P. 21]

Once introduced into the text, this use of free transitions between present action and memory (or imagination) develops rapidly. The reader learns, through stages of increasing difficulty, to follow the system, to distinguish without intervention on the part of the author between reality, dream, memory, and, finally, paroxysmic vision. Without such an apprenticeship, subtly incorporated, it is doubtful if most readers could undergo or share, in the way intended by the author, the objectified experiences and emotions of the protagonist.

The shock produced by the confrontation of two times or two levels of action can occur not only when a present or real event plunges Mathias into the realm of memory—as the sight of a sea gull had provoked the sketching scene—but also when he "emerges" from an inner vision. When Mathias first observes the girl leaning against a pillar on the boat deck, he is carried back to the violent scene witnessed early that morning in one of the streets of the port of embarkation: "Going down a narrow street [. . .], Mathias thought he heard a plaintive cry." Suddenly, without transition, this scene is forcibly brought back into the present, to the young girl leaning against the deck support:

From the timbre of her voice—pleasurable, moreover, and without any trace of sadness—the victim must have been a very young girl, or a child. She was standing against one of the iron pillars holding up the corner of the top deck; her hands were held behind her, in the hollow of her back, her legs were held stiffly and somewhat apart, her head held back against the column. [P. 29]

The first sentence describes a girl victim seen in memory, the second a possible future victim standing in front of Mathias. Without deviating from his ostensible third-person narrative mode, the author makes the reader share the protagonist's psychic disturbance. The interplay of past and present, between interior and exterior, that has become Robbe-Grillet's hallmark, will, in *The Voyeur*, evolve significantly.

As the action of *The Voyeur* moves toward the "hole" in time where Mathias' crime occurs, the shifts between reality and phantasm multiply.[3] Most of the inner visions, instead of

3. Critics have often spoken of a "blank page" in *The Voyeur*, at the place where Mathias' crime occurs. This would be the unnumbered page 88 (note the double figure eight), the one preceding the roman numeral II indicating the second part of the novel. It is impossible to state whether this blank page occurs at the "blank" in the narration, or bears the "blank" (unprinted) number 88, other than by coincidence; if Part I had been slightly longer, at least part of page 88, including the number would have been printed, and no completely blank page would be used in the book's make-up. In any case, "objective chance," as the surrealists call it, seems to have made the format of the book (in the French edition, at least) correspond to the structure of the novel. The "suppressed" action of *The Voyeur* recalls similar ellipses in a number of modern novels. In *Crime and Punishment*, for example, Svidrigailov has committed a crime that he suppresses, as

retreating, like the foregoing, into the past, become anticipations of the future. The determining principle of these anticipations, as in the case of the memories, is found in an implicit psychology whose traits, though never stated outright by the author, may nevertheless be discerned. The reader learns that Mathias, after a series of failures, "was greatly in need of" the money he expects to earn from selling his watches, and that if "things did not go well, [. . .] he would have to [. . .] look again for a new trade." It is clear that fear or failure haunts him, driving him to undertake mental operations such as the calculation of the time available for each sale. The answer that he works out (four minutes per watch) causes him to imagine an "ideal sale": this imaginary scene, despite many clues in the text, may easily mislead a first reader into mistaking it for a present "reality." Gradually, however, the imaginary quality of the scene becomes apparent, so that when

---

has Stavrogin in *The Possessed*. Stavrogin's crime, quite similar to Marthias', was not divulged until after Dostoevsky's death; Thomas Mann's notable preface to this posthumously published "Confession" could well serve as a moral defense of *The Voyeur* as well. In Faulkner's *Sanctuary*, the scene of Temple's rape by Popeye is not described, and yet this implicit central event weighs heavily on the rest of the novel. The mystery story has used such ellipses; a striking example is Dorothy Hughes' *In a Lonely Place* (but not the better-known film, with Humphrey Bogart, made from the novel after radical and damaging changes in the plot). In *The Voyeur*, psychological verisimilitude reinforces literary ellipse, since Mathias has, plausibly, a compelling need to repress or force back into his unconscious mind all those images of a crime whose insistent upsurge into consciousness constitutes the essential problem of the protagonist and the basis of the plot. Robbe-Grillet has stated, in connection with the "blank" or "hole" of the suppressed act: "The principal action, the murder, is 'en creux' (suppressed) in *The Voyeur*. Everything is related before the hole, then again after the hole, and everything is done to try to bring together the edges of this troubling void. But [. . .] it is the void that engulfs, that fills, everything" (*Les Cahiers du Cinéma*, Sept. 1961, p. 18).

it is interrupted a few paragraphs later (as Mathias leaves the boat), before resuming in a much longer passage, the inexperienced reader begins to see these mental constructions more clearly as the quasi hallucinations of a protagonist struggling against a failure complex. The deceptive plausibility of his vision of houses and local costumes is aided by the presumption that he had spent his childhood on the island; he even plans to use real or false memories to awaken sympathy in his clients. It is therefore quite "logical" that he can invent scenes, backgrounds, and atmosphere that will correspond almost precisely with those of "real" scenes yet to come. Here are some of the time and scene shifts involved:

Mathias tried to imagine this ideal sale lasting only four minutes: arrival, sales talk, display of the merchandise, choice of the item, payment of the amount on the tag, departure. Even omitting any hesitation on the part of the client, any supplementary explanations, any discussion as to the price, what hope was there of bringing the whole thing off in such a short time?
The last house at the edge of town, on the road leading to the lighthouse, is an ordinary house [. . .].
Because of the green algae [. . .], Mathias had to choose carefully where to step [. . .].
It was now necessary to work out something a little less ghostly. It was indispensable to make the clients talk [. . .].
The door swung open, revealing the mistrustful face of the mother [. . .].
Things were going almost too fast. The fingers pressing the catch on the sample case [. . .], the notebook inside the cover, on the pile of watch boxes the end of cord rolled in a figure eight, the vertical wall of the slip running in a straight line toward the quay. Mathias turned away from the water, moving toward the parapet.
In the line formed by the travelers [. . .]. [Pp. 35–42]

Thus, as he leaves the boat, Mathias imagines trying to sell a watch to a woman who does not even open her mouth; he realizes that such a scene is "stupidly silent," and that "everything has to be done over again." He "goes back" to the door and "knocks" again. As if fearing to push the sale attempt too fast, he takes a long look at the curious design in the form of an eight on the door panel. At the "same" time, the need to watch where he steps (he is in reality climbing the ramp leading to the wharf) brings him back to reality, permitting the reader as well to orient himself in the "present" space and time. The phrase indicating the necessity of creating something a little less "ghostly" sets up an important new development of the scene, in which, though with difficulty, the client at last "speaks." The successful completion of the sale is still not reached; at the moment when Mathias "opens" the sample case in front of the woman, the rolled-up cord continues to obsess his thoughts, and he emerges from his inner vision in the middle of a phrase. Looking around for the girl leaning against the pillar, he sees no one about; he is the last to reach the wharf.

At times, the shifts from inner vision to outside reality occur in the passage from one sentence to another through an intermediary, bridging sentence applicable because of verbal ambiguity to either of the other two. A typical example of this procedure is found in the paragraph in which Mathias, during the landing, after emerging briefly from his trancelike state, is once more plunged into the imaginary scene of an attempt to make a sale:

Shoving his neighbors accomplished nothing. [. . .] Nevertheless, he felt himself giving in to a growing impatience. They were taking too long to open. [. . .] He knocked again. [. . .] The door [. . .] gave forth a dull sound. [. . .] He heard a noise in the vestibule. [P. 38]

The phrase "he felt himself giving in to a growing impatience" applies as much to Mathias immobilized by the slowness of the crowd as to Mathias listening at the door of the imaginary house.

The Voyeur makes use not only of remembered, or anticipated, scenes but also of false, or falsified, scenes, of which the greatest number are those that occur as Mathias tries to fill in the hole, or void, created in his activities of the day by the unexplained hour during which (as the reader is finally made aware) the meeting with Jacqueline took place on the cliff, followed by her rape and murder. The reader's confusion, on first contact with this type of scene, is increased by the fact that, as yet, he does not know or suspect what lies hidden behind all these inventions, even if he begins to recognize them as such. The author's intention is doubtless to reproduce in the reader the same kind of repression or censureship that Mathias himself is practising on his recent experiences. Mathias, "back again" at the crossroads, meets Madame Marek; the text then presents a series of hypothetical scenes. Madame Marek's admission that there is no one at her farm unleashes in Mathias a voluble and detailed account of a visit there—an account that will be repeated later with variations and finally "confirmed" by young Julien in a counterversion, just as false, when Mathias at last does visit the Marek farm in order to re-enforce and lend further credence to his indispensable alibi.

It is thus clear that Robbe-Grillet, moving freely between a traditional third-person mode and one "shifted" toward a virtual first person, objectifies his protagonist's universe and makes the reader share the highly charged vision of his hero. This narrative technique entails the use of several accessory procedures in the manipulation of dialogue and reported speech. In the normal "exchange" of remarks between characters, *The Voyeur* uses the customary system of dashes and quotation marks; at such times, Mathias utters at most one or two sentences. When, on the other hand, Mathias is supposed to engage in an extended speech, whose full quotation would cause him to speak rhetorically, and at length, repeating information already given, the author always converts such "speeches" into indirect summary: "Mathias explained that he no longer practised the trade of traveling electrician. He was now selling wristwatches. He had arrived that morning on the steamer" (p. 95).

This conventional technique of avoiding the literal citation of long speeches extends, in *The Voyeur*, to the fragmentary or irrational remarks that Mathias utters under stress. Earlier, in *The Erasers* (especially in the telephonic conversation of the bar proprietor, p. 257), Robbe-Grillet made full direct quotation of a chaotic speech; here, in *The Voyeur*, he chooses a more ambiguous method of presentation, which by its fragmentary, imprecise nature conveys the protagonist's disturbance better than would his actual words (note in passing that the technique used forms another contradiction of the theory held by some critics that *The Voyeur* contains *only* the viewpoint of Mathias). Here are two examples:

A chaotic sentence came from his mouth—unclear and excessively long, too sharp to be agreeable, gramatically incorrect—in which he nevertheless heard here and there the necessary formulas: "Marek," "good morning," "didn't recognize you." [Pp. 94–95]

Speaking even faster, the traveler resumed his monologue. [. . .] In order to fill in the empty spaces, he often repeated the same phrase several times. He was even surprised to find himself reciting the multiplication table. [P. 216]

Moreover, the only full quotation of a fairly long speech by Mathias sounds a somewhat false note (the scene in which he gives his sales talk, pp. 251–252). No doubt the comparative study of alternation in the novel between direct quotation and indirect summary of speech needs yet to be made. In Camus' *The Stranger*, for example, all the extended speeches of the supposedly laconic protagonist are given in paraphrase, reinforcing the *impression* that Meursault speaks very little, and in short sentences, whereas in "reality" the hero, as the text indicates, speaks a great deal and often at great length. Likewise Mathias, in *The Voyeur*, *seems* to speak little, despite the lengthy remarks which are given only in summary form. And, for quite different reasons, as will be shown later, the husband of *Jealousy* quotes in full the remarks made by his wife and Franck, while confining his own "remarks" to a special kind of indirect style.

With an understanding of the narrative modes and the principles of transitions between scenes used in *The Voyeur*, we are in a position to examine the problems of images, style, and structures in the novel. We can then seek to determine the unifying principle binding the whole together and giving it its aesthetic meaning.

Robbe-Grillet's novels are, as is generally conceded, very "formal." We saw that the action of *The Erasers* involved a kind of phase-shifted circle, that incidents of the beginning and the end were situated at the same or analogous points on the circumference, and that throughout the work a series of doublings were used to reinforce this correspondence. This almost baroque formalism diminishes somewhat in *The Voyeur*, without entirely disappearing. The circular 0 of *The Erasers* here becomes an eight (8, which, on its side, represents ∞, infinity). As in *The Erasers*, this basic form is repeated in a proliferation of supporting images scattered throughout *The Voyeur*, conferring on the very shape of the island, as well as on the novel and its objects and actions, a geometrical formal unity.

The first of the figure-of-eight objects is the cord that Mathias picks up on the boat deck; it is this cord, the last in a series of strings, cords, and pieces of rope collected since childhood, that will be used to tie up the victim of the crime. Next comes the mark left by the iron ring on the wall of the dock, selected as a "reference point" after being used to "pass a rope through"; then, the eight-shaped design on the doors of the houses on the island, suggesting "eyeglasses, or eyes." We may say that these images already represent the extreme limits of the correlation between the eight form and the action as a whole: on one hand, a physical means, an objective reinforcement of the action of the crime (cord, iron ring); on the other hand, a passive support of the theme of the glance or the idea of a *voyeur* (the eyes). Some twenty or more other variants of the figure of eight occur, including, more or less obviously: two barrel covers whose edges touch; Jean Robin's gestures as he describes the oscillations of the searchlight beam, movements "in which abounded circles, spirals, loops, figures of eight"; the loops made by the smoke from Mathias' cigarette; the doodles he mechanically draws in his notebook; the curves made by the gulls wheeling in flight (their "inexpressive" eyes reinforcing the theme of the fixed glance); the handcuffs that Mathias imagines; the arrangement of the stakes used to bind the victim, legs and arms spread apart; the adjacent circular impressions left by wet glasses on the counter. Even Mathias' bicycle has the form of an eight (two circles held by a chain); and, as Mathias explains to the café owner, "the general shape of the path taken around the island is a kind of eight" (a path parodied by the movie poster's title, "Monsieur X on the Double Track"). The action of the novel makes a sort of eight in time: Mathias completes the first loop when, on the afternoon of the first day, he misses his boat; during the following days, he repeats his itinerary and thus executes the second loop in the pattern. And it is at the point where the two loops of the actual road round the island touch, at the "crossroads," that Mathias, escaping as it were from the tyranny of the figure-of-eight form, evades his predetermined schedule to enter the "hole in time" created by the missing hour of the crime on the cliff.

Robbe-Grillet's earlier descriptive style, as it appeared in *The Erasers*, with its North European city, undergoes relatively few changes in *The Voyeur*, despite the radical shift of scene to a sun-bathed offshore island similar to the Ile d'Ouessant, a familiar spot to Bretons like Robbe-Grillet. Most of the now recognizable features of this style, after undergoing some evolution in *The Voyeur*, will be greatly diminished (for reasons to be shown later) in *Jealousy*, only to reappear in the following novel, *In the Labyrinth*, and—to a varying degree—in the author's subsequent works. While the "urban" aspects of *The Erasers* (canals, tramways, automatic restaurants) are absent from *The Voyeur*, common descriptive situations recur: the prose evocations of canals resemble those of the water in the port; the houses of *The Voyeur* "look alike," just as those of *The Erasers* "are all constructed on the same model." The main square in *The Erasers*, with its enigmatic (and almost symbolic or "metaphysical") statue, standing on a raised pedestal protected by an iron fence, has the same Chirico-like atmosphere as the small square in the town of *The Voyeur*, with its statue, pedestal, and ironwork whose shadow falls on Mathias like that of prison bars. In both cases, an allegory links the statue to the novel: in *The Erasers*, the subject is a warrior on a chariot (like Laius, Oedipus' father); in *The Voyeur*, it is a peasant girl (like Jacqueline) looking out to sea. Objectified images of confused thoughts (such as the police chief's twirling fingers in a notable passage in *The Erasers*) are repeated in *The Voyeur* by uncertain cloud forms torn to pieces by the winds, by the tangled paths found around the scene of the crime, which offer "a multiple, sinuous, fragmentary track, bifurcating, coming together again, continually criss-crossing, or even stopping abruptly in the midst of the shrubs." Even the black and white floor tiles, the blue cigarette package, the rooms with unmade beds, the obsessive designs on the doors, the shops with bizarre and "absurd" objects, and the café ambiance of *The Voyeur* come more or less directly from *The Erasers*.

But Robbe-Grillet's art always evolves. The style of *The Voyeur* develops that of *The Erasers* by a process of refinement. Those phrases of geometric or scientific inspiration which had attracted so much attention in *The Erasers* have their modified counterparts in *The Voyeur*: in the earlier work, we find such "typical" Robbe-Grillet turns of phrase as, oblique, chisel-shaped, flattened ring, 90° angle, re-entrant angle, a chair situated 30 centimetres away, vertical to the eye, curve, inversion, square grid, cubical, rectangular, transverse, rectilinear, obtuse angle, sinusoidal arcs; many of these same terms reappear in *The Voyeur*, along with new ones, such as, parallel lines, perpendicular planes, horizontal lines, on the bias, on the diagonal, variations in amplitude, inclined plane, period of contact, horizontal trajectory, cylindrical, fusiform, double-arched, inverted and intermixed sinusoids phase-shifted by a half-period on the same horizontal axis, and many others.[4] At the same time, the style of *The Voyeur* grows firmer and more precise, especially through the elimination of the more facile, conventional phraseology often used in *The Erasers* (with its effects sometimes reminiscent of Simenon, such as, "This idea amuses him immensely; his well-fed body is shaken by laughter"). The writer, in Malraux's term, is "wresting" his proper style from his own past.

Objects in a room, whose appearance and relationships were

4. I have already pointed out, writing of *The Erasers*, how geometric and scientific terms are used to "cleanse," to decondition, the objects described, according to Robbe-Grillet's theory of *neutral* objects. As for the origins of this kind of descriptive style, one source is surely Sartre's *Nausea*, where even the famous "parallelepipeds" may be found. One may also find striking resemblances between the Robbe-Grillet's geometric style and that of arithmetic books used in French schools. In *The Voyeur* (p. 191), occurs this passage: "It was a kilometric road marker of the usual model, a rectangular parallelepiped attached to a half-cylinder of equal thickness, and of horizontal axis. The two principal surfaces, squares terminating in a half-circle." An elementary textbook contains this description in one of its problems: "A kilometric road-marker [. . .] is composed of a base in the form of a rectangular parallelepiped on which rests a cylindical column. On the latter stands a sign-holder in the form of a cube" (*Arithmétique et travaux pratiques*, by C. Lebossé and C. Hémery [Paris: Nathan, n.d.], p. 152). This kind of precise description must have made a deep impression on Robbe-Grillet as a young student.

so minutely observed and described in the short "Instantané" or snapshot entitled "Three Reflected Visions" and in *The Erasers,* are used in *The Voyeur* mainly as objective correlatives, or "supports," for the imaginative projections of an obsessed vision. Describing the bedroom occupied by Mathias, the author begins at the door, passes slowly from one piece of furniture to another according to the strict perspective of a fixed observer (a procedure which, by correcting the lack of stabilized viewpoint in neo-Balzacian descriptions, creates a kind of "existential volume" within the room), then plunges the whole construction into a different level of "reality" by stating that it was in one of these wardrobe drawers that Mathias as a child kept his collection of strings and cords.

One of the most original techniques of *The Erasers* was its use of "frozen" scenes indefinitely prolonging a moment of fugitive time: Garinati mounting the steps to commit his crime suddenly comes to a complete halt, like an actor immobilized in the middle of a scene or an orchestra conductor stopping, with his raised arm rigid, in the midst of a melodic line. Note that in *The Erasers* the author insists upon these *comparisons,* thus depriving the scene of any literalness and making it into a kind of metaphor. The evolved form of the procedure of the frozen scene in *The Voyeur* is more striking; the text, "paralyzing" the action, objectifies interior mental states without recourse to comparison or metaphor, thus communicating them far more directly to the reader. As he had gradually prepared the reader for the many "false" scenes to come, Robbe-Grillet introduces him to the fixed or motionless scene by preparatory passages in which the immobility *is* described by means of a comparison. Near the beginning, Mathias looks at the young girl on the boat; her posture stirs up his first erotic fantasies, and he sees again in his mind's eye the violent scene witnessed that morning: the huge man with uplifted arm, the outcry of the victim behind the red curtains. The scene "freezes": "The whole scene remained motionless. In spite of the unfinished motion of his gesture, the man made no more movement than a statue" (p. 28).

It is important to recall that this first appearance of a "victim" will be followed by variations involving the girl on the boat, the café waitress, the girl on the movie poster, the girl in the picture glimpsed hanging on the wall of a bedroom, Jacqueline-Violette leaning against the tree in the photograph, Jean Robin's fearful wife (who figures in a scene closely similar to the first in the series), and, of course, Jacqueline herself, bound to stakes in the ground in the cruelly sadistic vision which Mathias is at last unable further to suppress (p. 246).

For it is obviously the emotion of fear, or more precisely the erotic reaction experienced by Mathias at the sight or thought of a fearful victim, which brings about the "freezing" of most of the fixed scenes. In the case of the barmaid, her fearful attitude toward the overpowering figure of the proprietor causes a sort of hypnosis, and Mathias is unable to make the scene "continue" in time:

The other characters were already immobile. Once the fearful movement of the young girl was re-absorbed, [. . .] the whole scene was solidified.

Everyone was silent.

The servant girl kept her eyes on the floor at her feet. The proprietor looked at the girl. Mathias watched the proprietor's glance. The three sailors looked at their glasses. Nothing revealed the pulsing of the blood in their veins—not even a slight trembling.

It would be useless to try to estimate how long that lasted. [Pp. 57–58]

Thus, through a series of short sentences, the text slows the action down to a halt. In a later incident, after the crime, the same proprietor suggests to Mathias that he take a trawler which is getting ready to sail to the mainland. The protagonist's inner tension, caused by the conflict between his desire to flee the island and his fear of causing suspicions if he shows a guilty haste, is embodied in another kind of frozen scene, in which external movements undergo periodic interruption. Through the glass pane of the café entrance, Mathias sees a fisherman (it is Jacqueline's "fiancé") walking rapidly along the jetty. Taking his eyes off the fisherman momentarily, he speaks to the proprietor, then looks out of the same window: although still striding along at the same fast pace, the fisherman seems to have stayed exactly where he was when Mathias looked away, as if, during the brief interval when Mathias was not observing him, he had remained frozen in space and time:

A glance through the glass pane of the entrance door causes him to experience the same surprise: the fisherman is at exactly the same spot where he had appeared to be an instant before, when [Mathias] took his eyes from him, still walking with a steady, fast pace in front of the piles of nets and lobster traps. As soon as the observer ceases to watch him, [the fisherman] becomes motionless, resuming his movement just at the instant when the eye returns to him—as if there had been no interruption, for it is impossible to see him come to a stop or start walking again. [P. 242]

The passage can only be the objectification of a psychic state linked to some fundamental mental disorder in Mathias. In *The Voyeur*, the author has stated that he created a protagonist "qui ne cadre pas avec lui-même," who "does not fit into his own pattern." We are brought to a point in our discussion where the question of the "psychology" of the main character must be considered, despite the misgivings expressed by Robbe-Grillet concerning this line of interpretation. For there is, in the novel, a systematic conception of psychological behavior which, however implicit, serves as the basis for the plot.

Robbe-Grillet's novels, in addition to their formal systems of internal correspondences, are organized around psychological themes which serve as underlying supports for the unity of the work. In a sense, the author illustrates Gaston Bachelard's principle—already mentioned in the discussion of *The Erasers*—that a literary work always depends for its unity on an overt or hidden psychological complex. In *The Erasers*, the Oedipus complex is at work throughout the story; in *Jealousy*, the transitions between scenes are caused by a paranoiac obsession that transforms suspicion into murderous phantasms; the soldier of *In the Labyrinth* suffers from a sort of fugelike amnesia; and the mythomania of *Last Year at Marienbad* seeks to defeat the "reality principle" of an abnormally suggestible woman.

What about Mathias, in *The Voyeur?* He too fits into the omnipresent psychopathology found in the works of Robbe-Grillet. To situate him in the spectrum of more or less abnormal personality types that appear to preoccupy the author requires that we first examine and dismiss several errors in psychological interpretation that have confused the meaning of the word *voyeur* and deformed the relationship between the title term and Mathias' own "case." Some critics, attributing to Mathias exclusively the geometric perspectives and descriptive minutiae of the novel's background, make of the protagonist a *voyeur-voyant*, as if it were *his* psychology (or even lack of it) that imposed such a vision on the world; in reality, as we have tried to show, Mathias projects his deformed visions upon a world already stylized by Robbe-Grillet. Speculation on the meaning of *voyeur* (which appears *only* in the title) led Bernard Dort to consider Mathias completely empty, "transparent," even "nil," and Roland Barthes to deprive him of all motivation, making him a character without either "motives, character development, or actions." Although Barthes left the door ajar to a psychological interpretation by speaking of the absence of "explicit intentionality," Maurice Blanchot wrote that there was a complete "destruction of interiority" in the protagonist, whom he wittingly calls (punning on the French term for a traveling salesman, "voyageur de commerce") a *"voyeur de commerce."*

But Mathias is almost certainly not the *voyeur* of the title, and his personality, far from being transparent or nil, or even

ambiguous, obeys the classic pattern, as found in many manuals of psychopathology, of cyclic schizophrenia accompanied
by an erotic sadism.

Let us first take the word *voyeur*. Once we reject the alleged relationship between the character of Mathias and what
Pierre Lagarde called "the minuteness, the meticulousness of
observation" of Robbe-Grillet's descriptions, we can try to
give to the term *voyeur* a more exact meaning, not limited to
the idea of geometry and visual minuteness. This other meaning would obviously be closer to what the word customarily
suggests: a *voyeur* is one who watches, more or less covertly,
erotic acts in which he does not himself take part. The only
critic to take this meaning of *voyeur* into account, Robert
Champigny, falls into a different error when he objects
strongly to the title on the grounds that Mathias, instead of
being a passive *voyeur*, commits sadistic acts as well as rape
and murder. All this is true, but why must we assume that
Mathias is the *voyeur* of the title? Is it not a similar confusion
that led Blanchot, Germaine Brée, and others to cast serious
doubt on the reality of Mathias' crime? If we insisted at all
costs on making Mathias the *voyeur*, we would have to admit
that the only act of "voyeurism" he commits is looking through
the window in the port city before leaving for the island, and
that all the rest of the novel (his torture and murder of Jacqueline, his lies and contradictions, even his state of panic) is
only accumulation of groundless phantasms.

But a careful reading of the text shows that Mathias, instead
of being the *voyeur*, is himself the *object* or victim of the real
voyeur of the novel. The theme of Mathias watched by eyes
is stated quite early: the expressionless eye of the sea gull, the
designs on the doors ("eyeglasses, eyes"), are directed at
Mathias, and do not represent a glance which emanates from
him. Mathias becomes chiefly the object of the look of young
Julien. At the Marek farm, when the boy turns his fixed gaze
on Mathias, with eyes afflicted by a "slight strabism," we read:

He was content to move his pupils only slightly, in order to keep his gaze fixed on Mathias. [. . .] Julien did not take his eyes off the traveler. [. . .] Without taking his eyes from those of the traveler. [. . .] The too insistent look of the young man [. . .]. [Pp. 196–201]

In the scene on the cliff when Mathias discovers Julien spying on his efforts to get rid of the evidence of his presence at the crime, Julien's *voyeur*-like activities exert further pressure on the protagonist:

Julien looked at him, saying nothing, with the same steady gaze. [. . .]
"An old rag," said Mathias, "that I found over there."
"A sweater," corrected the imperturbable voice of the watcher. [. . .]
Julien [. . .] looked at the candy sack, then the traveler, and again the sack. Mathias realized, at that moment, what made those eyes so strange. [. . . Julien] looked at him again. [. . .] Or could it be a glass eye that made his gaze so disturbing? [Pp. 207–210]

Finally, Mathias knows that Julien has *seen* his crime:

But he had to have something more than suspicions—even precise ones—to authorize such assurance. Julien had "seen." It was useless to deny it further. Only the images forever registered by those eyes could confer on them that unbearable fixity. [P. 214]

The *voyeur*, therefore, is Julien. Does he also represent Mathias at an earlier stage, innocent but drawn toward a *voyeurism* that might evolve into criminality? It is possible; Robbe-Grillet uses such correspondences (Wallas-Garinati in *The Erasers*, the soldier and the boy in the *Labyrinth*). The essential point is to reject the identification of Mathias as the *voyeur*, and to avoid drawing such conclusions as "It is therefore less a case of a *Voyeur* than of a *Menteur* (Liar)," in Roland Barthes' formula. It is not the first time, besides, that a title has referred to someone other than the main character of a work.[5]

Mathias fits the pattern of the sadistic schizophrenic, recalling in many ways the personality of the infamous "butcher of Düsseldorf" incarnated by Peter Lorre in Fritz Lang's film *M* (which also contains a number of "objective clues" to a

5. The original title of the novel was *Le Voyageur* (*The Traveler*), as one might deduce from reading the French text, where the hero is always referred to either as "Mathias" or "le voyageur," with the word "le voyeur" appearing nowhere other than in the title. But this rather ordinary title lacked interest, and the author proposed to his publisher the present title, *The Voyeur*, which contributed so much, undoubtedly, to the success of the novel. At the same time, the work contained a character and an action quite capable of justifying the definitive title, which had, moreover, a definite relationship to certain ideas already advanced by Robbe-Grillet concerning the primary importance of visual description and optical perspectives. The word *voyeur* had actually been used by Roland Barthes in an early essay on Robbe-Grillet, in which he wrote: "Modern description [. . .] sets the *voyeur* firmly in his place" ("Littérature objective," in *Critique*, July–Aug. 1954). The title *Le Voyeur* is in part, at least, a product of surrealist "objective chance." If it is true, as I think, that the only possible *voyeur* in the novel is young Julien, a certain lexicographical difficulty does arise, since, in the argot of brothels and "*maisons*," the *voyeur* is an habitual frequenter of pornographic spectacles. I quote from an interesting and pertinent letter which Jean Hytier wrote to me on this subject: "Now, for Julien, this is a first experience, and there is little chance that it will be repeated. Nevertheless, one can call him a *voyeur*, as one can Proust's young Marcel witnessing the relationship between Jupien and Charlus. It may also be that the author is not too scrupulous about the proper use of terms (aside from the vocabulary of the geometrician, the scientist, and the surveyor), but, in this case, the door is left open to any interpretation. [. . .] *Voyeur* would end up meaning almost anything. Saint-Simon uses the word, in the plural, to designate the curious standing around to watch whatever is happening. There is, in old French, a word *voieur* (which is the modern "*voyer*," "police officer stationed on roads or streets"—he was not on our hero's path!), but derived from *voie* (road), and not from *vue* (sight); it's too bad."

similar crime, including candy wrappers, cigarette butts, and the like). When the reader of *The Voyeur* begins, in the second part of the novel, to sense or glimpse the as yet unstated motives of Mathias' odd conduct; when he finally "sees" the sadistic act itself, censured, repressed, but constantly rising toward the surface to modify outside reality as the protagonist perceives it, the reader himself shares Mathias' guilty anguish and becomes the victim of a "simulated" schizophrenia. The secret of *The Voyeur*, as of *Jealousy*, is not to *analyze*, but to *create* a psychology, and to impose this psychology on the reader through objective presentation.

Nothing is more consistent, in *The Voyeur*, than the coherent relationship between Mathias' implicit psychology and the sequences of individual scenes: flashbacks, visions projected into the future, deformations of perceived reality, frozen scenes, sudden halts in the flow of Mathias' thoughts, images linked by serial associations, even the dislocation of language and syntax—all these may be explained by his complex, with its mixture of eroticism, fear of failure, and no doubt desperate desire to appear a normal man. Everything obeys the dictates of a sadistic psychophrenia which is not "explained" by Robbe-Grillet, but which is merely *there*, as a fundamental, determining state.

The role played by the photograph of Jacqueline which Mathias sees at Madame Leduc's house provides an illuminating example of the way in which the hero's implicit psychology serves as a principle of transition and scene linking. The first sight of this picture provokes in Mathias an immediate confusion between Jacqueline and Violette, doubtless the name of the girl mentioned in the press clipping he carries in his pocket.[6] Imagining an erotic scene of Jacqueline-Violette

6. In Graham Greene's *Brighton Rock*, which presents (as we have shown) certain parallels to *The Erasers*, we find a press clipping recounting a sadistic crime, the murder of little Violet, raped (*violat*ed) and thrown into the sea. It is tempting to see this clipping as the same

"tied" in cords, Mathias is unable to see anything in the room where he stands; instead, his vision takes him into an objectified hallucination of latent sadism:

At the foot of the pine tree the dry grasses were beginning to catch fire, as well as the bottom of the cotton dress. Voilette twisted away in the opposite direction and threw back her head, opening her mouth. Yet, somehow, Mathias finally managed to say goodbye. [P. 85]

Later, in his attempt to work out a solid alibi, Mathias goes back over his day's itinerary. Each time he reaches the moment when he first saw Jacqueline's photograph, the same powerful erotic drive, new reinforced by the repressed memory of the actual crime, draws him back into the abyss, into the "hole" in time which grows larger and larger, inexorably, despite all his efforts:

The whole first part had gone along at a rapid pace [. . .] the corridor [. . .] the big kitchen, the oval table [. . .] the fingers pressing on the catch of the sample case, the lid springing back, the black notebook, the descriptive brochures, the rectangular frame standing on the buffet, the gleaming metal leg serving to support it, the photograph, the path leading down, the hollow in the cliff sheltered from the wind, secret, quiet, isolated as if by the thickest walls . . . as if by the thickest walls . . . the oval table. [. . .] [P. 117]

Mathias' efforts at repression of his guilty memories cause him to bring his thoughts forcibly back to Madame Leduc's kitchen, to the scene of his sales demonstration, but, each time the photograph appears, he risks succumbing to a deadly stream of associations. Thus he goes over the scene again, trying in desperation to "block" his reaction to Jacqueline's picture:

---

one that Mathias carries in his pocket (and also as that which Sartre alludes to in *Nausea*).

[. . .] the lid springing back [. . .] the black notebook, the descriptive brochures, the gleaming metal frame, the photograph where can be seen . . . the photograph where can be seen the photograph, the photograph, the photograph, the photograph . . . (p. 117).

A similar explanation may be given for the other sudden stoppages or blocks in the text, such as the one in which Mathias at the sight of the fearful barmaid is unable to complete a phrase about her "frightened face" (p. 106), or the passage already referred to when Mathias repeats the same phrase and even stammers out a multiplication table (p. 216).

One of the novel's most striking scenes depicts the doubling or splitting of the protagonist's psyche, his schizophrenia. It is presented in the form of a psychic seizure so violent that Mathias is divided almost literally "in two," and falls down in a faint. To follow the passage correctly, the reader must recall that throughout the novel Mathias is designated either by his name, or by the term "voyageur," traveler. In this scene, he is standing at the counter of the tavern, opposite a mirror. Thus the elements of doubling (words, images) are already present, and by using them Robbe-Grillet expresses Mathias' abnormal mental state (he has only just committed the crime) as he succumbs to a schizophrenic crisis:

Mathias finished his absinthe. No longer feeling the little sample case between his legs, he lowered his glance to the floor. The case had disappeared. He thrust his hand deep into the pocket of his coat, to rub his grease-stained fingers against the rolled-up cord, while raising his eyes to look at the traveler. The proprietress thought he was feeling his pocket for change. [. . .] He then turned toward the large woman, or toward the woman, or toward the girl, or toward the young barmaid, then put down the valise in order to take hold of the case while the sailor and the fisherman squeezed, jammed their way, stood between the traveler and Mathias. [. . .]

Mathias rubbed his forehead with his hand. It was almost dark.

He was sitting, on a chair, in the middle of the street—in the middle of the road—in front of the Café des Roches Noires.

"Well, are you better now?" asked a man wearing a leather jacket, standing near him. [P. 222]

If, at the time of his first appearance in this café (p. 107), before the news of Jacqueline's death had spread, Mathias had managed to keep his composure in spite of the tensions caused by the rumors and hints already circulating around him, now his world collapses. The retelling of the crime, together with the recital of the local legend of the young girl sacrificed and thrown over the cliff for the benefit of "travelers," has violently affected him; at the next moment, in the passage quoted, he begins a series of dangerous alterations (large woman, woman, young girl, young barmaid) which he tries to block. The resulting tension splits, as it were, the two halves of his personality, and he sees or feels himself as two distinct individuals, between whom the sailor and fisherman can pass. (The role of the mirror above the bar in this scene is no doubt that of an implicit objective reinforcement.) Thus, torn by terror and anguish, Mathias loses consciousness. The effect on the reader, needless to say, comes less from an intellectual understanding of this complicated construction than from direct contact with the text. The mental state of the protagonist is objectified in distortions and impossibilities that make the reader feel, for the time, that he is suffering from, Mathias' syncope.

The general sense both of the word *voyeur* and the novel which bears the title *The Voyeur* is now clear. Far from being a "novel of the irremissibility, or of the non-existence of everything, even the crime" (Blanchot), in which Mathias' crime "is a crime which he has not committed, that time has committed for him" (Gaëtan Picon), the work is, rather, the story of a pathological case whose mental derangements we are made to share by specific literary means. The world in which the protagonist exists is a world created and stylized first by

Robbe-Grillet, and not a universe perceived exclusively by his hero. Nor is Mathias a "transparent *voyeur*" whose alleged absence of personality can be used to explain (in a way never made clear by the proponents of this view) the style and images of the book. The psychic mechanisms of the hero deform the surrounding universe; but—and this is a crucial point—even the deformed scenes that result must necessarily pass into the style and assume the structural forms characteristic of the author, whose rigorous "invented exactitude" is clearly discernable throughout.

Is *The Voyeur* an immoral novel? The question seems inappropriate to a work by Robbe-Grillet, but critics have raised it, especially Emile Henriot, for whom the book suggested an atmosphere of criminal courts concerned with perverse acts, or the psychopathic ward of an institution. At the end of the book, Mathias leaves the scene of the crime unpunished, and there is no hint of future retribution. What conclusion should we draw from this fact? Robbe-Grillet has said that he envisions a literature produced in and for a "society reconciled with itself." Is the ending of *The Voyeur* an example of such a literature, conceived for an advanced society that would no longer insist upon conventional retribution? Is there a suggestion of a parody à la Hitchcock, of an outcome that the reader is not to take "seriously"? Are we to see in the image of the cage-shaped buoy, with its iron grills, that looms in the harbor at Mathias' departure not only an objectification of the protagonist's fear of prison, but even a foreshadowing of a possible future incarceration? The novel gives no answer to these questions; it is simply open-ended.

It seems doubtful, also, that Mathias' sadism in *The Voyeur* represents an updated form of protest against novelistic sentimentality. In *Portrait de notre héros*, R.-M. Albérès characterized this protest as "liberating," and suggested that the truly "sincere" novelist would have to assassinate David Copperfield or bring about the rape of Little Dorritt. This conception of inverted metaphysical sincerity à la Marquis de Sade would appear to bear little relationship to the almost abstract act committed by Mathias. *The Voyeur* contains no philosophic demonstration, no attack on sentimental or other values, no intellectual message. Is its ending, nevertheless, a defiance, a refusal, a proof of the artist's independence? Is its very absence of explanation tendentious? While any conjecture is possible, it would seem that the most satisfying view would see any possible punishment of Mathias, any moral redemption, as adding nothing to the novel's structural unity, and would falsify its style and tone. In any case, it is surely apart from moral or social preoccupations that the reader of *The Voyeur* undergoes a new and astonishing literary experience.

4 The Paroxysm of the "Absent-I": *Jealousy (1957)*

> Consciousness . . . can only take on the form of the cavity which it fills.
>
> R.-M. ALBERES, *Portrait de notre héros*

It is exceptionally difficult, in reading literature—never an easy undertaking—to isolate and examine the basic aspects of an unusually complex work. Yet the more resistant to analysis the work appears to be, or the more disconcerting its structure, the more necessary and important the critic's task becomes. Alain Robbe-Grillet's third novel, *Jealousy* (whose French title, *La Jalousie*, conveys an ambiguity not retained in the English word), well illustrates the point. This compact, powerful narrative, which marked a decisive step in the development of the New Novel, requires and deserves the closest scrutiny. Why? What does this highly unusual novel offer?[1]

Robbe-Grillet himself, in a statement printed on the back of the first French edition, has described the general form in which the narrative content of *Jealousy* is organized. The story with its three characters—the husband, the wife, the presumed lover—is "narrated" by the husband, a tropical planter

1. Chapter 4 appeared in slightly different form under the title "New Structure in the Novel: *Jealousy* by Robbe-Grillet," in *Evergreen Review*, Nov.–Dec., 1959. The quoted passages from *Jealousy* and their page numbers are from Richard Howard's translation, used by permission of Grove Press, Inc., and of Calder & Boyars, Ltd.

who, from vantage points in his banana plantation house, surrounded on three sides by its wide veranda, suspiciously keeps watch over his wife. Guided by this author's statement, the reader is able to find his bearings fairly quickly in a narrative of the "first" person which contains not a single "I," "me," or other verbal reference to self. At the time *Jealousy* appeared, the serious study of the fictional use of narrative pronouns had barely begun, especially in France. The subsequent success of a narrative "you" in Michel Butor's prize-winning *La Modification* (*A Change of Heart*, 1958), led numerous critics to start an investigation of the problems raised by the use of "I," "he," and the like in novel technique; today, classifications and theoretical analyses of "point of view" in fiction are a major concern of novel criticism around the world, reinforced by the parallel study of cinematic viewpoint, with its analogous attention to camera angle, framing, tracking shots, subjective camera, and other filmic devices.[2]

The narrative orientation of *Jealousy*—its use of what one

2. Among the important studies of viewpoint in the novel are: Wayne Booth, *The Rhetoric of Fiction* (Chicago: University of Chicago Press, 1961); Bertil Romberg, *Studies in the Narrative Technique of the First-Person Novel* (Stockholm: Almquist & Wiksell, 1962); Georges Blin, *Stendhal et les problèmes du roman* (Paris: J. Corti, 1954); J.-P. Sartre, *Situations II* (Paris: Gallimard, 1948); Michel Butor, *Répertoire II* (Paris: Minuit, 1964); Françoise van Rossum-Guyon, *Critique du roman* (Paris: Gallimard, 1970); and Jean Rousset, *Narcisse romancier, essai sur la première personne dans le roman* (Paris: 1973). See also my articles, "Roman et cinéma: le cas de Robbe-Grillet," *Symposium*, Summer 1961; "De Stendhal à Robbe-Grillet, modalités du point de vue," *Cahieres de l'Association Internationale des Etudes Françaises*, June 1962; "The Evolution of Narrative Viewpoint in Robbe-Grillet," *Novel*, Autumn 1967; and "The Alienated 'I' in Fiction," *The Southern Review*, Winter 1974. Cinematic analogies with novelistic viewpoint are discussed widely, by such critics as Marcel Martin, Jean Mitry, and André Bazin. (See especially the issue "Cinéma et roman" of the *Revue des Lettres Modernes*, Summer 1958.)

would term the *je-néant* or the "absent I"—is one of several conventional headings (such as description, vocabulary, images, use of dialogue) which might conceivably be used to study the novel.[3] Since what dominates everything else in *Jealousy* is the *structure* of the novel, the greatest clarification may be achieved through concepts especially applicable to this structure. The difficulty is that this idea of structure proliferates, disintegrates even, under examination, rejoining other categories from which it resists separation: the plot and its "chronology," the apparently chaotic sequence of scenes, the

3. In proposing the French term "*je-néant*" ("absent" or "suppressed" first person) to designate the narrative mode of *Jealousy*, my intention is not only to refer to the lack of any first-person pronominal or other form, but also to emphasize the phenomenological and existential implications of the procedure. According to Sartre's argument in *L'Etre et le néant* (*Being and Nothingness*), consciousness exists only as the result of a process of "*néantisation*" or reduction to nothingness directed toward objects and events. Sartre writes: "Being-for-itself (*le pour-soi*) has no other reality than to be the reduction to nothingness of Being; its only characteristic arises from its abolition of the individual being-in-itself (*l'en-soi*)." R.-M. Albérès explains this passage as follows (in *Portrait de notre héros* [Paris: A. Michel, 1945], p. 156): "The phenomenologist, studying ontology according to the structures of consciousness, recognizes in the world only Being-in-itself and Being-for-itself, that is, *things* and *consciousness*. The law of consciousness (Being-for-itself) is not to be what it is but rather what it is not, since consciousness is always consciousness *of* something else. Human consciousness can only be this *néantisation* or reductive process which calls the world into existence." Such a philosophical demonstration of the abstract bases of the *je-néant* narrative technique, in which the protagonist's consciousness is always other than itself and always attached to the "something else" of sensory and other perceptions, fits in with Robbe-Grillet's own theories of "*objets-supports*" or objective correlatives for mental states. The suppressed first-person mode, which appears to be Robbe-Grillet's invention in literature, is now found in the fiction of other important novelists, such as Claude Ollier and Jean Ricardou.

repetitions and the variations, the role of "formal themes" and objects, the use of "objective psychology."

Paradoxically, in the case of this fundamentally antichronological novel, a "linear" résumé of the plot permits us best to penetrate into the labyrinth of its structure. A few words of caution are necessary: this method is in no sense a proposal to "rectify" the chronology of the plot; its excuse is solely that it provides a means of studying a new novelistic technique. It is a laboratory experiment in analysis, not an "explication" of the novel.

The chronological novelty of *Jealousy* fits into the framework, moreover, of many trends in the treatment of chronology in the modern novel, most of which, in turn, go back to the beginnings of narrative literature (as in the "flashbacks" in Ulysses' storytelling in Homer). Readers interested in a general survey of the variations in the use of time in twentieth-century literature may consult *Temps et roman* by Jean Pouillon, or the article by Jean Onimus on "The Expression of Time in the Contemporary Novel" in the *Revue de Littérature Comparée* (July–Sept., 1954).

What is involved in *Jealousy* is not a retreat into the past (Proust), nor the construction of multiple duration (Gide, Dos Passos, Sartre), nor the blending of several chronologically ambiguous plots (Faulkner), nor the use of interpenetrations of past and present (Huxley, Graham Greene), nor the construction of a false time to prepare for a surprise dénouement (as in certain detective stories), nor the now-conventionalized mixture of past and present made familiar by the flashbacks of the movies.

If one had to state briefly exactly what *is* involved in *Jealousy*, one might say, at the risk of oversimplifying the novel, that the work attempts to create, as objectively as possible, the *mental content* of a jealous narrator: what this man, during a rather short and concentrated period of time (a few days, a few weeks at most), sees, hears, touches, and imagines. During the "time" of the novel the protagonist observes, lives, suffers, and remembers the events of the plot, and makes of them, through his dynamic imagination, the "experience" which is the novel itself.

The result is a great formal freedom (variations of scenes, reiterations of themes with shifting emphasis, developments of episodes, metamorphoses of external elements and objects) bearing an analogy to musical structure, in which the composer may feel free to return at will to any previous theme, or to rearrange the order of his themes (always, of course, in terms of the musical integration appropriate to the composer's style). But, like all analogies this too is inexact, and risks falsifying the true essence of a literary structure made not of the materials of music (sounds organized by rhythms and expressed in harmonies and discords) but of forms of language, phrases imbued with psychological reminiscences and incrusted with semantic layers of meaning. Furthermore, the formal liberty of *Jealousy* is primarily a matter of its apparent or exterior chronology; interior, or psychological, chronology pursues, as we shall see, a rigorous line of development in the direction of progressive psychological tension.

Jealousy is composed or structured, then, on the basis of the interior order of a man's vision—that of the jealous husband, who, though he may "progress" in time, that is, though he may *live* the episodes that he describes (or better, that the text *presents*), at the same time *relives* other episodes, reexamines them, compares them, directs new questions at them, and transforms or metamorphoses them by the action of his imagination. There is an overall linear chronological movement from a beginning of initial suspicion toward a final appeasement following the apparent failure of the affair between wife and lover. But it is a linear progression which is almost immediately interrupted, twisted by repetitions, sidetracked by reversions into the past, troubled by anticipations and recapitulations, and which seems to reach a dead end in the fourth of the nine parts of the novel. After Part IV we find nothing really "new" in the plot—apart from the absence of A. Yet the high point of the novel, the crisis of jealousy that is reached in Part VII, is attained only after further astonishing and brilliant developments of already familiar materials, and is in turn followed by a *diminuendo* and *coda* of exceptional beauty and virtuosity.

Two levels of action may in general be distinguished: the level of the scenes which—apparently at least—"happen" at the same time that the narrator presents them to us (without, however, their forming a chronological sequence in themselves), and the level of the scenes which the narrator (in accordance with principles to be examined later) recalls, recreates, or even imagines.

What may appear to be chaotic, then—the textual order of scenes—is in reality, a perfectly coherent artistic unity. Admitting this, we may without prejudice to the work extract from it a linear plot. This implies no setting in order, no rectification. What is involved is forging a tool of research and investigation for an enterprise of understanding a difficult fictional structure; later, when it has served its purpose, the tool will be laid aside.

To salvage and place, with any degree of exactitude, the "facts" of the plot of *Jealousy* in chronological order, it becomes necessary to clarify the images seen in the distorting mirror of the husband's vision, in which events and objects are caught and reflected. We must constantly separate ourselves from this jealous husband that we *become* as we read, whose tormenting emotion we share, whose perceptions and ideas haunt us, who drags us with him into his eternal cycle of obsessive visions that annihilates all chronology. It becomes necessary, in a word, for the reader, having become a man sick with jealousy, to be cured of his disease, to be brought back to normal.

What "linear" plot do we find, then, taking all necessary precautions, in *Jealousy?* A dedicatory notice that the author composed for a copy now owned by the collector Artine Artinian speaks of "a narrative without plot," in which there are only "minutes without days, windows without panes, a house without mystery, a passion without anyone to feel it." Does this radical reduction of the text correspond to what a close reading finds therein?

The book unfolds in a tropical banana plantation, perhaps in the Antilles, but not in Africa (though the description of the region in many ways suggests Africa rather than the Antilles). We are installed (after a few pages no one can doubt this) in the mind, in the sense fields, of a narrator or pseudo narrator who from the first sentence trains upon everything that surrounds him the most minute attention: the form and structure of his square house, its veranda columns that function like a kind of sun dial, the geometrical arrangement of his banana trees, the smallest details of his exterior world. This man at the center of the narrative, who never refers to himself (does one refer to himself in his own thoughts?), directs this scrupulous attention even more minutely at his wife A. (Is this absence of the complete name a kind of psychological shortcut, or an effect of timidity in the narrator?) But when A turns her head toward her husband, he no longer dares look toward her, and the text that we read "whirls" immediately in another direction, stopping on a baluster of the veranda, or upon some sector of the plantation.

From the beginning of the novel, the husband's anxiety concerning his wife's actions is felt in the manner in which he watches A: as she writes a letter; as she reads, in a veranda chair, a novel given to her by Franck, a neighboring planter; as she hastily orders removed from the dinner table the place set for Christiane, Franck's wife, when Christiane (who suffers from some vague illness) fails to arrive with her husband. A seems to listen with special attention to Franck's conversation. His energetic manner disturbs the husband and seems to impress his young wife.

Fragments of conversation accumulate: Franck talks about the mechanical breakdowns of his truck, and the shortcomings of native drivers; both Franck and A discuss the novel she has begun to read, and the narrator appears to discern in their ambiguous remarks references to a jealous husband, an aggressive lover, an unfaithful wife (who even gives herself to Negroes)—an elaborate story whose scene is laid in Africa and whose possible parallels with the present situation will furnish the narrator occasions for painful conjectures.[4]

4. This "African novel" in *Jealousy* offers numerous similarities to *The Heart of the Matter* (1948) of Graham Greene, whose works seem to have furnished Robbe-Grillet with various fictional elements. The following points of resemblance may be mentioned between the inner novel of *Jealousy* (as well as the work as a whole) and *The Heart of the Matter*, in which we find: the Post Office calendar and the wife's photograph on the husband's desk (p. 8); a lizard on the wall (p. 58); the cockroaches on the wall, and the game of squashing them (pp. 66, 74); Scobie's struggle against jealousy on seeing Wilson kiss his wife (p. 80); the malaria attacks, with atropine and quinine (pp. 81, 91); the dishonesty of an employee (pp. 137, 162); Scobie's unexpected entrance (p. 241); and doubtless other details. Robbe-Grillet has not sought to hide the resemblance between the inner African novel of *Jealousy* (despite its "description of a tornado" and its "revolt of the natives," which have no parallel in Greene's novel) and *The Heart of the Matter;* but until now no critic has taken the trouble to verify the relationship. These parallels, together with those pointed out between Greene's *Brighton Rock* and *The Erasers* in Chapter 2, show the fascination felt by Robbe-Grillet for Green's novels, which, Robbe-Grillet once said to me, "often made me want to rewrite them."

The use made by Robbe-Grillet of reduced models of the work itself in the form of inner novels, legends, pictures, and the like relates to the general question of inner duplication, or the procedure of

These conversations continue on the veranda, at the cock-
tail hour and after dinner. A has arranged the porch chairs so
that she remains beside Franck, while her husband, placed
ahead and to one side of her, cannot see the two of them
without turning his head sharply backward (which he does
not dare do until the night is too dark to permit him to see
anything). Cries of animals moving about in the darkness reinforce the tense and violent atmosphere of the tropics, heavy
with expectancy and hidden energy.

Implicit brutality, energy, and sexuality are expressed in a
major scene which, although never exactly situated chronologically, occurs according to some indications even before
the loan of the African novel to A. At dinner, a centipede appears on the wall opposite A. Franck is the one who gets up to
squash it, first on the wall and then against the molding near
the floor. The erotic meaning hidden in this action manifests
itself in certain reactions and gestures on the part of A that
show a distinctly sexual implication: accelerated breathing,
hand clenched on her dinner knife. (Aside from this scene, A
never allows the slightest emotion to show, which further
emphasizes the importance of the shock felt at this moment.)
The spot left by the centipede on the wall opposite A becomes
an index point for the beginning of the sexual attraction between Franck and A, and the scene of the squashing of the
myriapod (subjected later to extended developments) becomes
inextricably associated with their possible physical relations.

The ensuing "episode of the ice bucket" produces in the
narrator (or rather in the *reader*) the impression that A and
Franck are planning some sort of project. The three are drinking on the veranda—mixed drinks which A has brought out.
Neither she nor the houseboy—is it because she arranged it
thus?—has brought the usual ice for the drinks. A's remarks on

"*mise en abyme*," first described by André Gide. See my article, "Un
Héritage d'André Gide: la duplication intérieure," *Comparative Literature Studies*, June 1971, pp. 125–142.

the lack of ice cause the husband to rise from his chair and go to fetch some. He passes through his study, which also serves as his office, and looks out through the *jalousies* or slatted blinds to observe A and Franck. They are motionless but appear to be speaking in a low voice. In the pantry, the houseboy is filling the ice bucket preparatory to bringing it to the veranda, and gives only a vague explanation of what his instructions were from A concerning the ice. When he returns to the veranda, the husband sees (but only in the first repetition of this scene in his *memory*) in Franck's pocket a sheet of blue writing paper—a letter from A?—which Franck tries to conceal.

The project becomes more evident when Franck, still complaining of frequent breakdowns of his truck, states that he plans to drive down to the coastal city to enquire about the purchase of a new vehicle. A proposes immediately to go along; she needs to make, she explains, a number of purchases. Franck explains that Christiane is prevented from going by her poor health and her child; but in any case they will be back after nightfall, if they leave early. Everything appears normal, but whenever the narrator revisualizes this scene of the project, it appears to him in a more ambiguous light, as his suspicions grow.

So A departs with Franck, at six o'clock in the morning, in Franck's blue sedan. There follows the long day which the husband spends alone in the empty house. Here, in Parts VI and VII of the novel, the protagonist's paroxysm of jealousy reaches its culmination. Haunted by visions of his wife, the narrator prowls through the rooms of the house. In his study the photograph of A becomes confused with postures of A in her veranda chair, sitting next to Franck. Scenes return mixed, altered, emphasized differently: the letter that A writes in her room, the episode of the ice, the conversation about the African novel, the plans for the trip to the coast, the squashing of the centipede. The unbearable erotic significance of this last scene appears again in the husband's efforts to remove the trace of the animal from the wall, by means of an eraser and a razor blade, an operation that blends immediately with an action of A in her room, when she appeared to be erasing something from a letter. A's room is subjected to a systematic search, including the bureau drawers and the drawer of the writing table. The subject of the picture on the Post Office calendar above the writing table produces in the husband proto-criminal confusions (to which he reverts again) in which are mingled the motif of a ship tied at the dock (a theme related to his fear that A will leave him) and images of someone drowned (that curious object floating in the water). Later, in returning to this fantasy, the husband will see in the picture a man wearing a tropical helmet like Franck's.

In spite of the presence of elements ostensibly posterior to the day the narrator spends alone in the house, we can situate during this time, at least from the psychological viewpoint, the scene that constitutes the apotheosis of the crushing of the centipede. Night has fallen and A has still not returned. Sitting on the veranda, the husband listens to the trucks passing in the distance and watches the oval movements of the insects whirling in their orbits around a hissing gasoline lamp. The turmoil of his thoughts, objectively reinforced by that of the whirling insects, revolves around images of A and Franck: on veranda, at the dinner table. Actions begin to become mechanized; one feels that the husband is hastening his memory to reach some kind of climax: and once again it is the crushing of the centipede. But this time, the husband sees Franck crush the animal against the wall of a *hotel room*, then return to A, who waits for him in a bed behind a shabby mosquito net, her hand clenched on the white sheet. Rhythmic phrases of an equivocal nature then carry the narrator's image into the half-erotic, half-murderous vision of a car wreck in which A and Franck are engulfed by crackling flames, in a noise similar to the crackling sound produced by the centipede, or to that made by the hair brush as A strokes her long black tresses. This imaginary scene of the lovers *in flagrante delicto*, followed by their imaginary death in flames, constitutes the psychological apogee of the novel.

What does the husband do later, that night, in his solitude, after these anguishing visions? Does he spend the night in A's bed, upon which he pictures her in erotic posture? Does he engage in autoerotic practices? The text, with verbal ambiguities suggestive of unspoken implications, allows us to suppose what we will.

The following morning, A has still not returned. The husband breakfasts on the veranda. A native from Franck's plantation (who had come once before, perhaps sent by Christiane to spy on Franck's actions) arrives: his mistress is upset at Franck's failure to return home. At lunch, the narrator sees in the dining-room windowpane the distorted reflection of Franck's car pulling into the courtyard. A gets out, holding in her hand a tiny package (is that all she has bought?). The husband, despite his hasty movements, is unable to see whether A has kissed Franck before turning toward the house; the posture of the couple allows such a supposition. Before setting out for his plantation (he seems hurried) Franck adds to the explanations furnished by A a few details concerning the reasons for their absence: car trouble forced them to spend the night in town at a hotel. Franck appears ill at ease with A, who seems to tease him. Franck alludes ambiguously to his being a "poor mechanic" (was there a sexual disappointment on the part of A?). Henceforth, Franck's behavior changes; he is always in a hurry to return home; his dinner visits become rarer.

The novel moves toward a mood of appeasement, contributed to by partial repetitions and variations of scenes which are perhaps (in the "real" sequence of actions) prior to the trip: A's return from a visit to Christiane, driven home by Franck; more or less motionless postures of A in her bedroom and elsewhere. The plot or story is, so to speak, over. The husband's crisis, with its visions of sexuality, its images of fear and revenge, has passed. The rise and fall of the protagonist's recollections begin to diminish in an attenuated rhythm of contradictory variations, blurred outlines, and confusions. The narrator's uncertainty now affects each return to a former scene, and even makes a contradictory hodgepodge of his conception of the African novel (that hateful instrument of infidelity), which he destroys mentally in a paranoiac passage.

But at least, the reader feels, the husband consoles himself with the fact that his wife is still there. The fantasies of her escape and flight have not turned into reality. Perhaps there is even no real danger from Franck. The tropic night may now engulf the house and the characters.

When does the narrator see or envision these scenes? It is impossible, and contrary to the intentions of the author of *Jealousy*, to establish a timetable. Following the strictest logic, one would be forced to think (since there are, almost from the beginning of the novel, frequent allusions and intercalations concerned with "later" events) that the whole narrative takes place in the *memory* of the narrator after the "end" of the plot, when the husband, already in possession of all the elements of his experience, tries to see things in such a way as to decide the truth or untruth of his wife's unfaithfulness. But this conception fails to explain the essential feeling of *immediacy* which prevails in most of the scenes. Obviously what is involved is not an exact chronology (even mental), but the restructuring of inner or psychological time. The narrator lives and relives in a time system that goes in two directions. Elements of memory and of "real" time (or of the present) are fused within him in a time system that is outside real time. Hence the chronology of the novel has quite new dimensions. Linear time is distorted so that it may pass into this new continuum, only to emerge, altered, developed, or even diminished, at unforeseen moments, in a process in which each element continues to remain alive, to evolve, to modify the whole. An examination of these procedures will show how Robbe-Grillet gives artistic coherence to scenes which seem to be floating in a loose, chaotic fashion in new zones of literature. It may be stated at the outset that the principles of order and association which prevail can derive only from an implicit psychology, expressed in objective correlatives.[5]

5. A declaration by Robbe-Grillet in the *Nouvelles Littéraires* of Jan. 22, 1959 is relevant to what might be termed the attempt to "reconstruct" the chronology of *Jealousy* made in this study. The novelist states that "to try to reconstitute [. . .] the chronology of *Jealousy* is impossible, impossible because I intended it thus." Now I certainly have no desire to find in Robbe-Grillet's work something which is not there, and I think I have sufficiently emphasized the atemporal quality of the sequences of scenes in the novel. But none the less, the author of *Jealousy* has followed, in writing his work (and in his own words) "a rigorously premeditated plan," and in this plan there is a general chronological movement very similar to the one I present here. There are also in the novel (and I point them out) chronological *impasses* or dead ends: for example, the major scene of the killing of the centipede (transformed into an erotic paroxysm) seems to occur in the narrator's vision while his wife is absent, and yet this scene already contains elements of the *explanation* of her absence furnished by A upon her return (the hotel, the mosquito netting). In this sense, it is quite true that one cannot construct a linear chronology for the novel (in contrast with certain works of Huxley or Graham Greene, for example, where there are only rearrangements of time without fusions). On the other hand, it seems to me impossible to understand *Jealousy* completely, or to explain the structure of the novel, without bearing in mind the principal "stages" of the plot: the letter, the episode of the ice, the plan of the trip to the coast, the trip itself, A's absence and return, Franck's subsequent manner. The genius of the author is revealed in the way in which he brings to bear on all this the transfiguration and detemporalization that changes this "story" (rather banal actually) into a new fictional form. The author's remark that he "intended it thus" applies chiefly to the total aesthetic effect of the work, to which the reader must return after any analysis such as the one presented here. I do not think that I am either at-

In creating the psychological tensions that bind together the elements of the novel, the author constructs corresponding chronological tensions. These are not only the repetitions and variations of the principal scenes (the incident of the ice, the centipede, and the like) but also a number of smaller variations in external time which form supports or correlatives for the psychological variations, or even contrasts to them. Thus, reiterations of almost identical scenes are mingled with observations on the number of banana plants that have been cut in a certain trapezoidal plot of ground situated opposite the house. The first time the trapezoid appears, "several plants have already been cut there"; the second reference concurs; and all seems to progress normally (although intervening scenes have varied radically in their time sequence) when one reads that "all the banana plants have been harvested" in this sector. Nevertheless, at the next reference (when the feeling of duration has been produced in the reader by many pages of text) "none of the plants" has as yet been cut in the trapezoid, a contradictory or refractory condition, so to speak, which still persists toward the end of the novel, when the harvest is described again as not having yet begun in this field. These variations are seen to be an even greater barrier against linear chronology when one understands that we are never told precisely which cutting is meant, in connection with this plant which grows up again with great rapidity.

In similar fashion, the variations in the positions of the workmen during the "ballet of the logs" they are maneuvering in repairing the bridge over the stream that flows through the valley, in sight of the house, constitute equivocal and contradictory time markers. Against the background formed by the more or less linear progression of these maneuvers, occur scenes from different stages of time; and yet the last appear-

---

tempting the impossible, then, or revealing secrets that are not to be discussed.

ance of the workmen shows them again on the bridge ready to *begin* their task. To reinforce the psychochronological tension thus produced, a fixed theme (with respect to the bridge) appears here and there: a native is crouched upon it, watching the water as if searching for something (in the same posture as the man on the calendar in A's room). This vaguely disturbing theme of a possible drowning doubtless represents a projection of an unexpressed desire of the narrator.

The indices or markers in this system of time variations form also, in their interlocking designs, a mobile chronological network. Examples are the way in which the author uses references to the place A has reached in her reading of the African novel, to the presence or absence of the spot left by the centipede on the wall. Only such temporal markers permit in many cases a distinction in the order of adjacent scenes: Franck taking his hasty leave *after* the return from the trip with A sets down a glass in which there is left no trace of ice; but a few lines further we read, "At the bottom of the glass that he sets down is the last unmelted fragment of a small piece of ice, rounded on one side." This sentence returns the scene violently to a former incident, although in the same paragraph a different index, the arrangement of the logs for the bridge, seems to progress rapidly toward the future with respect to the immediately preceding scene. Terms such as "then," "now," "since," "still," "at that moment," and especially the term "but," strewn among the parachronisms of the narrative in an absolutely nonlinear manner, give to the supposedly normal rhythms of the sentences countermovements of a very complex periodicity. If one adds to this the effect of the imaginary scenes (retrospective or future), one emphasizes again the quasi impossibility of a complete clarification of the thoughts, perceptions, actions, and emotions of the narrator, which are often metamorphosed into a state of psychic visions.

In an attempt to explain the apparent incoherence of structure in *Jealousy* several critics have pointed out a parallel between the description in the novel of a native chant and the composition of the narrative itself. The reader will recall the passage describing this "song of the second chauffeur":

[. . .] it is difficult to determine if the song is interrupted for some fortuitous reason—in relation, for instance, to the manual work the singer is performing at the same time—or whether the tune has come to its natural conclusion.

Similarly, when it begins again, it is just as sudden, as abrupt, starting on notes which hardly seem to constitute a beginning, or a reprise.

At other places, however, something seems about to end; everything indicates this: a gradual cadence, tranquility regained, the feeling that nothing remains to be said; but after the note which should be the last comes another one, without the least break in continuity [. . .] then another, and others following, and the hearer supposes himself transported into the heart of the poem . . . when at that point everything stops without warning. [Pp. 66–67]

Such a parallel, however, runs the risk of falsifying the unity of the novel, and constitutes in reality a mistaken conception of the true role of the chant or song. This fluid song is only ambiguous because we *do not know its rules.* Likewise, the sequence of scenes in the narrator's mind is only superficially equivocal; even if the narrator himself appears not to understand the necessity that joins together the scenes he envisions, he obeys none the less, in conjuring them up, inexplicit but well-defined psychological rules. One might even say that on the surface, things happen *as if* there prevailed in the narrative an incoherence similar to that presumed to prevail in the native song. But to conclude from this that the novel presents a disjointed, random sequence of scenes, or a series of unmotivated actions, or a willfully embroiled chronology designed only to confuse the reader or to attempt to surpass other novelists (such as Huxley, Joyce, Faulkner) in concocting chronological confusion, would be a serious mistake.

Most of the corrections that must be made in what serious critics have written about Robbe-Grillet's work have to do with two basic errors. One is the mistaken idea that the author seeks to create (according to the formula attributed to the native song in *Jealousy*) disjointed literary structures without "causality." The other is that Robbe-Grillet wishes to dehumanize the novel. We have just seen the danger presented by confusing the deliberate use of an appearance of acausality in the creation of literary effects (here the depiction of the mental state of a jealous husband), and "true" acausality, even admitting that the letter can really exist. A similar critique may be made of the attribution to Robbe-Grillet of a novelistic theory of dehumanization.

Robbe-Grillet has himself often categorically denied the too widespread idea that he wishes to depersonalize the novel. Apart from any question of psychology, the large role of the visual in his art (which some critics cite to argue his basic coldness) is envisaged by the author as a means of placing in the center of a narrative a "human eye" which, far from excluding man from the universe, "in reality gives him the principal place, that of the observer."[6] Still stronger is the rejection of the accusation of dehumanization in the article "Nature, Humanism, Tragedy," in which Robbe-Grillet (without naming the novel) speaks of the technique of *Jealousy:* "How can they [the critics . . .] accuse a novel of turning against or away from man when it follows from page to page each of his steps, describing only what he does, what he sees, or what he imagines?"[7] The confusion which allows this misunderstanding concerning Robbe-Grillet's alleged "dehumanization" to persist rests primarily on an erroneous conception of his ideas

6. "Notes on the Localization of Point of View in the Contemporary Novel," *Revue des Lettres Modernes,* Summer 1958.

7. Translated from "Nature, Humanisme, Tragédie" (*Nouvelle Revue Française,* Oct. 1958), in *Evergreen Review,* Summer 1959, p. 100, under the title "Old 'Values' and the New Novel."

on the *neutrality* of objects in the universe, and also on the attraction felt by some modern thinkers toward the very idea of acausality itself. These misconceptions are shown clearly in critical discussions of the possible role of *symbols* in Robbe-Grillet. Now the idea of symbol—an idea so contaminated in our time that in appropriating to itself too many meanings it has lost all meaning—is, indeed, a kind of *bête noire* for Robbe-Grillet. What has troubled the critics is that the author, having denounced all symbolism, has used (in their opinion) a highly developed personal symbolism (figures of eight in *The Voyeur*, the centipede in *Jealousy*). The contradiction disappears if we carefully examine the author's literary processes in the light of his theoretical statements. First, after rejecting completely any *inherent* meaning of objects (as well as all ideas involving the mystical symbolism of hidden correspondences), Robbe-Grillet reconstitutes an emotional or psychological use of the object, which he describes quite clearly: "the eye of [. . .] man comes to rest on things with a hard insistence: he sees them, but refuses to make them part of himself, refuses to enter into any conniving or doubtful relationship with them. [. . .] He may [. . .] make them a *support for his passion*, for the line of sight that he directs at the world."[8] It is therefore in an objective correlation between emotions and objects, as seen by Robbe-Grillet's characters, or in the use of objects as supports for feelings, that one must seek the secret of the "refusal of psychology" attributed to the author, which is in reality only a refusal of *psychological analysis*. To create, not analyze, the psychology of his characters: such is the essential goal of Robbe-Grillet's art. The irony is that the author of such a novel as *Jealousy*, capable of producing in the reader unprecedented direct effects of human emotion, should be accused of coldness, of excessive attention to descriptive detail, mainly be-

8. *Evergreen Review*, Summer 1959, pp. 100–101; my italics.

cause he has refused to practice the conventional style of psychological analysis "expected" in the current novel.

Literary antipsychology is not an exclusively present-day development, and the reaction against the tradition of Stendhal, Balzac, and Proust (or their Anglo-Saxon counterparts) is far from having run its course. In France, the influence of the so-called American "behaviorist" novel on the antipsychological writings of Sartre and Camus is recognized. There is little point in retracing such influences, or in pointing out the development of mixed forms, in which "objectivity" and interior monologues are combined with multiple viewpoints and chronological rearrangements. With the influence of Kafka added, certain modern novels present an adulterated *mélange* which exerts a strong attraction on readers and critics who have developed a taste for a more or less irrational novel, placed under the sign of a pseudo metaphysics of complete acausality. According to the devotees of acausality (who would like perhaps to appropriate an author like Robbe-Grillet, whose work might appear to fit their theories), the alleged meaningfulness of the world is but a façade which contemporary thought has fragmented into pieces whose only relationships are mere "synchronicities," unmotivated arrangements, or simple contiguities. The classic simplicity of David Hume's anticausality (which was at once absolutely logical and completely unbelievable) disappears in a new "modern" complexity. Many echoes of these contemporary ideas may be found in certain defenders of Robbe-Grillet. Yet the relationships between objects and characters, in this author, belong as little to the realm of meaningless juxtaposition as they do to that of concordant symbolism (or even to the so-called "uninterpretable" symbolism of an Auerbach). Robbe-Grillet's objects, although cleansed of all mystical relationship to the human soul, and although placed in a neutral universe, become, in his own terms, the supports of his characters' passions—ob-

jective correlatives, one may say, which the fictional characters must have in order to live—an existential necessity. Robbe-
Grillet's objects are optico-audio-sensorio-verbal structures
that surround the characters and receive, as they penetrate
into the visual field or the psychic interiority of a character
(though remaining descriptively "objectal"), the psychic discharge engendered by the "life" (or the *situation*) of the character. Robbe-Grillet's art is then neither an art of incoherence
nor an art of dehumanization. His objects are neither without
human meaning nor arranged in a series of synchronous juxta-
positions in a literary universe without causality.

Under careful study, all the scenes of *Jealousy* are found to
obey, in their sequence, very precise rules of *liaison* or linking.
In the dramatic art of the French seventeenth century, critics
like the Abbé d'Aubignac discovered an elaborate system of
liaison de scènes, followed more or less consciously by Cor-
neille, Racine, and other classical playwrights: scenes linked
through the *view* of one character (who, for example, when
leaving the stage sees another arriving, or vice versa), through
the common *presence* of an actor in successive scenes, through
noises overheard by characters entering or leaving the scene,
even through the *intentions* of one or another character as he
enters or exits. This system arose from a need of continuity in
dramatic action, and represented a classical predilection for
coherence as characteristic of the seventeenth century as the
taste for disjointed acausality (at least for some) is of the
twentieth. Psychologists will someday perhaps explain (they
have so many things yet to explain) the psychic bases of artistic unity, for it takes all forms, including that of so-called "unmotivated" arrangements.

In *Jealousy*, there is first of all a general (and obvious) liaison between scenes through the narrator's *view*. Our aware-
ness of this is almost instantaneous, and helps relatively little
in understanding the structure of the novel. What must be

sought are the implicit motives or reasons for these shifts of the husband's view. The reader becomes aware of the latent psychological force behind these shifts when the visual field is abruptly changed. The best example is the often repeated turning aside of the glance provoked in the husband when A raises her eyes toward him, an action which invariably causes a sudden turning of the viewpoint:

The black curls of her hair shift with a supple movement and brush her shoulders as she turns her head.

The heavy hand-rail of the balustrade has almost no paint left on top. The gray of the wood shows through. [P. 2]

Such a shift is soon felt to be habitual by the reader, who thus shares directly the husband's inability to look A in the eyes, when, watching her in her room, he sees her start to glance out toward the veranda, the garden, or the bridge, or notices that she has moved up to look out through the slits in the Venetian blinds of a window.

But this turning aside of the glance, caused by a movement of A's head, sometimes opens up in the continuity of the text a large "hole" in time, unrelated chronologically to the exact time of A's action, and in which events occur with the rapidity of a dream, of a memory, or of imagination itself. In the example quoted, A has just entered her room. She has turned toward the door to close it, then toward the narrator. Immediately the narrative eye looks elsewhere, and, for several pages of narrative, surveys the general orientation of the house in its surroundings. (The incidental function of this passage as exposition is obvious and needs no comment.) But when the husband again looks toward A he sees his wife still with her back against the bedroom door (thus at a moment that could only be a second or two later than the original instant, already "old" textually, when he glanced away), and the continuity of the former movement resumes when A takes several steps forward into the room toward her bureau.

Often, between scenes apparently linked by the view or sight of the narrator, we find intervening verbal terms (of which several have already been mentioned) which almost imperceptably mask nonlinear transitions in time or space. Not only do the terms "now," "moreover," and "besides" almost always produce temporal displacements, but also phrases such as "on the left," "nearby," "in that direction," and other spatial references such as "at the same distance, but in a perpendicular direction" send the reader out of a given visual zone to plunge him into a different time. These terms and phrases are the verbal equivalents of the inner disturbances provoked in the husband by psychological movements and changes. Interestingly for the study of the technique of the novel, almost all the transitions between scenes occur at the beginning of a paragraph. The rare exceptions pass almost unnoticed except on the most minute reading, and represent only very brief alternations between tightly linked elements.

What are the principles that govern these movements in time, these cyclic returns that seem woven into the present (even when they anticipate the future), these apparently fortuitous liaisons of view and shifts in the field of vision? Space changes become indistinguishable from time changes; both must be explained together as a unified process. Yet time dominates, and the constant (and violent) oscillation in "normal" time puzzles many readers of *Jealousy*. To understand how different events and different times are linked in the eternal present of the narrator, we must penetrate into his character. All the temporal displacements occur as a function of his personality, in a more fundamental way even than the immediate shifts in his glance, or in his physical movements on the veranda, in the corridor of the house, behind the blinds in his study, in his wife's room, or elsewhere.

The reader's task is less to uncover a "solution" to the narrator's personality that will explain the novel, than to undergo himself the literary experience of the text in such a way as to share this personality directly, to understand (nonverbally) and accept this man's visions and actions as if they were (for the duration of the work) his own. Human diversity will doubtless always prevent certain readers from "succumbing" to the functioning of a novel like *Jealousy*. Corrupted by their reading of analytical novels, some readers will always insist that the novelist *explain* to them (in the explicit terms made fashionable by the psychology of the day) his character's thoughts and actions; these readers will no doubt refuse to experience the jealous husband's emotion. They will always demand verbal clarifications and commentaries. For them, *Jealousy* will be a novel that functions weakly, or not at all.

One proof of this may be found in the absurdity of the criticisms that have been formulated against the narrator-husband of *Jealousy*. Critics have categorically denied his versimilitude. Many have protested against the minuteness of his description of the banana trees and his counting of them (is it not psychologically plausible, however, that this hyperattentive man should apply to his plantation the same exaggerated attention and scrutiny that he practices in other respects?). The narrator has been called a monster rather than a human character. Robbe-Grillet has been rebuked for not letting his protagonist act, for restraining him from "participating" in his own story. Critics have claimed that the narrator does not even appear in the novel, that he never speaks, and that, moreover, if he did speak his words would resemble closely the chaotic verbiage of the "protean monster" that Samuel Beckett depicts in *The Unnamable*.

But it is most inexact to state that this jealous narrator "never reveals himself." The whole novel is his self-revelation. One may even argue that the husband speaks, but without citing his own words (is this not the impression one frequently has of his own words, when one recalls a conversation?). He speaks several times, and there is every reason to suppose that his speech is perfectly conventional, without the slightest resemblance to Beckett's verbal chaos. Here is the narrator "speaking" to his wife, at the dinner table:

> To be still more certain, it is enough to ask her if she doesn't think the cook has made the soup too salty.
> "Oh no," she answers, "you have to eat salt so as not to sweat." [P. 12]

During the incident of the ice bucket, the narrator directs a question to the houseboy; we read: "To a vague question as to when he received this order, he answers: 'Now,' which furnishes no satisfactory indication" (p. 31). When A returns from the trip with Franck, she "enquires what events may have occurred at the plantation"; the narrator's reply is given in the form of indirect discourse: "Besides, there is nothing new." Then the husband himself asks one or more questions: "She herself, questioned as to her news, limits her remarks to four or five pieces of information" (p. 63).

Certainly the husband is reticent, not only with respect to his own words, but also as far as his "inaction" concerning his jealous suspicions is concerned. But far from being a "monster held on a leash," he may be viewed as obeying in all probability a fundamental timidity based on implied psychic impotency in his sexual attitude toward A, accompanied by fear that his wife will leave him. Timidity and impotence, fear of aggressiveness like that of Franck (who would perhaps be capable of overcoming a certain coldness in A which in itself might partly explain the husband's difficulties), overmeticulous attention directed at the world, constant fear of abandonment by A (expressed in various fantasies of *fugue*): the husband appears, thus described, as an almost classic type from manuals of psychosexual disturbances, a human being of almost too familiar "versimilitude."

Using then an operating principle (found in a sort of psychoanalysis of the narrator) to follow the liaison of scenes in *Jealousy*, we can take up again the problem of the novel's structure. Although the sense of sight dominates in *Jealousy* (the author has often commented on the priority of the visual in the novelistic universe he favors), many liaisons may be identified as effected by means of sounds, which engender relationships, correlations, and metamorphoses. Examples are the noise of the gasoline lamp during A's absence, the noises of trucks on the highway behind the house (expectation, fear of Franck), and the important complex of sounds including the crackling of the comb or brush in A's long hair, which is found again in the noise made by the buccal appendages of the centipede and the crackling of the flames engulfing Franck's car imagined by the narrator at the climax of his crisis.

A revealing example of transitions effected by means of a sound is the following in Part IX: The narrator has returned to the moment—before A's departure for the coast with Franck —when his wife is still engaged in reading the African novel (whereas the preceding scene was one that *followed* her return from the trip). The passage develops thus:

. . . she looks for the place where her reading was interrupted by Franck's arrival, somewhere in the first part of the story. But having found the page again, she lays the open book face down on her knees and remains where she is without doing anything, leaning back in the leather chair.

From the other side of the house comes the sound of a heavy truck heading down the highway toward the bottom of the valley, the plain, and the port—where the white ship is moored alongside the pier.

The veranda is empty, the house too. [. . .]

It is not the sound of the truck that can be heard, but that of a sedan coming down the dirt road from the highway, toward the house.

In the open left leaf of the first dining-room window, in the middle of the central pane of glass, the reflected image of the blue car has just stopped in the middle of the courtyard. A and Franck get out of it together. [Pp. 138–139]

At the beginning of the passage, A's posture reflects a certain combination of independence and impatience tinged with *bovaryisme* that is characteristic of many of the scenes before (and perhaps even after) the planning of the trip with Franck. Is A dreaming of escape? The sound of a truck accentuates this fear of A's flight, which the narrator sees in terms of a possible flight toward the port (where the truck is headed), then on the ship anchored there (an allusion to the picture on the calendar in her room). From this idea of flight the husband passes to the time of the actual absence of his wife, during the trip (the whole house is empty). Then the dominating noise that binds the scenes together leads to the scene of the return in Franck's sedan, a scene to which the narrator constantly reverts in an effort to search out elements that might change or confirm his suspicions.

This fluid progression in time could scarcely be more human, if not logical. Contrary to the opinion of certain critics, Robbe-Grillet is not attempting in any way, in such passages as this, to confuse or mix up time; one might even argue that he is attempting to clarify time, in the sense that he seeks to extract from its continuum all possible emotional relationships. To return inwardly to the smallest details of a vital experience, to replace them in all possible contexts, to scrutinize them from all viewpoints, to make them come alive again in various ways, to enlarge them imaginatively or reduce them to schematic outlines and dry résumés: all these procedures in the narrator's mind are but functions of his situation as a victim of jealousy. Everything in this so often misunderstood book is entirely plausible.

The art with which Robbe-Grillet has linked the scenes of *Jealousy* reaches its height of subtle development in Part V, which is a section of reprises and reinforcement of themes preparatory to the great scenes of A's absence and the husband's climax of jealousy. Part V begins with the native song of the second driver (who may himself be suspected of a sexual association with A) which, as pointed out, constitutes a kind of résumé or epitome of the structure of the novel and which schematizes the forms of future returns and anticipations. There follows a scene that finds A in her room, writing a letter (the beginning, as it were, of the whole story); she seems pensive, hesitating over the few lines she has written. She turns her head toward the window; the husband shifts his glance to follow the movements of the workmen on the log bridge (that mobile time marker). He looks again at A as she writes. She rises, moves toward the window, again causing the narrator to look away toward the distance, past the bridge this time to the trapezoidal planting sector, where the number of cut trees, as mentioned earlier, varies in such a way as to set free from linear chronology the time of any specific moment. Shortening his glance, the husband notes that the native workers are looking toward the house; he too "dares" look back toward A's window, and see her holding up before her the letter that she has been writing. At this point there occurs in the text the first antichronological transition of Part V that might appear arbitrary or disconcerting: suddenly Franck is sitting in his chair on the veranda, and A has gone to get the drinks.

Before us again, is the episode of the missing ice, and the narrator's self-imposed errand to bring some. But this time, the scene takes place in a rapid résumé, except for the appearance in Franck's pocket (on the narrator's return) of a letter written on the telltale pale blue paper. This new detail causes the progression into the psychological present of a scene that has already been "lived." Obviously the husband now finds an explanation, by reviving a scene in his memory, for a stage in the relations between A and Franck, and discovers in this new version clearer clues to A's betrayal. The husband asks himself indirect questions, which constitute a type of "thinking" about this scene that originally (in Part II) unfolded without such mental action. Why had the boy not brought the ice: "Could she then have told him not to bring it? It would have been the first time, otherwise, that she had failed to make herself understood to him." The entire reprise of the scene forms the answer which the husband constructs to the question that he asks upon seeing (still in his memory only) A in the act of writing a letter: when could she have transmitted this letter to Franck?

From the depths of this scene which takes place in the narrator's memory, A looks again toward him. Quickly he turns his eyes toward the log bridge; now, the arrangement of the workers has changed. (All the narrator's visions in this part are accompanied externally by maneuvers at the bridge.) Again it is the worker's looking toward the house which draws the husband's glance in that direction, but now it is to witness the scene of Franck's abrupt departure *after* his return from the trip with A. Setting down a glass without ice (that associative element), he leaves, muttering an excuse for being such a "poor mechanic" (the erotic meaning of the word will be developed later by the narrator). But, immediately, we read that in the bottom of the glass Franck has just set down there remains a small piece of ice of a certain form. We have returned once more to the other scene, to the episode of the ice, from which dates (in the husband's mind) the understanding between A and Franck.

A psychological force then begins to distort the husband's vision, to twist and dislocate his reconstruction of scenes between A and Franck. He repasses these episodes on the inner screen of his mind, whose images constitute the text that we read. Suddenly Franck and A, in their veranda chairs, have exchanged positions; other elements, such as the logs to be used in the new bridge, begin to change position. Transformations occur. By association perhaps with "mechanic," former actions return, mechanized: the houseboy walks "mechanically"; Franck's gestures (now he is seated at the table) become "exaggerated," with "rhythmic distortions." All these rapid reprises lead us inexorably toward a new version of the killing of the centipede. The boy's steps become more and more "jerky," he leaves the dining room moving his arms and legs in unison, "like some crude mechanism."

Although the scene of the crushing of the centipede now contains (as it does each time) new elements, it is still the letter that dominates the narrator's recall. Franck attempts (with a "mechanical" gesture) to push it back into his shirt pocket; it protrudes stubbornly; it is now definitely (after other foldings) "folded into eighths." It even becomes "covered with a fine, close writing."

The husband's torment produces a veritable stretto of chronological transitions. From Franck's pocket, seen at night in the dining room at the time of the crushing of the insect, the narrator's glance follows the shirt sleeve, moves to the crock situated behind Franck, falls upon the *extinguished* lamps, and thus emerges into broad daylight, for now the scene is a luncheon, and Franck is talking about his car. The car itself is "brought into the window" of the dining room by the conversation; but when the narrator looks at it, Franck is at the wheel, and A is getting out of the vehicle. Now two scenes of "return" are mixed, associated with Franck's sedan: the return from the trip with Franck, when A gets out holding a small package, and the return from a visit to see Christiane (or could it be to see Franck?), when A alights alone from the car.

There follows a whirling sequence of remembered images of the young wife: A listening to the native song, looking at her own image (is she bored, impatient?) in the mirror, combing her hair, plunging into her long tresses her "tapering" fingers (the erotic associations with A's narrow fingers occur frequently, especially in a visionary passage depicting A in an ambiguous posture on her bed), A writing the letter—the letter which, from one end to the other of Part V, forms the thread of Ariadne of all the husband's recalls, until the final disappearance of A into the zone of her bedroom, wherein she can no longer be seen from the outside (another image of the obsession with the possible escape of his wife which lies near the center of the husband's jealous complex).

Thus we observe that, in general, tacit psychological tensions of the narrator regularly form the basic principle of the transitions between the scenes of the novel. At the level of writing technique, we can distinguish transitions attributable to simple association (for example, A's dress brings to the narrator's mind an earlier conversation on this subject), to very advanced and complex relationships: liaisons that are more or less reversible in time, ostensibly based on sight, sounds, or movements of the narrator, often accompanied by ambiguous adverbial phrases. To these one could add associations of phrases (the "take a part," "break a heart" ambiguities; "everything has to start somewhere," "a poor mechanic"), formal resemblances of objects or patterns (the herringbone design of the corridor floor and the ripples on the river surface), and objects or places bound up with certain scenes (the dining-room window, which constantly brings back the scene of A's return in Franck's car).

Often, the technical execution of these liaisons involves a paragraph that is shared by two adjacent scenes. For example, at one point Franck and A are speaking of their plans for the trip. Then they discuss the African novel, speculating variously as to its possible denouement. The sentence "They sip their drinks" (a most irritating manner of drinking, one feels, to a husband who sees therein an excessive or conniving slowness) is repeated in refrainlike fashion. The passage then continues:

They sip their drinks. In the three glasses, the ice cubes have now altogether disappeared. Franck inspects the gold liquid remaining in the bottom of his glass. He turns it to one side, then the other, amusing himself by detaching the little bubbles clinging to the sides.

"Still," he says, "it started out well." He turns toward A for her support: "We left on schedule and drove along without any trouble. It wasn't even ten o'clock when we reached town." [Pp. 54–55]

The first of these two paragraphs could belong as well to the scene of the projected trip (or to that of the conversation concerning the African novel) as to the scene, quite posterior, of the return after the trip with Franck. Through this paragraph the narrator passes directly from one point of time to the other.

Still more striking is the metamorphosis of time and place that occurs when the husband sets out to erase from the wall, during A's absence, the spot left by the centipede. First using an eraser, then a razor blade, then the eraser again, the narrator manages to remove all traces of the fragments of legs and antennae remaining from the Scutigera. In the midst of this action, the situation of the erasure changes completely, and the blue letter paper which the husband had observed A working over formerly, doubtless performing some sort of erasure, becomes the paper on which the new erasing operation is performed. The ambiguity of the text is spread through two or three "mixed" paragraphs. Here are some of the stages:

The slender traces of bits of legs or antennae come off right away, with the first strokes of the eraser. The larger part of the body [. . .] becomes increasingly vague toward the tip of the curve, soon disappears completely. But the head and first joints require a more extensive rubbing. [. . .] The hard eraser passing back and forth over the same point does not have much effect now.

A complementary operation seems in order: to scratch the surface very lightly, with the corner of a razor blade. [. . .] A new rubbing with the eraser now finishes off the work quite easily.

The stain has disappeared altogether. There now remains only a vaguely outlined paler area, without any apparent depression of the surface, which might pass for an insignificant defect in the finish, at worst.

The paper is much thinner nevertheless; it has become more translucid, uneven, a little downy. The same razor blade, bent between two fingers to raise the center of its cutting edge, also serves to shave off the fluff the eraser has made. The back of a fingernail finally smoothes down the last roughness.

In broad daylight, a closer inspection of the pale blue sheet reveals that two short pen strokes have resisted everything, doubtless made too heavily. [Pp. 88–89]

Then the passage continues in this fluid fashion: the eraser causes a transition to the narrator's desk, where the photograph of A leads to a further vision of the young woman combing her hair, then to the scene where she performs, at her bedroom table, movements that the narrator interprets as the mending of a stocking, polishing of her nails, drawing with a pencil, or —more probably—erasing from a letter some "badly chosen" word. The husband appears to find in her motions an erotic meaning, and we read of "convulsions," ending in "a last spasm, much lower." Everything takes on for the narrator a significance traceable either to eroticism or to jealousy.

Jealousy probably contains more repetitions than any other work in the history of the novel. Robbe-Grillet has organized these repetitions of scenes and elements of scenes, however, so skillfully that they never lose force, but always gain. The scenes evolve, are transmuted, are developed (or foreshortened) constantly, following the inner rhythms of the narrator's emotions. Without these repetitions, the novel could scarcely exist, since it is largely in planned repetition (with variants) that the work finds its tempo and its form.

Some of these repetitions are of apparently innocent or trivial scenes: A sitting in the veranda chair with her novel (but is she not already dreaming of future infidelity?); A brushing her hair (but what an erotic fetish her hair represents!); A walking about in her room (but what a sacred place this room gradually becomes!). Imperceptibly varied repetitions occur in the background: the arrangement of the new logs for the bridge, the state of the trapezoidal sector of banana trees, the position of the shadow of the veranda column on the flagstone floor. The narrator is possessed by the need to examine everything many times, to turn, change, and modify each important scene.

We observed above, in following the metamorphoses of the letter written by A and the scenes linked to it (in Part V), how an object associated with the husband's jealousy can develop or evolve through a series of reprises. One could make a similar study of other elements: the African novel, the Post Office calendar, the arrangement of chairs on the veranda, the shape and size of the banana fields.

But the centipede is by far the dominant theme.

First, as a *spot*, the mark left on the wall by the crushed insect fits into the complicated design of other spots in the novel—Rorschach spots, so to speak, in which the husband seems to discover, or into which he projects, supports for his feelings. There is the oil stain in the courtyard (left by a car, perhaps Franck's), the dark red stain below A's bedroom window (could it be blood?), the paint spots on the baluster (which A wishes to have repainted), the stain on the tablecloth (at Franck's place), and even the mobile spot caused by the retinal image of A (whom the narrator has observed too long in the brilliant light of the gasoline lamp), which is seen everywhere against the house and the black sky. The spot is always a stain that needs to be removed or cleansed, since it represents for the husband the hateful stain of infidelity (hence the scenes of erasure analyzed earlier, the absorption of the oil stain in a defect of the dining-room window). Just as the narrator is incapable of suppressing his thoughts of A's betrayal, he is unable to get rid, definitively, of the other spots. Above all, he never succeeds in escaping from the spot left by the centipede, or in ceasing to place the scene of the quashing of this insect at the center of his complex, where it persists as the very image of the possible sexual relations between his wife and Franck.

The sequence of scenes related to the centipede follows a progressive order which illustrates convincingly the principle of psychological chronology in the development of an episode that has no fixed locus in "true" time. The spot, at its first appearance is: "a blackish spot [that] marks the place where a centipede was squashed last week, at the beginning of the month, perhaps the month before, or later" (p. 14). From the outset the time of the spot is fluid, floating. An almost unnoticed mention follows shortly: the light paint of the dining-room wall "still bears the mark of the crushed centipede" (only the word "still" betrays the narrator's concern). Next, the spot is oriented with respect to A's seat at the table. In the following paragraph, the first detailed description of the spot appears, but the time has already shifted, for it is now daylight, and the table is not set. With this description we sense the beginning of the transfer, the metamorphosis of the spot into a correlative of the husband's disturbance. Beneath the "objectal" precision of the style, words full of psychic nuances take on meaning: "doubt," "origin," "vaguer portions," the "question mark" that indicates the general shape of the spot. But all these are as yet only subtle preparatory touches.

Only when the spot is established and described do we reach the first version of the scene of the crushing of the centipede. The first time, this action takes place during the scene at dinner table when Franck and A propose (also for the first time) to make a trip to the coast together. Nothing proves, of course, that the two scenes are actually contemporaneous in "real" time; one would suppose, rather, that the squashing of the insect occurs before the planning of the trip. In any case, the mention of the projected trip leads instantly to the first narration of the killing of the centipede: a rather calm, objective version, but which contains the elements of future development. We note especially, in A's behavior, certain erotic signs: her half-open mouth trembling, her quickened breathing, her tapering fingers clenching the handle of her knife, her glance fixed upon the question mark outlined on the wall. Yet the centipede is described as one of "average size," and nothing, or almost nothing, in the conduct of Franck (who, after looking intently at A, rises to go and squash the animal) permits the supposition that he is discharging in this way some sexual aggressiveness, unless it is the fact that he, and not the husband (does the latter not suffer from an inferiority complex typical of the jealous man?) plays the male role of the killer of the dreadful insect which frightens (is that all?) the young wife.

The link between the centipede and the possible relationship between Franck and A is tightened during the first version of the scene of A's return. Explaining some of the events that occurred in town,

A tries talking a little more. She nevertheless does not describe the room where she spent the night, an uninteresting subject, she says, turning away her head: everyone knows that hotel, its discomfort and its patched mosquito netting.

It is at this moment that she notices the Scutigera on the bare wall in front of her. In an even tone of voice, as if in order not to frighten the creature, she says:

"A centipede!"

Franck looks up again. [P. 64]

Since A's remarks at the beginning of this citation are made as she lunches alone with her husband, it is evident how violent the distorting force is that plunges the narrator into the past when his wife mentions the hotel and its mosquito netting. The whole scene of the centipede unfolds again. This time, when Franck crushes the creature with his napkin, A's hand clenches the "white table cloth," and a (preparatory) phrase "returns to sit down" appears in the text.

The scene returns next to the "mechanized" recalls already referred to: a brief résumé of one paragraph (as far as the crushing of the insect goes), followed by a development of the image of A's hand, clenched this time on the "white cloth" furrowed by deep folds leading to Franck's place, where another stain stretches toward Franck's hand, which moves toward his shirt pocket, where it tries to push down inside the letter that obsesses the narrator in this section of the narrative (Part V).

Later, the husband sits at the table, engaged in attempting to make the dark oil stain in the courtyard disappear in a defect of the window pane. This effort to annihilate a stain leads once more to the spot left by the centipede, then to the presence of the insect on the wall. The action takes place again, but this time Franck has been taken away, removed entirely from the scene, which is described without any agency:

Suddenly, the anterior part of the body begins to move, executing a rotation which curves the dark line toward the lower part of the wall. And immediately, without having time to go any further, the creature falls onto the tiles, still twisting and curling up its long legs while its mandibles rapidly open and close around its mouth in a quivering reflex.

Ten seconds later, it is nothing more than a reddish pulp in which are mingled the debris of unrecognizable sections.

But on the bare wall, on the contrary, the image of the squashed Scutigera is perfectly clear. [Pp. 86–87]

After this removal of Franck from the action of the scene the husband undertakes the erasure of the spot mentioned earlier. His effort leads only to a persistent vision of A in the act of writing the suspected letter. The relation between the stain on the tablecloth in front of Franck and the spot left by the centipede returns, mixed with verbal elements of doubt ("perhaps," "almost," "not easy to fix with certainty"). A link between the centipede and the land crab served at the dinner eaten by the husband alone, during A's absence with Franck, is established, extending to the sounds emitted by the buccal appendages of the two animals, the crackling sound that will later be identified with the noise produced by the comb or brush passing through A's long hair.

The evolution of the incident of the centipede reaches its apogee in the great scene which constitutes the high point of Part VII (as well as of the novel itself). Alone in the house, waiting for A to return, the jealous protagonist goes through all the stages of a classical case of psychiatry, including hallucination, obsession, and the transfer upon reality of a feverish imagination. The discharge or projection of his ill-repressed jealousy is accomplished through an external hallucinatory vision which contains as well as expresses his inferiority complex, his fear of aggressiveness, and his pathological certainty that his wife is deceiving him with a lover who, unlike himself, knows how to act with the male brutality no doubt secretly coveted by the narrator. After several phrases of indirect discourse in which the husband "says" that A "ought to have been back long ago," after prowling through the empty house, waiting on the veranda by the light of the gasoline lamp (surrounded by the whirling insects that form a visible support for the turmoil of his feelings), after staring with morbid preoccupation at the calendar (projecting onto the man in the picture his hatred of Franck, as well as his desire to do him harm), the narrator enters the dining room.

There, suddenly again, is the centipede. But no longer the one of "average size," scarcely longer than one's finger, that figured in the first version of the scene. On the contrary, now the centipede is "enormous: one of the largest to be found in this climate. With its long antennae and its huge legs spread on each side of its body, it covers the area of an ordinary dinner plate" (p. 111). Again the scene unfolds "empty," without human agency. Franck does not appear, yet this impersonal crushing of the insect is expressed in a style so intense that it seems ready to burst. On the floor, the creature continues to emit the crackling sound that the husband now relates explicitly to the sound of the comb in A's hair, the comb held in the tapering fingers whose movements bring the narrator back to the swaying movement of the antennae of the centipede placed once more on the wall, as if refusing to be annihilated without the male intervention of Franck, whom the narrator has tried to obliterate.

Here the culminating anguish of the husband reaches its highest pitch in a "catathymic" vision. The crushing of the centipede takes on its fullest force as part of the scene which the husband envisions of Franck and A *in flagrante delicto*:

> Franck, without saying a word, stands up, wads his napkin into a ball as he cautiously approaches, and squashes the creature against the wall. Then, with his foot, he squashes it again on the *bedroom* floor.
>
> Then he comes back toward the *bed* and in passing hangs the *towel on its metal rack near the washbowl.*
>
> The hand with the tapering fingers has clenched into a fist on the *white sheet.* The five widespread fingers have closed with such force that they have drawn the cloth with them: the latter shows five convergent creases. [. . .] But the *mosquito-netting* falls back all around the *bed*, interposing the opaque veil of its innumerable meshes. [Pp. 112–113, italics mine]

If this vision seems to exceed the limits of objective correlatives or exterior emotional supports, it is doubtless because it resembles closely that psychopathic hysteria which transforms remembered reality into a nightmare of suspicion and repressed anxiety, and then projects this nightmare upon the world.

From the stage of fear of reality, the jealous individual must pass to a stage of aggressiveness. If he is fundamentally (like the husband in *Jealousy*) timid, inhibited, withdrawn (even perhaps suffering from psychic impotency), he will be satisfied—in spite of the intensity of his hatred—with an interior action, a passive vision whose true meaning or goal he may not entirely comprehend. In this connection especially critics of *Jealousy* who have reproached Robbe-Grillet for not allowing his protagonist to "participate" in his own story have totally missed the significance of the text.

Let us see first how, in terms verbally ambiguous (which also have their psychological function, since they represent one more effort to avoid the truth that he fears), the husband pictures to himself Franck in physical possession of his wife: "In his haste to reach his goal, Franck increases his speed. The jolts become more violent. Nevertheless he continues to drive faster" (p. 113). These abstract words, containing *no image*, following immediately upon the description of the hotel bed, apply directly to the lovers. But the phrases have already begun their metamorphosis toward the *image* of the destruction of Franck and A in a visionary holocaust into which the husband plunges them:

In the darkness, he has not seen the hole running halfway across the road. The car makes a leap, skids. [. . .] On this bad road the driver cannot straighten out in time. The blue sedan is going to crash into a roadside tree whose rigid foliage scarcely shivers under the impact, despite its violence.

The car immediately bursts into flames. The whole brush is illuminated by the crackling, spreading fire. It is the sound the centipede makes, motionless again on the wall, in the center of the panel.

Listening to it more carefully, the sound is more like a breath than a crackling: the brush is now moving down the loosened hair. [P. 113]

After this summit in the development of interior action in the husband, there follow images with a diminishing rhythm. The narrator searches the personal effects in A's bureau and writing table, in one of the rare "actions" risked by this timid man obsessed with dread of the possible escape of his wife, to be feared especially if he should make some overt reproach or take some direct action toward her. It is a fruitless search, since he finds no proof of A's unfaithfulness. But no matter: for this husband, it is enough that he should *fear* infidelity to provide the only basis necessary for jealousy such as his.

The text contains a last reference to the spot left by the centipede. Much "later," when a mood of appeasement has begun to come over the husband, he recalls it a final time, in a memory of A sitting at the table, with "her gaze fixed upon the brownish remains of the crushed centipede, staining the wall opposite her." The spot now rejoins the system of index points like the shadow of the column, the number of banana trees that have been cut, the arrangement of the logs for the bridge. The extraordinary psychological expansion of the episode of the killing of the insect, accomplished by new and powerful technical means, and executed in hitherto unexplored fictional dimensions, has reached its end.

5 The Maze of Fictional Creation: *In the Labyrinth* (1959)

In the labyrinth we will find the straight path.

HENRI MICHAUX

The publication of *In the Labyrinth* in 1959 appeared to mark a turning point or a metamorphosis in the evolution of Robbe-Grillet's work. Despite his earlier remarks about a "non-novelistic novel," the writer had produced, nonetheless, three novels in which, beneath the notorious "surfaces" so insistently announced in his theories, the "novelistic" persisted, in as "stubborn" a manner as did the famous "objects" of his phenomenological descriptions so carefully divorced by the author from all metaphysical implications. In those novels Robbe-Grillet utilized recognizable, familiar fictional formulas of traditional construction: *The Erasers* revitalizes a Greek tragedy based on a myth; *The Voyeur* causes the reader to share the viewpoint of a sadist; *Jealousy* immerses us in the obsessions of a mind which, tortured by desire, fear, and other emotions, distorts space and time. In each case, strong psychological motivations lead toward that "tragic" world which Robbe-Grillet constantly denounced and tried to avoid. His theories called for a detached, "cleansed" literary work, wherein, as in Flaubert's projected *Book about Nothing*, the art of articulations, of structures, of the *making*, would create and incarnate the work, yielding a pure fiction whose beauty and aesthetic value would be totally inherent.

153

The curious foreword to *In the Labyrinth*, with its insistence on the "strictly material reality" of the "things, gestures, words, events" of the work, its denial of any "allegorical value," repeats the earlier doctrine. But, as at the exit of mazes at rustic fairs (referred to in the publisher's note on the back cover of the French edition), there is a hole, a passage leading to the outside, a possibility of escape. The author deliberately cracks the absolutely sealed confines of his novel when he invites the reader to find in the book "no more, or less meaning than in his own life, or his own death." Is Robbe-Grillet opening the door here leading to those "metaphysical beyonds" which he had denied to fiction? Or is he warning the reader that any interpretation, any projection of outside values on a text must be done at the reader's peril? Is "no more, or less" much or little?

The reply to this question is perhaps not so difficult. Let us assume that a "Soldier's Story"—a simple one, the death of a lost infantryman, wounded and feverish—presents a basic human interest. One can easily imagine how other authors would treat the subject. What about Robbe-Grillet? He shows us his solution in *In the Labyrinth*. If the subject immediately becomes complex, baroque, labyrinthine in form; if multiple, interlocking perspectives create contradictory framings; if the soldier's as well as the narrator's worlds take on a Caligari-like appearance whose objects, scrutinized, deformed, organized in accordance with psychic fixations express "no more, or less" than what the reader attributes to them, none of this surprises us, coming from Robbe-Grillet. In a sense, reading *In the Labyrinth* is easier than reading the earlier novels: there are few, if any, difficulties in following the order of events. On the other hand, to fully appreciate the structure of the work requires patient attention and precise identification of the guiding threads that lead to hidden aspects.

It is always useful, in studying one of Robbe-Grillet's novels, to schematize the plot, even if it should appear to be a purely conventional one. What *happens* in *In the Labyrinth?* Who acts, who speaks, what does one see? What does the text give us?

A narrator begins by saying, "I am alone here, now, sheltered." But until the the final section (the fourteenth of the "chapters"), no further pronoun or other first-person form will recall his presence. As Doctor Rieux tardily reveals by first-person narration that he is the author of the text of Camus' *The Plague*, the doctor-narrator of *In the Labyrinth* finally clinches his identity by two words, a "my" and a "me," the latter as the last word in the novel. However, during the numerous scenes in the narrator's retreat, a closed room from which he emerges in various deceptive ways, we are continually drawn along by the suppressed first-person narration of this unnamed "I." Passages which in appearance are entirely objective, which produce upon the reader at first the impression of scenes shot by an impersonal camera eye like Dziga Vertov's, acquire a curious intimacy because of the hidden presence of the narrator, whose movements, however labyrinthine, affect our perceptions and our consciousness. From the outset, the labyrinth—the city in which the soldier is lost— looms as a maze of inert matter, seen in feverish vision. The oscillating movement from the narrator's room to the various "foci" of the labyrinth outside (the café, streets, corridors, apartments in which actions occur) figures metaphorically as oscillation between thought and things.

In the narrator's room, the door of which is left unmentioned until the next-to-last page of the book, there are a bed, a chest of drawers, a fireplace without a grate, a table with a lamp, and heavy red curtains (hiding a window?). On the table lies an object whose form suggests a cross, and which will engender an object series typical of Robbe-Grillet: it will be linked to the design on the wallpaper, to a torch, to a human figure, to the handle and blade of a bayonet. On the floor, shiny slipper tracks outline a triangle with rounded corners, one angle beside the bed, one by the table, one at the chest. A fly walking around the top edge of the lampshade projects on the ceiling, through a reversed *camera oscura* procedure (the small black point performing the same function, as in optics it may, as the *hole* located elsewhere on the lampshade), a moving image of the bare filament burning within the clear bulb. When this brilliant polygon reaches the folds of the curtains, a sudden rupture occurs. As if moving through the hidden window, the text opens onto an outside scene.

It is the labyrinthlike city: identical streets, regularly intersecting, vistas of identical buildings—a neutral, flat, empty décor beneath a falling snow consisting of equally spaced snowflakes, as if a rigid structure were descending slowly. A brief return to the room occurs, according to one of the various modes of scene linking to be studied later; then we are again outside. A soldier leaning against a lamppost materializes, beginning with a hip, a shoulder, an arm wrapped around the post. In a parallel montage effect, outside and inside sequences alternate rapidly: a description of the soldier's tired face is followed by details of the room; the soldier is carrying a package under his arm, but, a few lines further on, the box is "now" on the chest, with the suggestion that it may have been opened and wrapped up again. The narrator is, perhaps, like Jean Gabin in the well-known film *Daybreak*, remembering the past at the prompting of objects around him (Section I, pp. 9–24).[1]

On the wall above the chest, a steel engraving depicts a café scene: a counter, groups of distraught drinkers, a table where three soldiers sit. In front of them, a young boy squats on his heels, holding a package or box. The violent but frozen gestures of the crowd gathered about a poster can no doubt be explained by the title of the engraving itself: "The Defeat

1. Page references are to the 1959 printing of *Dans le labyrinthe*, (Paris: Minuit).

of Reichenfels." As the long and minute description of the picture continues, the text imperceptibly causes the scene to become animated. The customers have left; the boy is speaking to the soldier. Through the upper rectangular portion of a glass door—there is no door in the picture, as there is none in the narrator's room—can be seen the total blackness of a dark night.

The next series of scenes appear to be designed to bring about the meeting of the boy and the soldier at the café: they meet near the lamppost; the soldier tries to remember where he is to take the box; the boy disappears. A variant of the same scene: again the boy disappears in the diminishing perspective of endless lampposts. Finally, success; the soldier and the boy go into the café, passing in front of another person (the narrator?), and taking up their places as shown in the engraving (Section II, pp. 24–60).

The boy once more encounters the soldier leaning against the post. The soldier reveals that he has spent the night in a "barracks" in town (a scene that is developed further on as an incident much "later" in the action). The soldier's glance, directed high up toward a window opposite, brings about a return to the narrator's room, then a re-entry into the picture itself, where the soldier is again seen with the boy. Now they are again outside. The boy disappears into an apartment building; the soldier tries to follow him through dark corridors, passing a number of women whom he surprises or frightens by his presence. He meets the boy's mother, who helps him try to reconstruct the name of the street where, we learn, he is to turn over his box to someone. This name proliferates in Kafkaesque fashion (as often happens in Robbe-Grillet's works): rue Matadier, rue Montoret, rue Montalet, rue Bouvard, rue Brulard, and so forth. The soldier, who is succumbing to accelerating attacks of fever, closes his eyes upon a vision of falling snow (Section III, pp. 40–59).

The text shifts to the narrator's room. A mirror above the

fireplace then "frames" the soldier as he wanders through a maze of corridors looking for the boy's mother. Doors open and close abruptly, lighting the corridors briefly, then plunging them into darkness. Again reaching the woman's quarters, the soldier accepts food and drink. The room in which he finds himself is described in terms similar to those used for the narrator's room; but on the wall where the engraving would hang there is a photograph of a soldier leaning against a lamppost. For a short time the photograph too becomes animate: the soldier in the picture "returns" to the apartment and takes the place of the soldier protagonist. Giving confused explanations of his presence in the city, the soldier appears to the woman as a possible enemy spy. His reference to a barracks merges into a sequence of vain search for such a building, among nightmarish or feverish streets and intersections (Section IV, pp. 59–74).

The soldier is once more seen wandering outside in the snow. The point of view is from above, revealing tracks of footprints, circles (traced by the boy around the lampposts), and paths of pedestrians. In the narrator's top-floor room, the fly continues its movement around the lampshade. Above the chest of drawers, the oval photograph of the second soldier has replaced the engraving. The scene dissolves into a reprise of the episode of the soldier protagonist in the young mother's apartment. A limping man appears (there is a possible suggestion of a verbal link between *boîte*, box, and *boite*, limps), whose manner of holding his single crutch leaves some doubt about the validity of his affliction. This disquieting individual asks the boy to accompany the soldier in his search for the street where he is to hand over his box to someone as yet unknown. In the night, the soldier and his young guide pass through one after another of the round circles of light beneath the lampposts, in the falling snow (Section V, pp. 74–94).

The boy leaves the soldier in front of a door and disappears into the darkness. Several aborted scenes occur as the soldier tries to enter the building. Is he delirious? He meets a woman ("no"); he is in the narrator's room ("no"); he sees, in the corridor, an individual wearing gray suede shoes ("no"); finally, he speaks with a man in military uniform who leads him upstairs to a long room where soldiers are sleeping on cots. Looking down from a window, the soldier sees at the door below another soldier, his own double. The uniformed man has him lie down; worried about his box, he hides it under his pillow. Fragments of a dialogue between the soldier and the boy, which must have occurred later than the present scene, appear now in the text; the reader, moreover, remembers that this exchange had already appeared (in the third section). As the soldier falls asleep, the scene dissolves into the café scene of the engraving (Section VI, pp. 94–110).

The waitress becomes the focus of attention: she is the young woman we saw in the apartment building. Now the soldier is again there in her room, examining the oval photograph. The boy's mother speaks of the army's defeat at Reichenfels. The man with the limp enters. The boy again accompanies the soldier to the barracks, passing in front of the building housing the narrator in his top-floor room. As in a dream, the soldier reaches the "false" barracks. He wakes with a start, but wakes into another dream: someone has given the alarm in the trenches. As his fever worsens, he wanders through a nightmare maze of corridors and streets; through the windows of an apartment he sees a crowd of people pointing at him as if he were a spy. He flees into a stairwell—which leads up to the narrator's room. The fly continues to walk in circles on the lampshade, observed by someone lying on the bed (Section VII, pp. 110–126).

The soldier awakens in his "true" bed, at the barracks. Despite his fever, he is determined to leave and turn over the box to its intended recipient. The man in charge brings in an orderly who announces that the doctor is coming. He must change his wet uniform, put on a dry capote. Using the pretext of going to the toilets, the soldier makes his escape down the stairs. At ground level, he is confronted by the man with the crutch (how can he have walked so far, if he is really lame?), who questions him threateningly about the contents of the box. The soldier brushes the man aside and leaves. In one pocket of the new cape, he finds a glass marble (Section VIII, pp. 126–141).

This round glass sphere, described in terms appropriate to a glass eye, is now in one of the boy's hands, at the café. The boy undergoes a doubling procedure; the text alternates between two boys, one who has led the soldier to the café and a different one who has led, or will lead, the soldier to the barracks. The boy is heard denying that the lame man is his father. Verb tenses suddenly shift violently, oscillating between past and present. The soldier is again outside, talking at a street corner with a person who may be the narrator about his efforts to find the man to whom he is to give the box. Alone, the soldier wonders if it would not be better to get rid of it; as he approaches a sewer opening, the boy appears, asking why he wants to throw away his package. A noisy motorcycle is heard (Section IX, pp. 127–160).

As if called into being by the noise, a sequence materializes wherein the soldier, in the midst of an attack, tries to save a wounded comrade. Then he is again alone, carrying the box through the street, imagining that he is throwing it away. Another barracks appears, and another scene of a suspicious crowd watching him. A motorcycle with sidecar drives up, carrying enemy soldiers armed with a machine gun; they shoot at the soldier. Wounded in the side, he drags himself, with the boy's help, into a doorway (Section X, pp. 160–170).

Again the scene returns to the café. It seems to take place at an earlier time, just before the defeat, perhaps in another town. The talk among the customers is of treason, corrupt officers, enemy agents, spies. The soldier learns he is being sought. More recent scenes surge into the text: the soldier again enters the room in the young woman's apartment. He is wounded; a doctor (the narrator?) bends over him. Following a "no" (always an indication that a false or wrong turn in the labyrinth of the text is being rejected), the text moves back to the already related scene of the wounded comrade entrusting him with the box, before returning to the "present" room where is he stretched out wounded on the bed (Section XI, pp. 170–189).

Feverish, dying, the soldier expresses anxiety over the box. The young woman relates how she, the boy, and the doctor have saved him when he was shot down in the street; the boy has picked up the box. The lame man comes in and a violent discussion ensues. In his delirium, the soldier tries to get up and leave. A number of fragmentary scenes whirl around in his mind. In one of them he tries, as the narrator had done much earlier, to examine closely a crack in one corner of the ceiling. Thoughts of soldier and narrator fuse in an ambiguous identity (Section XII, pp. 189–205).

In a conversation with the young woman, the soldier reiterates the wounding and death of his comrade, the transfer of the box, the telephone call that fixed the meeting place in this town (was it from the other soldier's father?). Images of the first and second soldiers blend. Finally, fixing his attention feverishly upon the minutest details of the room where he lies fatally wounded, the soldier protagonist dies (Section XIII, pp. 205–211).

The narrator, whose identification as the doctor is now made clear in the words of the text, draws together the threads of the story. Upon the soldier's death, the young woman turns over the box to him. He takes it to his room, where it lies as in the first pages of the book. He has now opened it and gives an inventory of its contents: letters from the fiancée of "Henri Martin" (presumably the soldier wounded in the trenches), a watch, a ring, a bayonet. As the narrator recapitulates the story, events pass once more into the present tense: we are once more in the café, where the soldier sits beside the young boy. This scene solidifies and becomes the steel engraving. In the narrator's room, on the table, lie scattered sheets of paper—the text of the book? The word "door" finally appears in the description of the room, and through the exit thus created, the narrator emerges from his labyrinth, ending the text with the phrase "and leaving the whole town behind me" (Section XIV, pp. 211–221).

The analysis of the novel, with its minute visual descriptions and its interlocking multivalent structures so familiar to readers of Robbe-Grillet, yet here accompanied by an intermittent lyricism that strikes a new note in the author's work (especially in the pathos of the delirious, suffering soldier), requires, first of all, a working theory that can explain its narrative mode and identify the point of view from which the reader is to "see" the text. Since the majority of the scenes involving the soldier, whether he is alone, or with the boy, his mother, or the customers in the café, do not clearly reveal the presence of a narrator, we are tempted to believe that only the scenes in the closed room, with their technique of the suppressed first person (similar to the mode of *Jealousy*), are seen subjectively, the others unfolding according to a traditional, impersonal, almost Balzacian viewpoint, with the occasional unexplained presence of a narrator at some street corner, in the young woman's apartment, in the café, or elsewhere—a narrator who takes on substantial form in the text only in the guise of the doctor who figures in the last episodes, and who lets fall the words "my" and "me" after two hundred pages of pronominal silence.

The impression of impersonal narration is, however, an illusion; even when he is invisible, the narrator is always present. The "framing" of all scenes of the soldier, whether he is leaning against a lamppost, seated in the café, or lost in the corridors of an apartment building, corresponds to a personal point of view, directed at the hero from a specific angle, at a fixed distance. Moreover, beneath the ostensible realism of events depicted by this imaginary, hidden observer, the reader continually senses the thoughts and emotions of a personal consciousness closely attached to the actions and feelings of the soldier, projecting itself into his memories, deliriums, and feverish dreams. It is a participatory third-person mode which we may call "symbiotic." The specific quality of this technique stands out if we compare its effect with that of *The Voyeur*. In *The Voyeur*, the mental content of the protagonist, Mathias, is objectified and projected upon the "outside" world, modifying and transforming exterior reality. The reader, if the text functions correctly, passes directly into Mathias' psychic states with no intervening membrane of another consciousness. The text of *In the Labyrinth*, on the contrary, is not to be read thus independently, but only as the mental content of an omnipresent narrator within the fictional field, and who is, in a sense, the real protagonist of the novel.

The narrator's presence is continually evident in other ways. Not only does he evaluate and arrange the content of all scenes; he also chooses their order, going so far as to cancel or reorder them. He often gives the impression that the work is a kind of journal, a workbook for a novel, some fictional project involving the working out of a story through a series of hypotheses, of tentative solutions, of false starts and revisions. Hence the use of "no" in many passages where scenes termed "false" by the narrator himself are wiped out or erased, as well as such remarks as "this scene leads nowhere," or "doubtless it is here that the scene of the silent gathering takes place." The frequent passages in which the narrator seems to lose his momentum and retreats almost out of breath to his room add to the impression of the novel as a work journal, as do the many recapitulations, schematic résumés, and the final summary demystification in the inventory of the banal contents of the soldier's box.

We may even interpret *In the Labyrinth* as the text of a narrator who *never* leaves his room (except in the final sentence of the book), and who invents the whole story using the objects around him, such as the bayonet and the picture on the wall. How, otherwise, can we explain the animation of the picture, the fact that it contains the soldier protagonist, as well as the boy companion? A literal "account" of the picture (an old steel engraving, obviously) could lead to little more than a comparison between old and recent battles and defeats. Is the narrator indeed "interpreting" the engraving? Is he, like the camera in certain fantastic films, penetrating into the picture and discovering inside a new fictional world?[2]

Whatever we may conclude, it is quite evident that the narrator is engaged in creating a fiction designed to be self-contained, a sort of harmonious "pure" novel whose meaning is to remain implicit. If it is not the *Book about Nothing* of which Flaubert dreamed, it is, nevertheless, a novel in which the art of construction dominates the psychological interest or the emotional appeal. The paradox of *In the Labyrinth* is that in spite of its rigorous formalism and its emphasis on structure, it is in many respects the most moving of Robbe-Grillet's novels.

Understanding this phenomenon requires detailed analysis of a number of aspects of this highly articulated work, in which the art of transitions, modulations, formal relationships, chronology and de-chronology attains a state of near perfection. Only then is it possible to explain the curious power exerted by this story deliberately emptied of meaning, devoid of allegory or mystery, and more strongly expressive than any

2. As, for example, in the first part of the English film directed by Wendy Toye, *Three Cases of Murder* (1954), entitled "The Picture," or in the sequence of Sidney Gilliat's *She Played with Fire* (1957) in which "the dreamer penetrated into a château, then into a picture depicting the château, then into the château represented in the picture" (*Positif*, May 1961, p. 57).

conventional war novel of the pathos of a man reduced to his serial number in a world which, behind its literary *trompe-l'oeil* décor, rather exactly depicts the contemporary world.[3]

Among the focal points of the labyrinth in which the story unfolds—the closed room, the lamppost, the young woman's room, for example—there is a central point at which the various threads of Ariadne converge: the picture. This engraving, which depicts a place and a situation identical or analogous to those of the scene in the café, may at first appear to constitute another of those "interior duplications" or inner models found in the works of Robbe-Grillet as well as in those of other writers of the New Novel.[4]

But the picture in *In the Labyrinth* does more than outline in miniature the general sense of the work: animated, or frozen, it becomes an integral part of the "diagesis" of the novel. It organizes the decisive moments of the novel's action, within the fictional field, just as the entire text fixes the totality of this action between the first and last pages.

The following somewhat simplified outline may furnish a possible unified reading of the work: A narrator—the author, his double, his *persona, an* author and not necessarily Robbe-Grillet—is shut up in his room, for the purpose of *creating* a work of fiction (it is the Mallarméan situation of the poet facing the blank page). He rests on the bed, or walks about. What elements, what objects around him will permit him to draw his work forth from inner nothingness? The furniture, the tracks left by his slippers as he moves about the room, a bayonet (a war souvenir?) of ambiguous form, the pattern of the wallpaper (a multitude of small drawings, suggesting

3. Robbe-Grillet wrote in "The Death of the Novelistic Character," *France-Observateur*, Oct. 24, 1957: "It is certain that the present era is that of the serial number."

4. See note 4, Chapter 4, and especially the article on modalities of viewpoint and interior duplication, "Un Héritage d'André Gide: la duplication intérieure."

snowflakes falling, or other images), the moving pattern on the ceiling cast by the fly walking around the lampshade (the black body of the insect projecting the bright image of the filament, in an analogy perhaps with the way in which the obscure or invisible presence of the narrator projects into the text the scenes that he imagines), and finally, by a chance which will lose all the quality of chance in becoming the very essence of the story, the steel engraving (an old picture of a café scene following some forgotten defeat, in which the reactions of three soldiers and the townspeople have been caught and fixed for all time by some anonymous artist): these are the narrator's materials.

The narrator's task is then to unify these elements, finding relationships capable of linking them, to depict one scene here, another there, to make corrections, to backtrack in order to develop a better solution, to sketch in tentative and approximate scenes, even those that will turn out to be "false" or defective—to behave, as it were, like a prisoner caught in a labyrinth, seeking a way out. Movement through the maze becomes the very design and form of the work itself.

When he encounters an impasse, the narrator takes a different path. He finds himself often back at the same spot, but always as the result of following another route. Since he attaches himself closely to each step that his protagonist takes, even though he keeps his distance (as creator viewing his own creation), his hero also lives the life of the labyrinth. He will even die in the labyrinth before the narrator has filled in all the spaces in his plan, before he finishes his narration and emerges from the maze through the final opening.

In simple terms, the narrator borrows the subject of his novel from that of the picture: he brings to life the dead engraving on the wall of his room. The work thus appears as the working out of a complicated set of answers to a set of commonplace questions: who is this soldier, sitting at a café table after the defeat mentioned in the title of the picture?

Who is the boy sitting at his feet, and what could be the origin and contents of the box that he holds tight in his arms? And, since the narrator is himself involved in the story, what can his role be? The fact that all these questions find quite normal and unsurprising answers at the end of the book fits in with the rhythm of recapitulations which the narrator makes increasingly as he terminates the story. When all the lines of the pattern of the novel have been traced out, he can thus quickly put the last touches to the text before opening the door to his room, free himself from creative confinement, and leave behind on the table the scattered pages of his work.

This interpretation leaves unexplained, however, the strange fascination exerted by the novel and the story it contains, that combination of curiosity, wonderment, and minute, excited attention which the reader experiences at each episode. What causes the anxiety-producing atmosphere, comparable to that of a novel by Kafka read "at the level of the text," without reference to critical interpretations based on sociological, psychological, or metaphysical "meanings"? If it signifies nothing explicitly, how can the novel so move us?

Two strategic procedures are, it seems to me, largely responsible for the creation of this "magic" effect which critics perceived almost unanimously in *In the Labyrinth*. The first consists (in a manner analogous to Camus' technique in the first part of *The Stranger*) of presenting the hero—a "simple" soldier lost after a defeat, who tries to turn over as he has promised a package of personal effects to the father of a dead comrade—only *in situation*, as Sartre would say, according to what he *is* and *does* at a given moment, without framing his actions and psychological states with commentary on his thoughts or emotions, or with psychological analysis or explanation. The second procedure consists in describing the soldier and the world around him using a style that transforms the aspects of a banal universe—an unspecified European city with its apartment buildings, its corridors, its street corners, its cafés—into an intense, dreamlike background bathed in a new and unfamiliar light. To these techniques must be added the creation of intricate formal relationships between series of objects, analogously structured situations, and free movement in space and time, all of which usually characterize the works of Robbe-Grillet. Using imaginary or false scenes lying as it were outside the space-time of the novel, the author escapes from the strictures of the past-present-future and here-there-elsewhere vectors which rigidly determine the traditional fictional field.

The autonomy of space and time in *In the Labyrinth* is by no means arbitrary or undisciplined; nor is it designed merely to astonish the reader. It is constantly subjected to internal restrictions. The image of the labyrinth serves to impose on the author strict criteria for the linking of all scenes, as well as for the shifting and displacement of objects and events in the maze of the novel's transitions.

We may now identify some of these techniques of scene linking. It will be remembered that in *Jealousy*, for example, all the scenes of the novel can be shown to be related to preceding and following scenes by a variety of psychological associations in the mind of the implicit narrator. A different order of connections prevails in *In the Labyrinth*. Here the rhythm of scene ordering depends on such factors as similarity of form or structure, as well as the place occupied by a scene (or its repetition, or variation) in the over-all pattern of events or in the reader's time scheme. An individual scene has, first, its internal form; this form is in turn related to that of earlier and later scenes, according to transitional principles that depend in turn on the general structure of the work, determined by the central image or metaphor of the labyrinth: impasses, false paths, detours, backtrackings, failures, mistakes, stops, retreats, and finally, exits, openings to the outside. The more chaotic the various elements appear on the surface, the more will analysis reveal their deeper unity.

The first paragraph of the novel embodies a fundamental movement of *oscillation*, which, alternating between positive and negative opposites, will lead later to a synthesis of contradictions. The passage is particularly notable in that the modulation between the two poles occurs in the word "swinging" itself, which whirls repetitously around at the center of the image:

I am alone here, now, sheltered. Outside, it is raining, outside, people walk with their heads bent [. . .]; outside [. . .] the wind is blowing in the leaves, bending whole branches in a swinging, in a swinging, swinging, which throws its shadow on the whitewashed walls. Outside the sun is shining, there is not a tree, nor a shrub, to give shade, and people walk in the bright sunshine, sheltering their eyes with one hand, looking straight ahead, a few yards only in front of them, a few yards of dusty asphalt on which the wind draws parallel lines, forked patterns, spirals. [P. 9]

Further on, the French term *balancement* used in this passage for "swinging" is reinforced by *balanciers* (balance scales), which move in "parallel oscillations, identical, but contradictory" (p. 94). The initial passage thus constitutes an overture that announces the basic themes of contradictory movements, apparently irreconcilable elements (rain, sun), limited viewpoints, and multiple patterns of possible paths, as well as an indeterminate chronological framework for the events that will follow, going from the autumn rain that precedes the winter of the novel, to the spring dust and sunlight that will follow.

The patterns in the dust form the transition to the narrator's room, wherein the "only dust"—the only reality?—"comes from the room itself." Here we encounter the first panoramic descriptive movement of the many that will follow, turning about the room until the curtains are reached. When the narrator's glance touches their edges, or falls upon the corner of the room where the curtains start, the idea of a window, or the presence of the word itself in the text, causes a modulation of the passage from inside to outside:

The vertical wall [. . .] is hidden from the top to the bottom [. . .] by thick red curtains of a heavy, velvety cloth.
Outside it is snowing. The wind blows the fine dry crystals along the dark asphalt sidewalk [. . .]. But the regular noise of heels [. . .] cannot reach here [. . .]. The street is too long, the curtains too thick, the building too high. No noise [. . .] ever filters through the walls of the room. [Pp. 11–12]

Beyond, stands the table lamp[. . .]. On the upper ring of the shade, a fly walks slowly around [. . .]. It throws onto the ceiling a misshapen shadow, in which no feature of the insect itself can be discerned: [along with . . .] the image of the incandescent filament of the clear electric bulb. This little polygon with one side missing [. . .] when it arrives at the vertical wall [. . .], disappears into the folds of the heavy red curtain.
Outside, it is snowing. Outside it has snowed, it was snowing, outide it is snowing. The tightly packed flakes fall softly [. . .]. The snow as it keeps falling flattens the landscape, removes its depth, as if this unclear scene were merely poorly painted, in *trompe-l'oeil*, on a bare wall.
At the junction of the wall and the ceiling, the shadow of the fly [. . .] reappears and continues its circuit. [Pp. 14–15]

The only thing visible on the ceiling is the image of the filament [. . .] moving slowly forward [. . .] until the moment when, reaching the vertical wall, it disappears.
The soldier is holding a package under his left arm [. . .], something like a shoe box [. . .].
The box, wrapped in brown paper, is now on the chest of drawers [. . .]. Just above, hangs the picture [. . .].
Outside, the sky is still the same mat white. [Pp. 20–23]

Each time the point of view turns to the curtains, or to the corner of the room where they hang—whether because the narrator moves his glance, or the shadow of the fly arrives there—the point of view pierces the hidden window and falls upon the outside scene, or the soldier. Meanwhile, other transitions occur: the soldier's box, first situated outside (in the time of the "story"), and then lying on the chest in the room (in the "now" of the narration, when the story is being created); or the white ceiling of the room, transformed into the white sky over the town.

The view of the same box in two different but textually adjacent moments of time is similar to a type of modulation effected through similarities between different objects. The text flows smoothly from one image to its twin in a kind of "linked dissolve" or montage by analogy. When the image of the light-bulb filament, projected on the wall at one moment by a hole in the parchment lampshade, expands in the dim light of the room, we read immediately: "It is once more the same filament, that of an identical bulb or one only slightly larger, that is burning uselessly at the intersection of the two streets, in its glass cage" (p. 16).

Thus transported to the outside, the scene remains there until a new modulation brings it inside again, through the similar patterns of snow tracks around the lamppost and the shining paths on the waxed floor of the narrator's room. In other instances, forms like that of the rectangular mirror hung over the fireplace and the oval frame around the photograph in the young woman's room (also over the fireplace), or even the form of "someone stretched out on the bed" may serve as a bridge between distinct places and different times (see pp. 59, 66, 80–81, 126).

Among the transitional devices is a highly developed system of "false scenes" (so termed in the text, p. 202). The reader will recall that in *The Voyeur* false scenes occur as a result of Mathias' desires, or his fears that he may fail to sell his watches, or his need to fill in a suspicious lapse of time. In *Jealousy*, the husband's jealous obsessions create many false scenes. In *In the Labyrinth*, the procedure is used to open up false paths in the maze that the narrator is inventing, to sketch possible solutions, to abandon unwanted possibilities, to erase imaginary developments. If the narrative line suddenly intrudes upon a scene like that in the café, it is often obliged to seek, in a backward movement, the path that led it there.

The series of attempts to place the soldier in the café (beginning on p. 31), just following the first "animated" café scene in which the soldier and the boy are first seen, may be explained in this manner. A "first" encounter between the soldier and the boy leads nowhere, and the boy runs off toward the distant lampposts. The text "reflects" upon this: "Yet it is the same boy, with his serious manner, who led him to the café [. . .]. And it was a similar scene, under an identical lamppost, at an identical street corner" (p. 36).

This new attempt also fails, and the boy flees in a whirlwind of snow. The text "hesitates": "And yet, it is surely the same boy who precedes the soldier when the latter walks into the main room of the café" (p. 38).

The whole sequence ends with a final return to the café table and the soldier sitting in front of his glass—which, significantly, he does not have in the picture. Although this third attempt seems "successful," the earlier efforts leave in the text a residue of uncertainty that further colors the repetitions and variations of the story, especially when an almost identical episode, but one probably located in another city and taking place before the soldier has received the box from his dying comrade, comes in as a doubling reflection of the earlier scene. (See p. 170.)

The soldier's arrival at the "barracks" is similarly structured; the relation between the earlier scene and this one leads to such ambiguous passages as: "This boy is the one who was in the café, it would appear, and he is not the same as the other, who led the soldier (or who will lead the soldier, later) to the barracks. [. . .] In any case, this is the boy who guided the soldier to the café" (p. 143).

Considerably "earlier," we had witnessed a scene which

ought to have come *after* the night at the barracks (pp. 42–43: "Where did you sleep?" [. . .] "At the barracks"). Some fifty pages later, the attempt to develop this "announced" scene leads the narrator to a series of trial versions having a form analogous to the corridors in which the soldier wanders, lost:

> The soldier is alone, he looks at the door in front of him. [. . .] He notices now that the door is ajar: a door, a corridor, a door, a vestibule, a door, then finally a lighted room, and a table with an empty glass [. . .] and a lame man leaning on his cane, bent forward precariously. No. Door standing ajar. Corridor. Stairway. A woman running upstairs. [. . .] Door. And again a lighted room: a bed, a chest, a fireplace, a table with a lamp [. . .] and the lampshade which throws a white circle on the ceiling. No. Above the chest, hangs an engraving in a dark wood frame. . . . No. No. No.
>
> The door is not ajar. [. . .] Then the door frame swings wide open. [. . .] No. [. . .]
>
> The door opens violently. [. . .] In the middle of the [corridor] stands a man. [. . .]
>
> "Come in," he says. "This is the place." [Pp. 95–85]

It is as if the narrator, lost in the maze of his story construction, seeking a way forward, turns first (as indeed the soldier's thoughts might plausibly do) to the scene in the young woman's room (no); then, to his own room, to the picture that was his point of departure (no, no, no!); before finally choosing a different direction, finding the "right" path. At each turn, at each intersection of narrative paths, there is the risk of being trapped in one of the focal points of the story, of remaining prisoner there, incapable of progressing.

The falseness of other scenes is caused by a slippage in the chronological order of events. The narrator betrays a consciousness of this procedure when he states (for example, on p. 179): "No doubt it is at this point that we must place the scene of [. . .]." False scenes are "resolved" by blending them into nothingness or into unreality, by confusing two places or two identities (on p. 69, for example, the animation of a photograph leads to a merging of the images of the two soldiers), or by the creation of a sort of virtuality or negative presence. This procedure, which resembles Mallarmé's use of objectified absence (first pointed out by Albert Thibaudet), allows the narrator to confer a sort of fourth or fifth dimension to the space-time of his labyrinthine story, by treating as real, without completely materializing them, constructions that are merely *possible*. A striking example is the apparition in the text of what is first described as a "real" barracks, in contrast to the pseudo barracks in which the soldier had been forced to take refuge:

Without noticing it, he has perhaps passed in front of a barracks. [. . .] However, he has noticed no building in the traditional style: a low structure [. . .] stretching some hundred yards in length. [. . .] The whole mass stands at the back of a vast empty courtyard, covered with gravel. [. . .] A guardhouse, here and there, shelters a soldier holding his rifle at rest. [P. 73]

After the negative phrase "he has noticed no building" comes the verb "stands," creating the nonexistent building and giving it form and volume. Now, after projecting the image of this virtual barracks, the narrator takes it apart, destroying it completely in a series of superimposed montages. The text first states that the soldier "has seen nothing of the sort," that he has walked past "no iron fence," that he has entered no courtyard; the image of the barracks continues to diminish in intensity, but now, instead of proceeding by negation, the (imaginary) barracks are "literally" altered, or camouflaged, or reduced to the banality of some ordinary building:

The guardhouses have been removed, naturally, as well as everything that might distinguish the building from the rest of those around it; only the iron bars protecting the windows remain. [. . .]

The building could be, just as well, a fire station, or a convent, or a school, or business offices, or a simple town house, whose ground floor windows are protected by iron bars. Reaching the next street corner, the soldier turns right into the adjoining street. [P. 74]

Here, as is often the case with such false scenes, the imaginary or the unreal arises not only from some lost wandering of the narrator in the labyrinth of his creation, but also from the desires and fears of the soldier-protagonist. It is as if the surface of the text were a kind of interface between the objective (what the soldier sees or imagines) and the subjective (what the narrator thinks and invents). In this symbiosis, the text is alternately drawn toward the soldier (on whose behalf it is being composed) and toward the narrator (whose obvious anguish we sense). The soldier is looking for shelter; it is then plausible that he should "see" the barracks. But he must never burst into the narrator's room (no, no!); hence, the brutal rejection of any episode that runs the risk of bringing him there (see pp. 97, 117).

A study of the process by which the picture is animated, or frozen, reveals procedures analogous to those just analyzed. In the engraving, the café has no windows, and this absence of any "visible opening" is mentioned at some length (see p. 48). As in the case of the problematical barracks, a window or a glass entrance door materializes out of its very absence:

The three walls depicted in the engraving show, in fact, no type of visible opening. [. . .] The entrance door, with glass panels as is customary, with, in white enamel letters glued to the glass, the word "café" and the name of the proprietor in two curving lines[. . .], this entrance door can in fact only be located on the wall not shown in the drawing. [P. 48]

Once already (p. 31), and often later (p. 49, for example), the *presence* of this absent doorway permits the text to pass from static picture to moving action. Several times, the action returns to the café by means of a shared object, such as the table where the soldier is sitting, or a stove like the one near the counter. These textual strategies make Robbe-Grillet's transitions in *In the Labyrinth* differ considerably from the simple animation of a picture to which the fantastic film has accustomed us. In the cinema, it is usually the picture itself that begins to move; we are expected to admire the "realistic" effect of small, painted characters suddenly acquiring normal dimensions, speaking, walking about, and the like. In the novel, on the other hand, the transitions are brought about by means of words, phrases, paragraphs; the impression is one of being carried *elsewhere*, into the space and time where the scene unfolds, has unfolded, or could unfold. Words, rather than images, and despite the use of a "visual" vocabulary, control the scene, projecting it on the reader's imagination; no comparison with pictorial characters, animated puppets, or the like, is possible. It is as if we were present at the extension of the scene which the picture is supposed to depict, accomplished by memory, reconstruction, or pure invention.

Just as the scenes are linked in the manner described, so the fourteen "sections" of the novel are modulated and articulated technically and thematically. Thus, to lead into the first description of the picture (prior to its animation), Section I ends on the negative theme of *emptiness*. At the same time, the items specifically negated are those which will assume, shortly, the greatest presence and importance: "And the whole scene remains empty: not a man, not a woman, not even a child" (p. 24).

This technique of *erasure* (both destructive and productive) may be seen again at the end of Sections II and IV. Other sectional modulations employ the analogous procedures of reduction of scale (III and the final disappearance of the narrator), oscillation (V), frozen action (VI), sleep, dreams, fainting (VII, X, XII), anticipation (IX), enlargement or extreme close-up of an object (VIII), delirium (XI), and death (XIII). Each time, the beginning of the following section is linked to the end of the preceding by a variant of the "dissolve," or by "analogical montage," to use the cinematic vocabulary that appears singularly appropriate to many aspects of *In the Labyrinth*.

All the scenes of the novel, from the shortest (several lines in length) to the longest, as well as the larger sections of the work, are, then, carefully articulated in a project of concretizing the situation of a fugitive whose story and fate a narrator-observer tries at the same time to invent and to understand. An elaborate use of alternatives reinforces, at the level of the story as well as of the background (identical corners, reflected images, multiple lampposts, similar tracks in the snow or on the floor), the broad theme of the labyrinth of multiple possibilities, ambiguities, contradictions. Nothing remains stable: each object, through its form or function, relates to another. Each detail fits into the pattern of similarities, relationships, associations. As one result, many passages are characterized by a use of serial phrases almost to the point of idiosyncrasy. Going beyond the well-known "ternary style" of Flaubert,[5] Robbe-Grillet employs rhythms of three, four, or more elements. Here are a few examples:

> neither the wind, nor the rain, nor the dust
> the polished wood of the table, the waxed floor, the marble of the mantlepiece
> the lines of the floor [. . .] or of the bed, or of the curtains, or of the ashes
> several hours, several days, minutes, weeks
> a square, a rectangle, other more complicated forms
> parallel lines, forked lines, spirals
> spirals, twisting lines, forked undulations, moving arabesques
> on the floor, on the bed cover, on the furniture

5. Cf. the study by Ion Braescu on Flaubert's ternary style, in *Recueil d'Etudes Romanes*, No. 30 (Bucharest, 1959), pp. 279–286.

from the bed to the chest, from the chest to the mantlepiece,
   from the mantlepiece to the table
neither wings, nor body, nor legs
a uniform, uninterrupted, vertical fall
a hip, an arm, a shoulder
the color fading from the cheeks, the forehead, the lips
an office chair, or an ordinary chair, a footstool, or an armchair
traces of wet mud, or paint, or grease [Section I, pp. 9–24]

This procedure, similar to the *entassement* technique of baroque poetry, reproduces in the style and in the words themselves the little impasses and tentative movements in alternate directions, immediately canceled and replaced by other movements, at right angles, toward other possibilities, that characterize the labyrinth. Even when the series seems linear ("a hip, an arm, a shoulder") the reader, made cautious by so many false steps and retreats, hesitates to accept it as such, or accords it only a provisional acceptance, while awaiting fresh indications. Unconsciously, he is led to see in each phrase, however simple, a miniature maze.

One type of relationship important to the structure of the plot elements is doubling, often associated with metamorphosis. Such are the "double" groups: picture-café, picture-photograph, narrator's room and room of the young woman, soldier-protagonist and soldier-husband (of the young woman) or soldier-comrade, young woman-waitress. A single individual at times seems to undergo a sort of doubling: the lame man who is queerly able to move across town to the barracks, the boy who guides the soldier to the café but also leaves him before reaching the tavern. At one moment, the soldier leaning from the barracks window sees himself (or his double) in the street below:

The soldier leans out a bit farther. The sidewalk seems farther down than he had expected. [. . .] An indistinct mass makes a motion in the doorway. One would say it was a man wrapped in a large coat, or in a military cape. [. . . He recognizes] clearly a shoulder with its strap buttoned, an arm bent at the elbow around a rectangular package, of the size of a shoe box. [P. 103]

The bayonet-dagger that the narrator near the end of the story takes from the soldier's box is "doubled" from the start, since it appears very early, emerging from a pattern in the dust of the room, taking on form and volume in a kind of lengthy descriptive metamorphosis that leads to its identity after various false starts. Here are some of the steps in the process:

On the right, a vaguer form, already covered with several days' deposits. [. . .] It is a kind of cross: a long body, about the size of a kitchen knife, but wider, pointed at one end and swelling out slightly at the other. [. . .] One would say a flower. [. . .] Or it might be a figurine in human form. [. . .] It could also be a dagger. [. . .]

A similar motif adorns as well the painted wall paper. It is a pale gray paper, with vertical stripes only slightly darker [. . .], a line of small designs, all identical, of a dark gray: a flower design, a species of clove, or a miniature torch. [Pp. 13–19]

As to the wallpaper itself, the innumerable, minute spots which form its motif no more resemble in form a torch than they do a flower, or a human outline, a dagger, the flame from a gas lamp or something else altogether. One would say only that the spot were silent feathers falling vertically in a uniform fall [. . . like [. . .] particles in suspension in a still liquid, like little bu bles in a charged liquid, like snow flakes, like particles of d [. . .]

Only the table top, under the conical lampshade, is illumin as is the bayonet placed in its center. [P. 80]

Emergence, metamorphoses, polymorphic possibilities, tiple relationships (with snow, dust), and finally, ide this deadly weapon gradually acquires an emotional cha uncertainty, anguish, and doubt. Hinting perhaps at th of the soldier, it also prefigures the probable—quite banal—contents of the box.

Just what is the role of this box, which provoked so many comments among Robbe-Grillet's critics? It would be easy to find in popular tales, in adventure stories and even psychological novels, ambiguous, "closed" objects (in both the literal and figurative sense) with symbolic or even Freudian significance whose absolute identity remains mysterious or problematic. From magic coffers or bottles enclosing powerful, supernatural genies to modern psychiatric talismans (such as the steel balls that Queeg in *The Caine Mutiny* constantly fondles), the *objet troublant* follows its course. The box that must not be opened under penalty of disaster, and whose prototype was Pandora's box, is doubtless associated with strong unconscious drives. It is the same with objects having some mysterious function, of which an old but still meaningful example is the cup and lance of Chrétien de Troyes's *Legend of the Grail*. It is often forgotten that the current "explanations" of these objects are all scholarly speculations proposed long after the time of the work itself: religious symbols (the cup and lance of the crucifixion, talismans of Celtic myths, survivals of Eleusinian rites), sexual symbols (lingam and yoni), or evocations of social or historical patterns (such as genealogy). No trace of these identifications may be found in Chrétien's text. The fact that Perceval asks *no* questions about the meaning of the objects is indeed essential to the story: the refusal of the young knight to make any inquiry brings about the disappearance of all who participate in the Fisher King's ceremony, leaving the chateau empty of guests, objects, and setting. If we admit, as we can without difficulty, that all the modern explanations of the Grail ceremony only impoverish a beautiful, mysterious story—by limiting its meaning to a single idea which suddenly seems to explain nothing—we can appreciate the value and the role of an *object* whose function in the novelistic field is to *support* an emotion that, having only a situational existence, has no symbolic or metaphysical links with any other level of reality.

The fact that the box of *In the Labyrinth* is finally opened and its contents described (commonplace things: letters, a watch, and the bayonet) would seem at first glance to differentiate it from such hermetic objects as those in the Grail legend, or, to take an example from Robbe-Grillet's own works, from that other object, the eraser (in the novel *The Erasers*), whose meaning remains ambiguous or nonexistent, at least within the text. But the final "revelation" of the contents of the box in *In the Labyrinth* occurs only belatedly, so to speak, during the delayed and almost casual recapitulation that precedes the narrator's *detachment* from his narration. While, from a "realistic" viewpoint, the box could certainly be, throughout the story, nothing more or less than what it is at the end, it does, prior to that point, provoke a psychological disturbance among the novel's characters as well as in the reader, producing innumerable anxiety-generating structures that embody perfectly syndromes of anxiousness, flight, and progressive delirium. Moreover, it was necessary for Robbe-Grillet to give an inventory of the contents of the box if only to prevent symbolic interpretations among critics of transcendent persuasions who always discern in the smallest mystery a metaphor, a correspondence, or a religious symbol. Ironically, one of these still persists in the belief that the box in *In the Labyrinth* encloses the soul of the soldier, who obtains, before his death, absolution from the priest (doctor), in a kind of medieval-modern allegory. Perhaps a simple question might be put: suppose we ourselves met in the street a soldier carrying such a box—would it not immediately provoke our curiosity? And would this anxious curiosity lose anything of its *original* force up to the time of our discovery, later, that the box held only a collection of uninteresting objects?

To understand the undeniable success of *In the Labyrinth*, we may have recourse to a number of the principles that are elucidated in the course of this book, and that are in part ideas put forth by Robbe-Grillet himself and in part theorems that can be deduced not only from his novels but from the nature of the novelistic genre. It is again a question of finding the "justification" (in the technical sense) of the formalism of such a work (the over-all system that determines the relations among objects, scenes, metamorphoses, distortions), its de-chronology (which, especially since Faulkner, has increasingly invaded the modern novel), and its content (the soldier's story, or the story of the narrator who tells it). Robbe-Grillet's formal universe, from *The Erasers* on, is one in which objects "reply" to one another not in the manner of Baudelairean correspondences or symbols (which are always evidence of a mystical unity lying beneath appearances), but as real or possible objective forms whose relationships of geometry or other features are charged with psychic forces emanating from the characters of the novel or from the reader himself. It is a sort of "aided" phenomenological system. That "life itself" may not often present such formal correspondences is irrelevant to the creater of fiction.

The violation of normal chronology has its own justifications. In the first place, a few would contest the argument that mental content is rarely, if ever, chronological, or that the interplay of memories, visualized projects, and reconstructions of the past have their own psychological, emotional, and even obsessional chronology that contradicts the linear progressions of the traditional novel. In the second place, *In the Labyrinth* is organized about a spatial maze that has its analogue in time. A story is elaborated, or reconstructed, in a kind of *tesserac* (as Ouspensky called a volume in four dimensions) of space-time and engenders, as it builds, imaginary extensions or accessory developments that remain within the work.

In *In the Labyrinth*, the dual story of the soldier and the narrator (a duality that affects, as we have seen, most of the other characters in the novel) awakens the interest of the reader, maintains it, and transforms it, toward the end of the work, into an unusually pure type of pathos, mostly by means rarely identified critically in literary studies, but which have played an important part in twentieth-century cinematic criticism, with its innovations in the field of formal and aesthetic analysis. Borrowing certain ideas and terms from critics like Edgar Morin or Cohen-Séat, one can explain the fascination exerted upon the reader by the story of *In the Labyrinth* by references to empathy, mimetism, emotional projection, and other psychic attitudes that the spectator of a film, like the reader of a novel, necessarily takes toward any character placed before him, even an unknown person. This spectator-reader identification, subject to oscillations of approach and retreat (sometimes in a sort of Brechtian "distancing") and rich in affective nuances projected upon the character (through resonances and sympathies due to one's personal history, for example), expands and increases while our basic *voyeurism* holds us close to the episodes of a narration rich in "depths" that seem to hide confused and uncertain meanings. The formalism of narrative structures, the specificity of events, assure that the reader's projective involvement will not be accidental, but will conform to the inner rules of the work itself. The reader acts with the protagonist, but also reacts toward him. In the course of this transfer of forces, everything he attributes to the protagonist he reads into him as actually inherent. The more "hollow," the more undefined the character, and the less the author has sought to "fill" him by means of commentaries or explanations, the more the reader can identify himself with the character, "filling" him with his own anguish and concern, his own past, his own desires, "charging" him directly with his own emotions.[6]

A "plot based on nothing"? Yes, and no. *In the Labyrinth*,

6. Cf. Edgar Morin, *Le Cinéma ou l'homme imaginaire* (Paris: Minuit, 1956); and G. Cohen-Séat, *Problèmes du cinéma* (Paris: Presses Universitaires, 1961).

more than any previous novel by Robbe-Grillet, is a work created in the process of its own writing. The "secret movements leading to some design" are not only in the author's intentions; they are concretized in the work itself. Yet to consider the novel merely as an allegory of literary creation would be as serious an error as to construe Robbe-Grillet's objects as symbols in the regular sense. The work itself is its creation: the novel comes into being before us. We watch (to use an analogy with the documentary film on Picasso) *The Robbe-Grillet Mystery*. We feel simultaneously the anguish of the soldier lost in the labyrinth and that of his creator in the act of fashioning him and watching him evolve. With the end of the novel, the reader, undergoing the same "purgation" as the narrator, can withdraw from these entangled constructions, leave these confused paths, abandon these dreamlike perspectives.

Some critics thought that *In the Labyrinth* marked the end of what they termed *"Robbegrilletisme."* On the contrary, Robbe-Grillet's art enters a new phase in this strong novel, and begins to evolve along radically new paths.

6 "Monsieur X on the Double Track": Last Year at Marienbad (1961)

To put myself into your story.

MALLARME

Desire, the image of the thing itself.

MAURICE SCEVE

Even before writing the scenario of *Last Year at Marienbad*, Robbe-Grillet was described by a number of critics as an author of "cinematographic" novels. When he began to write and produce films, the general question of the relationships between his literary works and the art of the film gave rise to further studies involving the comparative analysis of novel and film, raising new questions in a long-standing controversy.[1]

1. A good summary of the question appears in Pierre Brodin, *Présences contemporaines*, III (Paris: Debresse, 1956), pp. 93–97, 195–199. Brodin shows that Yvan Goll's view of the film as "visual poetry" and Pierre Mac Orlan's doctrine that film may "express the unconscious" related early films to poetry rather than theater or novel. During the Dada and surrealist periods, new sources of poetic invention were seen in double exposures, slow motion, speed-up, lap dissolves, and bizarre montage. The "cinematography of thought" theory in turn led to a comparison between "interior films" and stream of consciousness or interior monologue in the novel. Later, in 1944, Sergei Eisenstein (see *Film Form* [New York: Meridian, 1957], pp. 195–255) laid the foundations of film-novel study on a formal basis in his famous study of the influence of Dickens on Griffith's films, pointing out novelistic montage, camera angles, and the like. Among

Despite arguments to the contrary, many undeniable links exist between film and novel. We may detect mutual influences, converging techniques, transpositions and correspondences, and a whole array of reciprocal relationships with which criticism—both literary and cinematic—must, increasingly, deal. True, hasty identification of film and novel, false analogies, and doubtful parallels must be avoided, but not at the expense of refusing to recognize the common elements shared by these two expressive systems, such as similarities between a novelistic narrative mode and the camera angles chosen by the scenarist or film maker, methods of linking scenes, parallel modes of chronological ordering, and the use of objectified subjectivity in imaginary or false scenes. *Last Year at Marienbad*, both as a film and as a *ciné-roman*, contributes greatly to the study of such problems.[2]

Robbe-Grillet himself, who before writing his first film had

---

the many early studies, the best is still the chapter "Cinema and Novel" in Claude-Edmonde Magny's *L'Age du roman américain* (Paris: Seuil, n.d. [1948]).

2. The special issue of the *Revue des Lettres Modernes*, Summer 1958 (Nos. 36–38), "Cinéma et Roman," marked the first phase of "cinematic" criticism of Robbe-Grillet. My article "Roman et cinéma: le cas de Robbe-Grillet" (*Symposium*, Summer 1961) studies in great detail the numerous and extensive observations on Robbe-Grillet made in that issue by G.-A. Astre, Michel Mourlet, Jean-Louis Bory, and Colette Audry. Although Robbe-Grillet had as yet written no scenarios, most of the critics discuss his "typically cinematic style" (Audry) and try to demonstrate that passages from his works read like movie scripts. Audry transforms the opening passage of *The Voyeur* into this scriptlike paraphrase: "One has only [. . .] to open *The Voyeur:* The Camera, set up somewhere on the deck, first shoots the crowd of passengers whose glance, turned toward the jetty, conveys their impatience to land. [. . .] Mathias then notices a young girl who stares at him fixedly. At this moment there begins a slow dolly shot forward, the inclined slip [. . .], the quay, perpendicular to the slip, the whole geometric background" (p. 263). Obviously,

published a short text comparing novelistic viewpoint with camera angles in films, became involved in discussions of film-novel parallels, openly disagreeing, for example, with the actual director of *Last Year at Marienbad*, Alain Resnais. Alluding to a series of shots not retained in the final version of the film, Robbe-Grillet described them in an interview as *fondus* or dissolves linking "two moments of *present* time," thus contrasting with dissolves as used conventionally to express time lapses. The interviewer then intervened:

—However, in your novels, there is never any equivalent of the dissolve.

Robbe-Grillet: Oh, yes, on the contrary.

Resnais: I don't believe either that they are dissolves. It is the use of a phrase that causes the image to change. The dissolve does not give the same impression. [*Les Cahiers du Cinéma*, No. 123, Sept. 1961, p. 16]

Why such a contradiction? Let us examine the question, using specific examples. In studying the scene linkings in Robbe-Grillet's novels, I have pointed out transitions brought about by gestures or objects whose formal or psychological analogies tie together images belonging to different levels of fictional reality, or separated in the nominal space and time of the novel. In *Jealousy*, two different moments in time are literally "dissolved" together when Franck sets on the terrace table a glass without a "trace of an ice cube in the bottom," but which, a few lines farther on, and with no indication of any time change, still contains "a little piece of ice cube, rounded on one side" (pp. 108–109). In the same novel, as the husband narrator erases the spot left by the centipede on the dining-room wallpaper, the paper "dissolves"—in the course of a paragraph which could apply to either of the two—into

such a procedure becomes an easy game, to be played with almost any novel.

the sheet of blue notepaper on which the wife A has made an erasure (pp. 131–132). As early as 1958, Arnaldo Pizzorusso, in a perceptive review, used the terms *dissolvenza* and *sovrimpressione* to describe the passage from a café terrace observed by the narrator in a photograph of A to the actual terrace of the house: "All the other portions of chairs, discernible in the photograph, seem to belong to unoccupied chairs. There is no one on this terrace, as in the rest of the house."[3] One could scarcely contest the analogy here with the cinematic dissolve; yet Resnais's remark about the difference in *impression* made by the literary procedure on one hand and the filmic on the other remains cogent. At issue is the basic difference between words and image. Recent critics, like Wladimir Wiedlé, have shown that supposedly "visual" texts (such as Rimbaud's *Illuminations*) often convey imprecise images at best, and that even these are secondary. Moreover, one can read the sort of literary dissolve in which Robbe-Grillet passes from one object (the erased trace of the centipede, for instance) to another (such as the erased notepaper) with no prevision of the second object, even during the "bridging" phrases, recognizing only after the latter has appeared that there has been a transition—an effect quite different from the gradual replacement of image 1 by image 2 in the fade-out fade-in technique of the cinematic dissolve.

Literary criticism is faced at present with a new, and important, problem: to discover, for written narrational texts, terms and definitions which will allow useful and proper analogies with the cinema, without falling into the trap of obliterating the necessary distinctions between an art of words and an art of visual images. To refuse all analogies would certainly impoverish the study of both novels and films; the publication of scenarios, the increasing number of studies

3. *Letteratura*, Jan.–April 1958, p. 183, quoting from p. 126 of *La Jalousie*.

comparing the two genres, the development of the *ciné-roman*,[4] all prove that criticism must apply itself to the new task.[5]

4. The term "ciné-roman" dates from the beginning of the century. It may be found, for example, in the Sept. 13–19, 1909, issue of *Ciné-Journal;* see Jean Giraud, *Le Lexique français du cinéma des origines à 1930* (Paris: 1958), p. 77. For the relationships between film and script, see also my article, "Problèmes du roman cinématographique," in *Cahiers de L'Association Internationale des Etudes Françaises;* May 1968, pp. 277–289.

5. See especially the Oct. 1961 issue of *Premier Plan* (No. 18, entitled "Alain Resnais"), containing important brief statements by a number of New Novelists on the subject of film-novel relationships. Claude Ollier (p. 26) emphasizes the distinction between visual image and verbal description, declaring that the latter "has no cinematic equivalent." While Claude Simon (p. 32) admits many parallels between literary and filmic *viewpoint*, Jean Ricardou (pp. 27–32) stresses the dangerous analogies proposed by the writers of the "Cinema and Novel" issue of the *Revue des Lettres Modernes*, which I had myself criticized, writing with respect to literary "images": "A given description of the movements of waves, which the critics claim to be typically photographic or cinematic [in *The Voyeur*], is not at all such. It is a wholly literary structure, a wave propelled by an organization of words, and its 'realistic' appearance does not come from any so-called realistic or scientific precision, the only reality being the words, phrases, sentences, and paragraphs—that is, a literary reality. The visual image constitutes at best an epiphenomenon giving a sort of supplementary or even parasitic value to a creation which lies, first and always, in the realm of language" (*Symposium*, Summer 1961, p. 98). With respect to the idea that a novel can be a "paraphrase of a film," I asked the following question: what would the results be if several authors wrote out versions of a single film? Would there not be as many "cinematic" literary styles as there were writers? The same game could be played in reverse: ask several film makers to film an identical script: what would happen to the alleged correspondences and equivalencies? They would, of course, be engulfed in the film maker's individual styles. It is somewhat the same problem as that of "true" realism: in principle, all the pictures painted by "realistic" artists should have an identical, "neutral" style, or even be indistinguishable from "nature," like a perfect *trompe-l'oeil*. But such is far from the case; any amateur can distinguish between a Vermeer and

Is *Last Year at Marienbad* a film, a novel, or both simultaneously? Can the scenario be studied or judged apart from the film? For some, like Bernard Pingaud, the text is difficult, if not impossible, to read, or at best "of very little interest [. . .] for one who has not seen *Marienbad*"; for Jean Thibaudeau, the published text of *Marienbad* "is, in a way, the the extraordinary novel of a man inventing a film,"[6] just as *In the Labyrinth* may be seen as the novel of a man writing a novel. The text of the book is a modified shooting script, with the original pages, done in the French style of sound and images given on opposite pages, merged into a single running text. Comparing the *ciné-roman* to the original scenario (with its system of facing pages), we find that the melding of the two parts, done in a manner similar to the shuffling together of a deck of cards divided into two piles, has hardly affected the impression of simultaneity produced by the two-page system, while at the same time the "integrated" text creates a different impression. Mixing the sound text and the visual text on a single page serves immediately to convert a film into a narration. Since all of the text that is *not heard* in the film— everything except the dialogues—is written with neutral precision, almost "without style" (suggestive of the "neutral style" that Sartre once proposed for novels), while the speeches, and especially X's long monologue running intermittently throughout the film, are in a mannered style, neopoetic and almost baroque, the reader of the text becomes aware of a duality of tone that is not apparent when one sees the film. On the screen, everything described in the neutral style (descriptions of rooms, furniture, costumes, gestures, actions) is transformed by the camera into a poetic-baroque visual equivalent which corresponds to the style used in the

---

a Courbet, and experts in photography have no difficulty recognizing the work of individual photographers. If there is art, there is style, and style is specific to its medium.

6. Pingaud's and Thibaudeau's comments are in *Premier Plan*, No. 18, pp. 23, 34.

dialogues, giving the spectacle a perfect unity of tone. The reader possessing only the printed text, and who must by himself visualize settings, actions, and the like, is obviously at a disadvantage, while viewers of the movie will at the least have a common store of visual images determined by the film itself. The photographic reproductions in the book are a poor substitute for the screen and cover at best a very small number of scenes.[7]

Since *Last Year at Marienbad* was, after all, conceived and written to be filmed, it is best in my view to consider the work primarily in its cinematographic form, referring to the printed text only when it contains developments, specific information, or differences from the film capable of throwing additional light on the flow of images and the continuity of the sound track.

Is it possible to *relate* the story of *Marienbad?* Various critics, as well as Robbe-Grillet himself, have written résumés. But there is a wide gap between a résumé and an analysis of

7. I may be permitted to cite my own personal experience in this matter. During the summer of 1960, I read the script of *Marienbad* (in the two-page version, sound and image) as Robbe-Grillet was writing it. The final choice of settings, backgrounds, and actors had not been made. Naturally, I made an effort to "see" the images as described in the text. When I finally saw the film, I was at first struck by a strong impression of *déjà vu:* it was indeed thus that I had "seen" the film in my mind's eye. Later, trying to analyze my reaction, I realized that in reality I had seen little if anything "mentally," before seeing the film, but had only retained the memory of words (snatches of dialogue, vague paraphrases of scene descriptions), surrounded by a sort of halo of indistinct visual images which the film brought into precise focus. This suggests, I believe, that the power to visualize word images varies greatly from person to person, as the power to visualize, even without words, varies in the same individual from the waking state to that of dreams. This subjective variability makes it virtually impossible to speak precisely of the images evoked by words, whenever these words are not forcibly linked to specific photographic images, as, for example, in a film.

the work: the more one tries in a résumé to remain faithful to the unfolding of the film, the closer one comes to a total reproduction of the scenario. At a distance, an over-all action seems to unfold; close up, the instantaneous reality of the individual scenes dominates. Between the two limits, the observer finds himself relying on efforts at rational coordination, logical assembling of elements, or the use of a preconceived pattern of events to impose on the sequences and scenes an order that cannot be other than arbitrary, whatever organizing principle is followed: the existence or nonexistence of "last year," the degree of reality of the images, attribution to one or another character of the filmed mental "phantasms," and the like. Since the action develops not only outside, but in opposition to, such fictional coordinates, it becomes obvious that any "explanation" is doomed to failure. In view of this fact, how can Robbe-Grillet and Resnais both claim that *Marienbad* is "a victory for realism"? It is a question to be answered later.

As for the plot of the film, let Robbe-Grillet's account serve as a résumé. His preface to *Marienbad* is one of the most complete commentaries that the author has ever made on his works. Here is his summary, abridged:

The whole film is in fact the story of a persuasion: what is involved is a reality that the hero creates by his own vision, through his own words. [. . .]

It all takes place in a luxury hotel, a sort of international palace. [. . .] An unnamed man goes from room to room [. . .], walks down interminable corridors. [. . .] His glance moves from one nameless face to another nameless face. But it always comes back to one face, that of a certain young woman. [. . .] To her, then, he offers [. . .] a past, a future, freedom. He tells her that they have already met, a year ago, that they became lovers, that he has returned now to this rendezvous which she herself had made, and that he will take her away with him.

Is the stranger an ordinary seducer? Is he mad? Or is he merely confusing two faces? The young woman, in any case, takes it all at first as a game. [. . .] But the man is serious. Obstinate, solemn, certain of this past story which he discloses little by little, he becomes insistent, he furnishes proof. . . . And the young woman, gradually, as if regretfully, yields ground. Then she becomes frightened. She stiffens. She does not wish to leave the other man [. . .] who watches over her and who is perhaps her husband. But the story told by the stranger becomes more and more real; irresistibly, it becomes more and more true. The present and the past have, besides, finally become fused, while the growing tension among the three protagonists creates in the mind of the heroine tragic phantasms: rape, murder, suicide. . . .

Then, all at once, she is ready to give in. . . . She has already given in, in fact, a long time ago. After a last effort to escape, [. . .] she seems to accept her role as the woman that the stranger has been expecting, and appears ready to go away with him, toward something [. . .], love, poetry, freedom . . . or, perhaps, death. . . . [Pp. 13–14][8]

The preface to *Marienbad* states a number of principles of cinematic theory. The film is the ideal means, according to Robbe-Grillet, of expressing "mental reality." Images on the screen exist in an "eternal present"; they are the kind of inner pictures that each of us forms mentally, especially at moments of great psychological tension. They are the "inner cinema" of our life, made up of memories, projected desires, objectified hypotheses, and fears, which in a sense imply that communication between human beings may be termed an "exchange of views," an exchange of a visual nature that the movies can best represent. In the interview previously cited, Robbe-Grillet develops the same point:

ROBBE-GRILLET: The whole question boils down to whether the uncertainty that impregnates the images of the film is exaggerated in comparison with what we experience in ordinary life. [. . .]

8. Page references are to the 1961 printing of *L'Année dernière à Marienbad* (Paris: Minuit).

For myself, it seems to me that things really happen that way. There is, between these characters, a passionate experience, of the type which for all of us contains the largest proportion of contradictions, doubts, phantasms. *Marienbad* is the kind of obscure story which we all live in our emotional crises, in our love affairs, in our affective life. [. . .] And again I say, the main concern is realism. [*Les Cahiers du Cinéma*, No. 123, Sept. 1961, p. 12]

The great paradox here is that a supposedly "realistic" work (at least so far as its psychology goes) can have provoked among its critics such an abundance of differing interpretations, or of interpretative "patterns," whose irrealism is manifest, and whose effect is to destroy any realism of the film in the ordinary sense of the term. Resnais himself not only declared in many interviews that he accepted the "reality" of the previous year at Marienbad, related by X, but even published a graphlike drawing which divides the scenes into one week of past time and one week of present time, plus an indefinite or imaginary time zone. Critics opposed to the claim of "realism" came forward with wildly implausible schemes for making the work nevertheless realistic, succumbing to the nostalgia for linear chronology to the point of recreating a "tellable," if not entirely conventional, story.[9]

9. According to Resnais's schematic—printed first upside down in No. 123 of the *Cahiers du Cinéma*, then correctly (right side up) in No. 125, p. 48—the "present" action of *Marienbad* runs from Tuesday to Sunday. This action is constantly interrupted by a series of flashbacks ("last year") running from Monday to Saturday night in a *past* week. In addition, there are "second-power" flashbacks and scenes occurring in an "all-time" zone, apparently imaginary. Unfortunately, it is impossible, without Resnais's working script with its numbered scenes, to correlate the published scenario of *Marienbad* with the foregoing schematic; nevertheless, one can follow Resnais's conception of two actions in parallel montage structure, each moving "toward the future," up to the final scenes. Resnais has not concealed his own "belief" in the reality of past relations between A and X, though he has freely admitted that the finished film does not require acceptance of

Since both Robbe-Grillet and Resnais vaunted the "open-endedness" of the plot, we may profitably examine the most serious proposals made by the critics to decipher the "story" of *Marienbad*. Roger Tailleur establishes two "co-ordinates," past-present, and real-imaginary; each scene is to be located on these, according to its "time" and its "degree of reality." Tailleur does not share Robbe-Grillet's views on subjective uncertainty, however, declaring that "in life [. . .] man makes a clear distinction between the objective and the subjective, the tangible and the intangible, the present and the past."[10] One would expect then from Tailleur a version even more "normal" than the author's, logical and Cartesian, but such is not the case. For Tailleur, X is sincere when he reminds A of her past promise, and she is equally sincere in not recognizing him: the reason is that X and A have known and loved, somewhere last year, *doubles* of X and A! We seem suddenly transported into the artificial world of a modern Marivaux, where implausibility may be cultivated for its own sake. Tailleur himself admits that his explanation of the plot is most unsatisfactory, and he manages to treat other aspects of the film with perspicacity.

Claude Ollier, well aware of Robbe-Grillet's intentions, gives an engrossing commentary on *Marienbad*.[11] His review, entitled "Tonight at Marienbad," multiplies Tailleur's "co-ordinates" into a system of image types: memory-images, desire-images, false-memory-images, and so forth. Ollier also makes an interesting parallel with Adolfo Bioy-Casares's novel, *Morel's Invention*, whose hero attempts to intrude into the life of a woman, already dead, but who apparently comes to life in a kind of three-dimensional holographic film. Among the "multiple solutions" that Ollier proposes for *Marienbad*, he

his own interpretation of the plot, and that his famous schematic was only an operational solution used to facilitate the filming.

10. *Les Lettres Nouvelles*, July 1961.
11. *Nouvelle Revue Française*, Oct.–Nov. 1961.

selects the following: X, already "sure of his triumph" over A, is to take the young woman away with him as soon as the theatrical performance (in the film) is finished. When he enters the theater hall, the fact that his own words coincide exactly with the dialogue of the play being performed there brings about the automatic reproduction of past events, in such a way that we understand that X, since the beginning of the film, has been "replaying" the scenes which the spectator took to be unfolding in the present, scenes which the protagonist will eternally relive *each time* there is a performance of the play. By insisting on this notion of cyclic recapitulation, Ollier establishes the link between *Marienbad* and Bioy-Casares' novel. That the first film version did not have "The End" at its termination seemed important to Ollier; but, in fact, the insertion of the conventional term in later copies seems to have been less a concession to "professional habit," as Ollier thought, than a return to the original scenario of Robbe-Grillet, where it had appeared from the outset.

François Weyergans advanced as the most "fecund" hypothesis an explanation of the film as a special kind of dream, resulting from a "diurnal" rather than a "nocturnal" conflict among the three main characters, who stand for "the id, the super-ego, and the ego of a single person, that is, of the woman caught in a struggle between the pleasure principle and moral inhibitions": a sort of Freudian allegory or reverie interrupted when the woman's "id" pushes her towards "a quite real lover."[12] The interesting part of Weyergans' critique, to me, is that it recognizes a psychiatric content in the film; I will revert to this later.

The merit of Bernard Pingaud's explanatory schematic of *Marienbad* is that it presents formally, rather than anecdotally, the various ways in which the plot elements may be related.[13] Starting with the assumption that X did indeed meet A last

12. *Les Cahiers du Cinéma*, Sept. 1961 (No. 123).
13. *Premier Plan*, Oct. 1961 (No. 18).

The Master Builder

year and that she promised to join him after a year's respite, Pingaud enumerates the various theoretical possibilities that ensue. For instance, A may have forgotten X; X may be mistaken, as A may be, about the identity of an earlier lover (Tailleur's solution); X invents the past by his very insistence (more or less as Robbe-Grillet suggests in his preface); finally, the story has already taken place when the film begins, and is repeated as a theatrical performance (Ollier's theory). As he studies these "variables" in the structure of the plot, Pingaud also examines the shifts and distortions within individual scenes and sequences: images contradicting dialogue, phantasms, and the like. His conclusion that "the *entire* film is subjective" brings strong support to the statements made by the author himself.

In the spate of articles about *Marienbad* (probably the author's most widely discussed work), two main trends are evident: on one hand, a tendency to emphasize the originality of its conception and realization, and on the other, a desire to derive its techniques and ideas from previous cinematic practice. In considering avant-garde films, going back to Robert Wiene's expressionistic *Cabinet of Doctor Caligari*, one critic, Gérard Bonnot, found "all that" (meaning dechronology, imaginary sequences, and opposition between image and sound) in Billy Wilder's movie version of *The Seven Years' Itch*.[14] Bonnot shared Tailleur's objections to the supposed "mental realism" of the work, stating that "the mind, normally, always distinguishes between real perceptions and the imaginary." *Marienbad* becomes, in his view, a precious game played by two insincere jokers, unrelated to any "human cause," and even betraying "man's ability to stand up for any serious concern." The symbol of this sterile activity on the part of a contemplative authorial God looking at the world *sub specie aeternitatis* and without ever intervening, is the match game,

14. *Les Temps Modernes,* Dec. 1961 (No. 187).

whose wide-spread popularity in *Madame Express* and similar publications was deemed by the critic to constitute self-evident proof of the film's "sophistication."[15]

André S. Labarthe's comparison between the techniques of *Marienbad* and those of Italian neorealist films contained several original suggestions. He considers *Marienbad* "dated," calling it "the last of the great neorealistic films." His ingenious argument runs as follows: the neorealistic film, rejecting the classical scenario, substituted for it an "open" script, in which scenes succeed each other in many cases without apparent logical connection, separated by *"manques,"* or absent, unfilmed transitions. In *Marienbad*, writes Labarthe, we find "the same gaps in the scenario, the same ambiguity of events, the same effort required from the spectator." A certain paradox nevertheless arises: in neorealist films all flashbacks are banished as a matter of principle, since they serve to fill in the gaps, whereas in *Marienbad* flashbacks (true or false) are numerous. Labarthe solves the difficulty by arguing that Resnais and Robbe-Grillet (as Orson Welles had done in certain films) use the flashback not to "rectify the discontinuity of the narration," but to reinforce the present, since the pseudo flashbacks rejoin the present at its own level, and with the same discontinuities, as the scenes of the fragmented narration

15. The unforeseen stir caused by the "Marienbad game" has given rise to many comments. Resnais identified it as a variation of the old "Chinese" game of *Nim;* Robbe-Grillet thought he had invented it, like the gentleman who, it seems, had even tried to patent it and wished to sue the authors of the film. In the game, M invites X to play, places sixteen matches in four rows (7–5–3–1), and forces X always to pick up the last match, thereby losing. As to the metaphoric relationship between the game and the film as a whole, Resnais saw it as a statement of the necessity to "make a decision" (as A must do). Other conjectures are quite possible: M, who always wins at the game of logic, loses in the game of passion; or, perhaps, the idea that, whatever the order of events, the outcome is the same: the game thus becomes an internal analogy of the film.

which "take place" at the time in which we see them. It is a clever argument, which suffers somewhat if one compares the typical themes, settings, and characters of recognized neo-realist films with those of *Marienbad*. Labarthe seems on firmer ground when he turns to existentialism as a basis for the de-chronology of the film, calling the chronology of a plot or story "the last *essentialist prejudice*."[16]

If we set aside a number of other "explanations" of *Marien-bad*, mostly allegorical (the myth of Death, who gives, as in the Breton legend, one year's grace to his victim; a modern version of *Tristan*, or of the legend of the Grail; an allegory in which the palace and garden represent conventional society from which X and A seek to escape through great passionate love), we may then consider a new "possibility," more or less "realistic" (as Robbe-Grillet would have it), which would fit the author's description of the work as the "story of a per-suasion" and still permit us to accept the fact that the charac-ters do not distinguish between reality and imagination, as so many critics insisted they would do in a basically realistic plot. If we must at any cost—without going so far as to suggest two people who fail to recognize each other, or who have im-plausibly forgotten an affair scarcely one year old—make what we see on the screen correspond to what takes place in "real" life, as Robbe-Grillet claims, and if we wish to establish a realistic basis for the subjective panorama of images whose de-gree of reality we cannot identify exactly, we need to look more closely at the notion of *persuasion*, with its associated ideas of *suggestion, insinuation,* or even *simulation*. Resnais at one point suggested, as he had done earlier for *Hiroshima mon amour*, that all the characters in *Marienbad* are perhaps patients in a mental clinic, and that he had envisioned the film from a psychiatric point of view: Freudian corridors, nar-cissistic bedrooms, pistol shots serving as symbols of impotence,

16. *Les Cahiers du Cinéma*, Sept. 1961 (No. 123).

and X as psychiatrist treating his patient A—a possible amnesiac having "voluntarily repressed" her past. Resnais went so far as to claim that this disquieting setting "seeks to put the spectator into a light state of *hypnosis*."[17] Hypnosis is, of course, an extreme form of suggestion or persuasion; although it is a bit old-fashioned today, its literature contains a number of quite surprising and striking parallels to what happens in *Marienbad*.

I shall limit myself to a single text, published over a half-century ago, Dr. Joseph Grasset's treatise on hypnotism and suggestion.[18] The chief interest of this book is that it examines in detail the numerous modalities of suggestion, from deep hypnosis to persuasion and insinuation in a quasi-hypnotic or "waking" state, corresponding, in the case of A (and sometimes X), not only to the generation of images through suggestions from another person, but also the strange fascination exerted upon the spectator or reader by these same images, which appear, in the light of this study in psychopathology, closely linked to recognized and identifiable mental processes taking place most often in the unconscious zones of the psyche. Without accepting Bernheim's extreme views on suggestion, which he sees as the basis for all human action ("suggestion is action, it is struggle, it is all of man and humanity," Dr. Grasset quotes him as saying), we can admit, along with the many authorities cited by Dr. Grasset, that the line of demarcation between pathological states, such as deep hypnosis, and more "normal" states of suggestibility is not clear, and that the procedures of true hypnosis are only an accentuated form of procedures which make it possible with "malleable"

17. Interview in the *Cahiers du Cinéma*, No. 123; also, an article by Bonnot in *Les Temps Modernes*, No. 187, containing a number of quotations of remarks made by Resnais and Robbe-Grillet on the subject of *Marienbad*.

18. *L'Hypnotisme et la suggestion* (Paris: Octave Doin, 1909). Quotations from Bernheim, Charcot, Binet, and Janet appear on pp. 21–22, 27, and *passim*.

subjects, without the use of actual hypnosis, "to produce by means of suggestion," in Charcot's words, "a systematic group of associated ideas which take over the mind parasitically" so that, as Janet states, "suggestions, with their automatic and independent development, become veritable parasites of thought."

If susceptibility to persuasion and suggestion are of the same nature as yielding to hypnosis, it seems legitimate to apply the analysis of states associated with hypnotism to the study of the suggestions made to A by X in *Last Year at Marienbad*. A, by her obvious suggestibility, her apparently neurotic personality, and her slightly hysterical temperament (screams, fainting spells), seems to match closely the characteristic traits of the "suggested subject" as described by Binet, who is "not only someone temporarily reduced to the state of an automaton," but is also "someone who *performs an action that emanates from someone else*." A's reactions during the "persuasion" undertaken by X to convince her of the reality of their past relations are striking demonstrations of the observations made in Dr. Grasset's manual concerning the behavior of suggestible individuals. Here are various citations that can serve as psychiatric commentaries on certain scenes in *Last Year at Marienbad*, with an indication of their film parallels:

Hypnotism and Suggestion (Grasset)	*Marienbad*
Some individuals are so impressionable to suggestion that they can be dominated or controlled, even in an apparent state of wakefulness, by means of forceful affirmations [. . .] and who can be made to have visual hallucinations. [P. 73]	(A's special suggestibility, or malleability.)
These subjects [. . .] are in a state of wakefulness, in that they show none of the signs of natural sleep; but	(Numerous aspects of A's behavior, especially in the "imaginary bedroom.")

Hypnotism and Suggestion (cont.)   *Marienbad* (cont.)

in reality, they are in a state of suggestibility, they are *hypnotized in a state of wakefulness.* [P. 77]

A suggestion, with the time of its future accomplishment, has been planted in the subject's mind; the subject has absorbed that, and then, when the time arrives [. . .], the subject acts through auto-suggestion. [P. 80]

    "I shall leave tonight [. . .] taking you with me [. . .]." "The first stroke of midnight sounds [. . .]. A gets up [. . .] like an automaton."

In a state of fascination, the subject passively and automatically imitates the gestures of the hypnotist; this *état paraphronique* is marked by a sort of delirium accompanied by movements, attitudes, words corresponding to the fantasizing conceptions of the subject [. . .]. These subjects, seemingly awake, are carrying out the suggestions given to them. [Pp. 96–97]

    (A's actions when she follows, in various scenes, X's "instructions.")

Where are you?—What do you see?—You are now in a garden, or an apartment.—What do you see there? —You are at a concert. What do you hear? [P. 112]

    (X addresses similar evocative remarks to A.)

You say to the subject: You are a general; or, You are an orator. And thereupon, the subject does not limit himself to replying, Yes, or to striking the pose of a general. He *constructs a whole novel*, in which he speaks, acts, behaves like a general. [P. 112] These subjects compose true *novels*, using the suggestion as a point of departure, as a theme. [P. 176]

    (A's visions form part of a kind of *suggested novel*.)

One subject was given a hallucinatory suggestion localized around a photograph; then, a number of prints were made of this photo; the hallucinatory image was thus multiplied: each of the prints was seen by the sub-

    (The photographic "proof" presented to A by X, with its subsequent *multiplication* in A's bedroom [in Resnais's film].)

Hypnotism and Suggestion (cont.)

ject [. . .] according to the suggested image. [P. 155]

Suggestion brings about doublings of the *personality*, and other transformations. [P. 124]

[When the subject] obeys too slowly [. . .], the instructions must be repeated with great authority. [P. 129]

The illusion may go so far as to create an error concerning someone's identity. [. . .] At the operator's command, the laboratory becomes a street, a garden, or a cemetery. [P. 140]

The imaginary object appearing in the hallucination is perceived in the same way as it would be if it were real. [P. 145]

Verbal suggestion is the simplest kind; it can evoke an idea that manifests itself in a more or less complicated action. [P. 173]

[The operator] says to a patient [. . .]: "Come with me: we will leave on a trip."—And then, she described successively the places to which she goes; the corridors [. . .], the details of places that her excited imagination and memory cause her to see as real. [P. 175]

There may be a *resistance* [. . .] to suggestion. It is felt at the moment an order is given. We saw that F did not wish to hear that she would see her husband. [. . .] This resistance is common to all suggestions. [P. 243] It [. . .] comes into play when the suggestion goes against higher principles or moral consciousness. [P. 388]

Marienbad (cont.)

(The "Pirandellian" identity of A: is she, or not, the woman in X's story?)

(A's delay in assuming the postures described by X, in some scenes.)

(Various ideas "proposed" to A by X.)

(The apparent "reality" of many "unreal" scenes.)

(A's phantasms originate most often from *words* spoken by X.)

(A's visions, following suggestions made by X.)

(Compare the famous scene in A's bedroom [note that individuals are also called "A" and "F" in the manuals] when A refuses to obey X's suggestion when he says, "You went back to the bed [. . .]. You went back to the bed.")

Hypnotism and Suggestion (cont.)	*Marienbad* (cont.)

The subject becomes attached to the hypnotizer, becoming not only his slave, but his amorous slave. [. . .] Hypnosis gives rise to "a violent passion and an almost irresistible attraction, in the hypnotized subject, toward the hypnotizer." [P. 301]

(A "projects" upon X a classic type of "*transfert*.")

The hypnotizer may abuse the hypnosis of the subject in order to commit forcible seduction, or rape. Can a girl or young woman be, through hypnotism, put into a state that makes it impossible for her to resist rape? I think that we may answer: yes. [. . .] It is sufficient that she be, not necessarily hysterical, but neurotic and leaning toward hysteria, for the experimenter to put her into a state of absolute incapacity of resisting the crime committed upon her. [Pp. 372–373] This is possible, without having to say with Bernheim that "the seduction of an honest woman is nothing more, basically, than suggestion." [P. 374]

(In the printed version of Robbe-Grillet's scenario [P. 156], A is the object of a "rapid and brutal scene of rape." This is the climax of the work. In the film, the rape scene was replaced by an oscillating, spasmodic, "white" scene in which A yields to her seducer. [This is the chief point of disagreement between the published scenario and the film.])

Sometimes the subject makes an unconscious accusation of rape, falling victim to deception, and mistaking an hallucination for reality. [P. 378]

(The rape may be only a phantasm in A's mind (Robbe-Grillet: "tension [. . .] creates in the mind of the heroine tragic phantasms: rape, murder [. . .].")

Through autosuggestion [. . .] all madmen become victims of suggestion. [P. 385]

(Is X a victim of autosuggestion? Robbe-Grillet, p. 13: "Is he a madman?")

A subject may *lie* or *deceive through the testimony he gives*. [. . .] He may suffer [. . .] complete amnesia. This retroactive amnesia may be the starting point of false testimony [. . .]

(Compare the scene in which M is seen as "murdering" A.)

Hypnotism and Suggestion (cont.)

of replies contrary to the truth [. . .], of denunciations, lying self-accusations, and *imaginary crimes.* [Pp. 394–395]

The physiological states most closely resembling hypnotism [. . .] are: teaching and *persuasion* [. . .]. [P. 414]

Can a distinction be made between suggestion, an involuntary and unconscious phenomenon, and *simulation,* voluntary and conscious? [. . .] Brissaud has written, concerning simulation and mythomania in hysterical patients: "But, can anyone state firmly that it is possible to recognize the difference between *conscious* and *unconscious* simulation? [. . .] The difference between conscious and unconscious deception seems to me impossible to establish." [P. 416]

Hypnotism and suggestion "illuminate the life of the mind more clearly than all the voluminous treatises of traditional psychology" (Buchner). [P. 427]

One can also, by means of suggestion, *distort the subject's memory,* suggest to him the *memory of nonexistent things,* give him or her retroactive hallucinations, what Forel terms "illusory retroactive memory." [P. 260]

When one gives a subject a retroactive hallucination, one *creates* an illusion of memory, so that the subject *has actually seen* things that have never existed. [P. 396]

Marienbad (cont.)

"The story of a persuasion."

(Are the "simulations" of past events, in the case of A and X, sometimes insincere, or deliberately invented?)

(Robbe-Grillet: "It is my impression that things really happen this way." The film is therefore true "mental reality.")

"What is involved is a reality created by the hero's own vision, by his own words."

The purpose of these parallels is not to furnish an "objective" clue to the meaning of *Marienbad,* but only to show in some detail how the psychology inherent in the film corresponds to previous theories of psychic behavior of a similar nature. X is not, of course, a "real" hypnotist, or even a psychiatrist or mythomanic experimenter, and A is not, in reality, his subject, patient, or suggestible victim. Most of the problems of interpretation outlined earlier still remain, although Dr. Grasset's treatise does throw light on the question of distinctions between the real and the imaginary, which in some states that are not necessarily abnormal are shown to be less clearly distinguishable than one would think.

One reason why most of the "keys" designed to explain *Marienbad* fail is that they attempt to resolve *external* ambiguities (identity of A and X, time of their first meeting, and so on) in a work whose ambiguities are *internal.* Certain plays by Pirandello, for example, which at first may appear quite close in structure and meaning to *Marienbad,* are based on ambiguities that are *external* to the plot: even if we never learn whether Frola's wife, in *Right You Are If You Think You Are,* is "really" his wife, the answer to the question is by implication an objective event. In *Last Year at Marienbad,* on the contrary, the ambiguity is of another type: it is in the very consciousness of the characters. No external "solution" can validate the plot, but only the *plausibility of the states of mind evoked,* apart from any objective story. When Robbe-Grillet speaks of "mental realism," or when Resnais states that he wishes to depict emotions rather than individual characters, what is meant is that apparently contradictory images, often chaotic and "open" to multiple interpretations, correspond nevertheless to possible, plausible states of mind, whose psychological truth the spectator-reader consciously or unconsciously recognizes. Such a conception accepts the definition of the work as a drama of persuasion that organizes, according to specific aesthetic principles, sequences of mental images: insinuations, attempts at resistance, false memories, objectified phantasms, imaginary scenes of murder and rape—all producing, in *Marienbad*, a rich and turbulent psychic mix.

On this basis, the structure of the work may be analyzed in accordance with the chief procedures used to link successive scenes, to link dialogues and images, and to distribute thematic elements. Since the majority of these techniques are the same as those found in Robbe-Grillet's novels, we are brought face to face once more with the novel-cinema controversy: either Robbe-Grillet, in his first film, makes use of literary techniques, or else he had already used in his novels techniques taken from the cinema. In either case, the procedures of the film appear to be rather exact "equivalents" of his novelistic practices.

First of all, in spite of its baroque visual quality, its sharp, shiny, almost "varnished" images, mixed with "white," overexposed scenes, *Marienbad* exerts a strong *literary* fascination, due in great part to the lyrical quality of X's tirades. X's restrained but intense theatrical voice controls the torrential monologue with which he guides the plot, giving to his narration a slow, majestic rhythm and a striking unity of verbal tone. It is X's monologue that prepares us at the outset for the dechronology of events ("Once more"), and which, merging with the text of the inner play, establishes the inner ambiguity of the theme and of the forthcoming action. At the same time, snatches of conversation plant in the listener's mind, like musical motifs or fragments of future melodies that will be developed later, various plot elements whose parallels or analogies in the ensuing action make a thinly disguised résumé of the film:

A MAN, then ANOTHER MAN [. . .]: Don't you know the story? [. . .] It's all they were talking about, last year. Frank had made her believe that he was a friend of her father and that he was there to watch over her. It was a rather strange way of watching over her, however. She realized it, but too late, the night when he

tried to force his way [. . .] into her bedroom, with the absurd
pretext that he wanted to explain the old paintings hanging there.
[. . .] But there wasn't a single picture in her room. [P. 43]

Similarly, the episode of the broken heel (another sexual
symbol or fetish) appears first in verbal allusions (a "random"
remark, p. 42, another made by X, p. 89), before taking place
for the "first" time on the screen (p. 128). Inserted into this
series is a scene showing A holding her shoe in her hand (p.
82). Without developing the point further, it can be said that
in general each important incident is subject to one or more
comments in advance of its occurrence, so that the spectator
almost always sees "present" episodes in the light of some
earlier and almost subliminal suggestion that creates an unconscious feeling of *déjà vu*. In this way the spectator, or the
reader, becomes to a certain extent a "victim" of X's persuasion, sharing with A false "retroactive" memories that create a
pseudo past.

X's glance, as well as his voice, links many of the film's
images. The long dolly shot or forward camera movement at
the beginning, with its off-screen monologue, establishes a
"subjective camera" narrational mode that resembles the subjective mode of *Jealousy*. The procedure in *Marienbad*, however, never imitates the excesses of the notorious *Lady in the
Lake*, in which the camera-character (Robert Montgomery
with the camera strapped to his chest) displays his hands,
smokes a cigarette whose smoke we see curling before our
eyes. Nor is X's glance exclusive, or omnipresent: the camera
often shows the scene from A's viewpoint (in reality or imagination), or from the angle of a minor character (see p. 42,
for example), or even from that of a nonexistent "eye" placed
at an impossible point in space (when, for instance, the
camera hovers above the statue in the garden). The camera
eye often "associates" itself with a character through prox-
imity, filming from alongside the person in question, or di-

rectly facing him or her, or moving forward or backward with the actor's movements. Far from limiting himself to a strict rule of the observing camera substituting for the human eye, Robbe-Grillet—assisted by Resnais—manipulates the lens with great freedom, while preserving the fundamental subjectivity of the film. In the field of mental images, no law of perceptive plausibility requires maintaining the viewpoint of an observer fixed at one spot. Psychological "vision" or mental images can assume the form and perspective of what a third-person witness could see, even defying time and space, and without becoming the "point of view of God," which the critic Bonnot tried to identify as the mode of the film.

A complete study of the *liaisons de scène* or scene linkings in *Marienbad*—there are between two and three hundred in the film—would require a text as long as the scenario itself. What should be emphasized is that, as in his novels, Robbe-Grillet never makes arbitrary transitions. The chaos or disorder that certain critics or spectators see in the film—not as a defect, but as something to be praised—is not the illustration of some doctrine of rupture or metaphysical discontinuity; on the contrary, each scene is tightly bound to the preceding one, and to the following, by strict formal ties. It would be erroneous to see in the film's domino game a metaphor for its own structure; there, the rows of dominos, while obeying the rules of the game, proliferate nevertheless in a bizarre labyrinth described as "needlessly complicated" (p. 149). The complexity of the film, however, obeys hidden principles that are necessary to its existence. Everything moves toward a climax of dramatic tension, situated about three-fourths of the way into the film: the famous "white" camera movement in the corridors, followed by the scene of rape—or acceptance—in A's bedroom. Following this, the story, as in *Jealousy*, returns to its former rhythm, to a mood of calm.

The various types of scene linking or "modulation" include: the use of "voice dissolve" (X's voice becomes that of the actor, p. 31); change of camera field in accordance with a shift in the direction in which one character looks (p. 42); a "sound dissolve" or contiguity of two similar sounds (the broken glass, A's sudden scream); an action such as listening (A turns her head "like someone trying to see where an overheard remark came from," with the camera thereupon showing "what A sees, in various directions," p. 49); X's suggestions to A, usually followed by a more or less long period of delay in their execution, or by a dialectic contradiction between X's words and A's actions (the scene of A standing in front of the balustrade, responding to X's suggestions, p. 69); camera rotations, or panoramic movements joining together two "different" times in an apparent continuity, with the same characters seen in two separate adjoining rooms (p. 60); camera movements (often deceptive, because of a time- or space-shift) in response to overheard remarks (p. 52); linkings by association of sounds not contiguous in space or time (the pistol shots, the footsteps on the gravel path); phantasms brought into being by inciting suggestions (p. 93 and throughout the film); analogies between objects (pieces of broken glass and poker chips, p. 96); similar or identical phrases, used in differing contexts ("It's quite impossible," referring once to the match game and once to the fountain frozen in summer); a posteriori linkings, such as the close similarity between the "real" garden which A finally sees (p. 126) and the garden already seen "in imagination" several times before; linkings supported by an emotion, especially fear (p. 131), or a violent negation (the series of "No!" 's, pp. 130–138); changes undergone by the same set, such as A's bedroom, which becomes increasingly baroque as the emotional intensity of the scenes taking place there increases, or which corresponds more or less to X's descriptions in accordance with the extent to which A is convinced by X's persuasions at a given moment; and lastly, what may be termed linkings through opposition, or significant differences between verbal and visual description, caused by the tension between X's insistence and A's refusal to accept his suggestions, which she will yield to only later, in stages. Even the transitions between scenes that the text itself calls "sudden" may be explained by some implicit or hidden emotion. Every aspect of *Marienbad* is coherent with the rest; the flow of images and words moves on with an irrepressible and continuous drive.

Last Year at Marienbad may be seen as the extension and logical outcome of Robbe-Grillet's novelistic techniques, accompanied by, or transformed into, cinematic procedures that expand or reinforce them. The false scenes and objectified hypotheses of *The Voyeur;* the subjective world converted into objective perceptions of *Jealousy,* with its detemporalization of mental states, its mixture of memories (true or false), of desire-images and affective projections; the "dissolves" of images in the *Labyrinth:* all these recurr and attain a new high point of development in *Marienbad.* The theme of imaginative creation, linked with the idea of a suggestible person on whom the creation is imposed, authorizes an interpretation based on implicit psychology; the external trappings of a pseudo plot (existence or nonexistence of a "last year," ambiguous identity of A or X, refusal of the past or traumatic amnesia) are present only to provide the realistic "supports" necessary for the exteriorization of emotions, mental images, fears, desires, false memories, and the like.

The effort of the spectator, like that of the reader, has become to an ever-increasing extent an integral part of cinematographic and novelistic creation. "The hour of the reader" that José-María Castellet has declared for the new novel has as its counterpart the "hour of the spectator" for the new cinema. This collaborative effort, which has never been wholly absent in art, becomes more essential, more critical: not in the former sense of the "deciphering" demanded by the hermetic poetry of a Rimbaud or a Mallarmé—wherein the search for meaning, for multiple interpretations, constitutes a first requirement for the comprehension of a given work—but in the sense of participating in the *aesthetic functioning* of the novel or film. The reader, or spectator, of *Last Year at Marienbad* or of any subsequent film by Robbe-Grillet, is less like a listener at a concert than one of the performers themselves. Face to face with the complicated structures and often oniric images of *Marienbad*, the spectator must, without concerning himself with external relationships—in space, time, or "plot"—yield to their suggestive power, while at the same time projecting onto them all the affectivity of his own psyche. Robbe-Grillet's film is not only a *created* work; it is, in a new and significant way, a work which *creates* as it comes into existence.

7 Toward a New Cinema: *L'Immortelle* (1963)

> Art's only concern with the real is to abolish it, and to substitute for it a new reality.
>
> JEAN ROUSSET, *Forme et signification*

The cinema, like the novel—with each genre to some extent overlapping the other—is undergoing a radical revolution which seems destined to overturn the style and structure of traditional narration. Study of this double phenomenon leads to the search for a theory of *fiction* in which film and novel, like waves and particles in the physics of light, are closely bound together in a "unified field." If Robbe-Grillet's first scenario, *Last Year at Marienbad*, appeared to constitute an extension and fulfillment of the author's novelistic techniques, his second film, *L'Immortelle*, of 1963, may be seen as reaching a stage of artistic creation in which the visual images and the sound track of the work (despite the fact that they may be and were reduced to the printed form of a *ciné-roman*) attain a virtual existence apart from either the screen or the printed page. This "fluidity of becoming" (to borrow a phrase from Pierre Boulez, whose musical theories often parallel the doctrines and techniques of Robbe-Grillet), in a new cinematographic-literary space and time, requires a new effort of critical and creative understanding, in whose absence the work may appear empty and meaningless.

Even before the writing of *Last Year at Marienbad*, Robbe-

213

Grillet's work had been viewed by critics as cinematographic, or at the least, influenced by the cinema.[1] As soon as his films appeared, a contrary tendency led Robbe-Grillet and his associates to deny such relationships, arguing that visual images and words were so basically different that the idea of description alone prevented any assimilation of the genres of film and novel.[2] While Robbe-Grillet had earlier proposed the parallel between camera angles and narrative viewpoint as an obvious proof of interrelationships, he came later to accept the doctrine of Claude Ollier that "the notion of *description* has no cinematic equivalent."[3] But if we set aside specifically novelistic or cinematic elements (words on the one hand, images on the other), there is left the whole question of fictional structure, the *découpage* or division into scenes and sequences—with their duration, their camera angles, lighting, contrasts, and reinforcements, in short, their montage. Here, in the ordering of scenes, we find the chief interest of *Marienbad* or *L'Immortelle;* in the montage of scenes of varying levels of "reality" (and imagination), from various points in filmic space-time, lies the true form of the work, the "new reality" which gives it meaning.

The increasingly frequent use of terms associated with *découpage* in the study of the novel, or narrative viewpoint in the study of film, implies no dependency of one genre on the other. The idea of *découpage*, as the establishment in fictional structures of viewing angles, time spans, movements of characters and objects, and the like, belongs to both written and filmed fiction; if the word itself comes from the vocabu-

1. See Chapter 6, note 2.
2. Alain Robbe-Grillet, "Sur le fait de décrire une scène de cinéma," *Revue d'Esthétique*, Nos. 2–3, 1967, pp. 131 ff. See also my article, "Aesthetic Response to Novel and Film: Parallels and Differences," *Symposium*, Summer 1973, pp. 137–151.
3. Ollier, "Réponse à une enquête," *Premier Plan*, Oct. 1961 (No. 18), p. 26.

lary of the film, the procedure has always existed, in the theater, the novel, in painting.[4]

Admitting, then—with all proper precautions—that there can exist a close resemblance between novelistic and cinematic creative processes and techniques, especially in the case of a novelist-scenarist-cinematographer like Robbe-Grillet, what can this assumption lead us to discover in *L'Immortelle*, viewed as a work of *ciné-roman-fiction?*

First of all, *L'Immortelle*—like *Jealousy*, like *Marienbad*—embodies an inner experience, that of a "narrator" who lives, relives, recalls, imagines, re-examines, deforms, and restructures a series of events in which he figures, involving the gestures, the ambiguous attitudes, and the problematical actions of the characters who play the principal roles in his story. In this sense, the whole film is subjective. At the same time, we find (as in *Marienbad*) a certain number of scenes that appear to be either "objective" or taken from a different viewpoint: as a fisherman who may be a spy, a young boy, a Turkish woman. More important, we find that the succession of scenes follows no "linear" order, that the "chronological impasses" of *Jealousy* appear to become more numerous, as do the scenes of uncertain "degree of reality," as also in *Marienbad*. The film unfolds as if its author has freed himself almost, but not quite, completely from the strictures of traditional cinematic and literary space-time (based on "realistic" criteria inherited from the past), creating a new type of psychic experience in which past and future, along with the purely imaginary, combine in purely formal patterns, much as the modern composer may introduce his themes, introduce variations, return to previous motifs, and create an integrated progression of musical

4. Cf. Claude Simon's revealing statement in *Premier Plan*, No. 18, p. 32, on the close similarity of novelistic and cinematic *découpage*. Some interesting analogies with painting and drawing are found in Gérard Blanchard, *La Bande dessinée: histoire des histoires en images de la préhistoire à nos jours* (Paris: Marabout Université, 1969).

flashbacks, modulations, inversions, transformations, distortions, false counterpoint, and more.

The basic elements of *L'Immortelle*, as in all of Robbe-Grillet's works, come from the "real" world, not only the world of objects and décor (here, Istanbul and its Turkish setting) but also from the "real" world of human psychology (emotions, attitudes, and the like), whatever critics may say who view Robbe-Grillet's works as nonpsychological. We may, without concealing the ambiguities of the plot or the large part played in the work by the imaginary, the unreal, and the subjectively distorted, make a fairly coherent résumé of the story line. *L'Immortelle* does not require (as in the case of *Marienbad*) an arbitrary or tentative choice between one or another interpretative "screen" (the existence or nonexistence of the past year, for example). The distinctions between scenes as they occur in the "real" life of the protagonist of *L'Immortelle* and those subjectively seen in memory, illusion, or even hallucination are not extraordinarily difficult to make. Even the distorted chronology of the plot can, to some extent, once the twenty-odd initial shots of the "overture" have unfolded, be viewed as a more or less continuous progression in time, with the remembered or imagined scenes inserted into the story at moments when they could be thus seen or thought by the narrator-hero. The following, much simplified, account of *L'Immortelle* contains in addition some initial observations concerning the structure of the film:

I. *Thematic prelude.* The film begins, without realistic "justification" at the story level, with about twenty shots which announce key scenes and episodes: a car crash on a road near Istanbul, a young woman's face as she is seen in various postures, against various backgrounds, a man—the protagonist—looking out through the slats of Venetian blinds ("jalousies," in French), a Turkish cemetery, a fisherman on a wharf, a white Buick convertible, a Turkish-looking man in

European dress accompanied by two large dogs (Scenes 1–22).[5]

II. *The meeting.* The protagonist, a professor of French nationality (whom the printed text designates by the letter N, for "narrator") who has arrived at Istanbul for an indefinite stay and who is taking advantage of an initial free period to get settled in an apartment and to become acquainted with the city and its surroundings, loses his way during a walk along the Bosporus. He asks for directions from a beautiful young woman, who, though she appears to be in the company of a man in dark glasses holding in leash two enormous black dogs, gives N a ride home in her white convertible. En route, he invites her to a party to meet other new friends. She accepts. In the printed text, the woman is referred to as L; she is the heroine, and will have various names starting with the letter L: Lâle, Leïla, Lia, even Louise. The man in dark glasses is called, in print, M, suggesting, as in *Last Year at Marienbad,* "mari," or husband (Scenes 23–29).[6]

5. References to scenes from *L'Immortelle* are to the 1963 edition of *L'Immortelle, ciné-roman* (Paris: Editions de Minuit), in which each scene carries its number in the margin.

6. Although the initials L, M, and N appear in the printed scenario, it is obvious that they play no part in the film proper, since the spectator has no way of knowing of the existence of these letter designations. They have, nevertheless, some interest for the close student of Robbe-Grillet's creative processes. Already, in *Jealousy,* the Kafka-like reduction to abstract letters instead of names resulted in the heroine's designation as A, reflecting, perhaps, on the psychological level, a significant ellipsis in the husband's (that is, the narrator's) mind. The heroine of *Marienbad* is also called A in the script, in which the hero-protagonist becomes X, and the husband-figure M, suggesting "mari." The letters used in the printed scenario of *L'Immortelle* underwent the following evolution: in the "continuity," the hero is already N, and his "true" name is never given, while in the typewritten *découpage,* as well as in the film itself and in the printed scenario, a quite legible address on a letter that N receives (Scene 148) gives his name as André Varais (perhaps a hidden cross-reference to the

III. *The party.* When L joins the party at N's apartment, her behavior is ambiguous. Though she seems to know a certain Catherine, N is able to establish only that her first name is, or may be, Leïla; he can get from her no address or other information. Watching L standing at the window, while a whistle sounds from a distant Bosporus vessel, N sees or imagines one of the obsessional images of the film: L leaning against the deck railing of a steamer. The scenes that follow, of the gathering, employ a manipulation of the camera often utilized in the film: the lens moves from left to right, or from right to left, then returns in the opposite direction to reveal an altered situation, with objects or characters now missing from the scene, or suddenly appearing as if from nowhere. This subjective camera movement makes the spectator share the interior vision and mental time of N, whose awakening interest in L determines the ellipses and uncertainties of the sequence (Scenes 30–38).

IV. *The love episodes.* This section, forming a good quarter of the film's duration, depicts the progress of N's relations

---

"André VS" of page 157 of *The Erasers*, and to the nonexistent "André Valace" who signs letters at the Editions de Minuit). In his preface, Robbe-Grillet says that N stands for Narrator. M doubtless still indicates *mari* or husband, at least in N's eyes. L's initial is related to several first names, including the Turkish word for tulip (a drawing of a tulip figures in the film). But in the early continuity, and as late as the typewritten *découpage* used in shooting the film, the heroine is called A and the husband (?) called B. In the first printing of *L'Immortelle* in book form, L is still referred to once as A (Scene 139) and the man in dark glasses as B (Scene 297), these designations having slipped through the correction of the proofs. Jérôme Lindon has amusingly suggested that the apparently innocent L–M–N letter sequence, associated with triangles in geometry, may, if pronounced in French, be understood as *elle*, *aime*, and *haine*. If then L is at the top of the triangle, he adds, "she" is subtly placed between the man that she really "loves" and the man that she "hates." If this seems a bit Byzantine, he adds, we must not forget that we are, after all, at Istanbul!

with L: their meetings at his apartment, their intimacy, N's consistently unsatisfied curiosity about L, their walks and excursions, L's unexplained precautions, the threatening appearances of M and his dogs, the ambiguous role of several characters who may be M's spies, or may know about the private life that L keeps hidden from N. These scenes make up the principal "material" of the film, since what occurs later is most often N's subjective return, in memory or imagination, to one or another of them. The main shots depict the following scenes: the café above the port (with M and his dogs in the background and the arrival of L, who is in a hurry to leave), the ferryboat, the Bosporus sand beach, N's waiting for L in the courtyard of the mosque, the interior of the mosque, the ambiguous conversation with the old man in front of the mosque, the bazaar and the antique shop with the evasive merchant, the cabaret and the exotic dancer, the Turkish cemetery with its ruined columns, the garden in which L writes down her "address" and then throws the paper into the bushes, the canoe storage hanger and N's canoe trip with L out into the Bosporus, the great tower in the ruins with the stonemasons at work, the drives in L's car, the servant woman who seems to know where L lives, the boy who brings L a message in Greek. Intermingled with these are scenes of meetings at N's apartment: L's first embarrassed arrival; L stretched out on the divan; L imitating the erotic dance seen at the cabaret; L partially dressed, as if after making love, but uncertain and fearful; and various scenes of L fleeing from N, as if, suddenly, she were affected by extreme fear, upon hearing the distant barking of a dog, or even when N himself makes a vaguely sadistic gesture, placing his hand half caressingly, half threateningly, upon the nape of her neck (Scenes 39–108).

    V. *The unkept appointment in the cemetery.* In the previous scene (105), L had received from the boy a message that "he" was back and had hastily left N, making an appointment for later in a spot known to both. (This message is spoken in

Greek in the film; only the readers of the printed text, where it is given in French, are in a position to understand it, if they do not know Greek!) The place of rendezvous is the cemetery, where earlier scenes of meeting have occurred. N waits endlessly; night falls; car headlights flash past, revealing at one moment M and his dogs. L fails to come. This is N's first emotional crisis (Scenes 109–122).

VI. *The search for the vanished L.*   Haunted by memories and images of desire for L, N searches for her, retracing their past itineraries. He recovers the page from his address book on which L had ostensibly written her address; it is blank. He waits for a letter that never arrives. Seeking out Catherine, he questions her; the scene is intercut with shots from the original conversation between the two women at N's first party, but with glaring differences in the movements and attitudes of the girls. Catherine gives him an address, but he finds there only evasive individuals who deny any knowledge of L. He questions the old man at the mosque, the servant woman, the owner of the antique shop who had seemed to know L when N had purchased a statuette for her in his shop. He follows through the streets a woman resembling L; when she turns around, it is someone else. Finally, after a crescendo of such quests, N catches sight of L, at night, in a crowd, standing near M and his dogs. Against her protests, N leads her off, demanding an explanation. L takes him to her car. They get in, and L drives off rapidly (Scenes 123–219).

VII. *The accident, L's death.*   Refusing to stop at N's flat when she sees the fisherman (whom we know to be M's spy) keeping the building under surveillance, L drives faster and faster through the night, on a road leading from the city. In ever wilder fashion, she gives only confused, fragmentary, incoherent explanations. Suddenly, one of M's dogs appears in the headlights; L turns the steering wheel, as N's hand stretches out to take control (or does it?). We hear the screeching of brakes, the woman's scream, and the metallic shock heard before during the opening shot of the film. Then, by the light of a flashlight playing upon the scene, we see N, his right hand slightly injured and bleeding. Behind the steering wheel, L is dead, no doubt from a broken neck. Finally, a police car arrives (Scenes 220–230).

VIII. *The enquiry: posthumous jealousy*. This section presents systematically N's progress toward a delirium of obsessive, retrospective jealousy. Who is this woman who gave herself to him without ever revealing her identity, and who, found again after a mysterious disappearance, died before she could offer any explanation? Where did she live? What was her relationship with the man in dark glasses, one of whose dogs may have caused her fatal accident? What made L fear to reveal the slightest details of her private life? The enquiry conducted by N takes place at two levels: scenes taking place in the "real time" of the present (N's hand is still bandaged), and scenes belonging to a past being remembered, re-examined, reconstructed (N's hand, in these sequences, is not bandaged). At the "present" level we witness these scenes: N's discreet efforts to get information from the police; a new interview with Catherine, who speaks to him of "strange affairs," of women held prisoners by jealous Turks, and the like; a new interrogation of the servant woman who knew L; new questions put to the old man at the mosque; a meeting with the young woman who looks like L, and who relates to N a distorted version of his own story; the discovery of L's convertible in a used-car stand at the market; an attempt to learn from the boy what he had said to L on the day that he brought her a message. At the level of the restructured past is an increasingly delirious series of reconstructed scenes, most of which apparently occur in N's mind as he reflects in his apartment, stretched out on the divan: L on the deck of the steamer; L lying on the sands of the beach; many reprises of L at the steering wheel of her car before the accident; ever longer speeches of L on the theme of the deceptive façade of

Istanbul and its Pierre Loti décor; the scene in the café above the port, showing L and M, as N arrives; N's meeting with L inside the mosque; the purchase of the antique statuette, with a conniving exchange of whispered words between L and the merchant; the cemetery; the canoe hangar; and, with a mounting eroticism, numerous scenes of L, almost undressed, on the cushions of the divan of N's flat. The two levels are at times mixed, giving hallucinatory effect, as when N, with his hand bandaged (an ostensible sign of the real present) sees L looking at him inside the mosque (Scenes 283–284).[7] Unformulated ideas of women kept prisoners and beaten, of L as the slave of some powerful, jealous figure (M, or someone whom M serves as an agent), are communicated visually, raising to a paroxysm N's memory of a lascivious, ecstatic L, mad with desire and fear. Finally, as if making an unalterable decision, N rises from his couch and leaves the apartment (Scenes 231–339).

IX. *N's death, the final vision of "L'Immortelle."* A sequence composed of elliptical camera movements with involved splicing shows us N buying L's white convertible, in which he drives out to the road along the outskirts of Istanbul where the accident took place. As night falls, he hears L's voice urging him to drive faster, promising further explana-

---

7. Robbe-Grillet brings about this nontemporal confrontation between N with his hand bandaged and L after her death with extreme prudence. In the scene mentioned, L is at some distance from N, between the columns in the obscurity of the mosque, and her image disappears as N turns toward her. In the later sequences of the film, when L (after her death) incites N to drive faster and faster, urging him perhaps to his own death, we hear only L's voice on the sound track, and we understand at once that we are witnessing an interior delirium of N. In the first continuity, we read: "Seen from the front, N and A [that is, of course, L] sitting side by side, but N is at the wheel, and his hand is bandaged. A [L] stretches out her hand to the car radio." But Robbe-Grillet later eliminated this too literal picture of L's ghost.

tions. As may be foreseen (though when it occurs, the event still creates a powerful shock), M's second dog looms before the car, in the headlights. Without making the slightest effort to avoid it, as if fascinated, N drives straight at the dog. The car crashes against a tree. The accident noises, already heard several times, return, deformed. A gradually increasing illumination shows N behind the wheel, dead, in the same posture as L at the time of the first accident. A brief coda reintroduces, as in the prelude, scenes of L as viewed earlier, leaning on the guardrail of a steamer deck, her "immortal" face gazing out from the screen. Her silent, enigmatic laughter freezes into melancholy rigidity in the last shot of the film (Scenes 340–355).

The chief usefulness of such a "deciphering" of the film—which must at best be only tentative—is to provide an armature of events and episodes that will permit a closer analysis and understanding of the work built upon it. A structural examination can now better reveal the way in which this cinematic fiction is articulated: its modalities of viewpoint, the linkings and cutting principles that join shots and sequences, the chronology and dechronology of sequences, the distribution of thematic elements, the doubles and interlocking characters, the manipulation of repetitions and variations, the scene transformations and metamorphoses that permit passages from the objective to the subjective, and the like.

It is well established that the techniques of viewpoint, in the novel as well as the film, are closely related to the metaphysics of the novelist or scenarist, and we hardly need to be reminded by Sartre that a fictional technique "always implies a metaphysics." At the outset of his career, Robbe-Grillet endorsed the Sartrian existentialist doctrine that each image of a text or film must arise from a narrative consciousness: there must be nothing in the narrative which does not exist previously (or simultaneously) in the mental content of a narrator.

When the text is written in the first person, or—as in *Jealousy*, the purest example of this procedure—in the suppressed first-person mode of the *"je-néant,"* the proniminal mode itself guarantees in advance a strict adherence to this Jamesian principle, adapted to suit contemporary philosophic views. When the text is written in the third person, as in *The Voyeur*, we find that the protagonist's universe, in the case of Robbe-Grillet, tends to have two aspects: an ostensibly "real" world in which the protagonist moves, and the transformed or deformed universe created by the effects of implicit psychological tension in the protagonist's mind. This first aspect is, in fact, present even in the mode of *Jealousy:* although the subjective procedure conceals to some extent the "arbitrary," stylized world created by Robbe-Grillet's geometric descriptions and serial forms (figures of eight, V designs, and the like), it is this world that is in turn "seen" (and deformed) by the psychology of the narrator.[8]

In his films, as we see from the prefaces to *Marienbad* and *L'Immortelle*, Robbe-Grillet considers most, if not all, shots as a "view or mental image of a character." In *Marienbad*, this interior vision is sometimes localized in the hero, sometimes in the heroine; in *L'Immortelle*, it is almost exclusively the hero who "sees" what the camera shows, and Robbe-Grillet does not hesitate to explain the initial N as standing for "narrator." In both films, however, a number of shots are filmed from angles clearly unattached to the narrator's viewpoint, and such shots violate, if briefly, the theory of the visual narrative center. Furthermore, the content of a few scenes of *L'Immortelle*, if viewed as N's mental content, become logically impossible, as, for example, the scene of the boy speaking Greek, a language unknown to N (but which a spectator knowing Greek in the audience could understand, and which is given in translation in the printed text), or the

8. Cf. my article, "The Evolution of Narrative Viewpoint in Robbe-Grillet," *Novel*, Fall 1967, pp. 24–33.

Turkish spoken by the old man and the policeman. At times, moreover, the camera of *L'Immortelle* (as indicated in the text as well) adopts the viewpoint of a minor character: the fisherman-spy, the boy. M himself (Scene 13), a Turkish woman (Scene 189), or even L (Scene 33, the wharf "as L sees it from the apartment window"). As for absolutely "subjective" camera shots, where the camera lens replaces the eyes of the protagonist (whom we do not see) as he moves about, "turns his head," and so forth (the technique of Robert Montgomery's *Lady in the Lake*, often compared to the "*je-néant*" of *Jealousy*), they appear in a number of scenes: when N's hand caresses L's face or the nape of her neck, when N overtakes and converses with L's double (Scene 316), or when the woman who may be the boy's mother speaks directly to the lens (N), while the narrator's replies are suppressed (Scene 190). One new subjective camera technique, which seems to be Robbe-Grillet's invention, is used: in Scene 188, for example, as N enters a dark hallway, still searching for L, the shot begins in near darkness and brightens gradually, as if the pupils of N's eyes were becoming accustomed to the dim light, and were slowly enlarging.

L'Immortelle makes frequent use of a type of subjective shot invented around 1925 in Berlin by E.-A. Dupont in his film *Variety*, in which the scene is shown from the character's viewpoint, but with the camera placed behind his shoulder, so that his head or profile remains visible. Many shots of N's movements and glances are filmed thus, to such an extent that it becomes the dominant mode of presentation, comparable to the "*je-néant*" of *Jealousy* but avoiding the excesses of the pure "camera-eye" techniques of *Lady in the Lake*, and allowing the spectator to project himself into the protagonist (seen at least partially) in two ways at once: through the image of a visible character, and through that character's perception of the scene itself. The acting style of Jacques Doniol-Valcroze as N fits perfectly into this system. Denounced by uncomprehending critics as rigid and awkward, Valcroze's inexpressive face, voice, and manner were calculated to restrain and diminish the ever-present subjectivity of the hero. Since nearly everything is seen (psychologically) from inside the character, his exterior appearance becomes almost schematic, abstract; the spectator's attention must not be drawn excessively to the protagonist, but rather to what he sees, just as the "narrator" pays little if any attention to himself, but concentrates on L, or some other character. If at times the camera appears to film N and L impersonally, in the third person and at a certain distance, such shots are generally rendered subjective by other means, as, for example, by manipulation of the sound track: in Scene 61 we see N and L from the front as they leave the courtyard of the mosque, but the dialogue is a direct, unbroken continuation of one begun in the preceding scene, located at a considerable distance from the one now shown.

Just as the point of view of each shot (its psychological as well as visual origin) is systematically coordinated with the camera angle of the preceding shot and the one that follows (according to the axis of the take, the direction of camera movement, associative cutting, and the like), so does the principle of organization of sequences (their progression in the network of relationships between past and present, or between the real and the imaginary) involve elaborate structuring. Some typical examples will illustrate this original *texture* of the film, reflected not only in scene content, but in less obvious bonds that are nevertheless essential to its final form and structure.[9]

9. It may be pointed out that while the *liaisons* or linkings are purely implicit in the film, they are often mentioned explicitly in the printed scenario, especially when what is involved is a sequence of related camera movements. It is still up to the spectator or reader to detect the underlying aesthetic and psychological motivations for the individual shots, except in such instances as Scene 13, where Robbe-

First, a number of fairly simple shots convey ideas or emotions through supporting objects or objective correlatives. The scene (323) in which N sees L with her back against a wall, her hands resting on a large iron chain, embodies N's obsession with L as a woman kept prisoner, perhaps in chains, to be beaten. The next shot, an ostensibly touristic view of "the old citadel [. . .], enclosed by high walls," is followed by a very close shot conveying an intensification of concern with the idea of a prison, a harem of imprisoned women. Each barred window that N sees; each iron grill, is viewed obsessively. N before his mirror makes a gesture as if to caress, or destroy, a mental image of L, the same gesture that he has made in previous scenes as he reached out to touch L's face or neck. He glances aside, lowers his eyes, and suddenly the entire screen is filled by a shot of a carved table leg representing, as we read in one of the rare explicit metaphors found in the printed text, "two roses side by side, protruding like breasts" (Scene 246).

Certain thematic transitions bring about a new type of ellipsis of linear time and, eliminating dead time, allow the joining of successive events. Instead of resorting to the conventional "analytic montage" system of merely cutting out unimportant or boring sections of an action (when someone travels from one place to another, for example), or, in the opposite sense, making use of the "synthetic-montage" mass of uninterrupted or integral time (as Italian neorealism did with Antonioni, for example), Robbe-Grillet in *L'Immortelle* develops subtle associative scene linkings. A typical *liaison* of this type can be studied in three versions, thanks to the existence of an early "continuity" of the film, a typewritten working scenario, and the film itself. The differences are re-

---

Grillet informs us that the camera turns on its axis in order to show us "everything that the glance of the fisherman takes in," as he raises his eyes toward the window of N's apartment.

vealing. In the schematic first version, N emerges first from the antique shop, catches sight of M and his dogs, then turns around to fetch L and lead her off in another direction. An abrupt cut (without linking) shows a street at night lit by carabet signs, and the following shot takes us inside the cabaret, where N and L watch the exotic dancer. In the working script, numerous linking elements are introduced into the sequence: as N leaves the shop, he sees a pretty brunette filling a jug at a fountain; nearby, he observes M staring insistently at the girl, and quickly leads L away. Then follows the same nocturnal street scene with lighted carabet signs, but now a shot seen from below (subjective camera) shows the picture of a naked dancer, the same girl we had seen at the fountain, and the same who is seen dancing lasciviously in the cabaret in the next scene. The film itself (as well as the printed text) uses a less complicated sequence, in which the spectator is no longer required to *recognize* the dark-haired girl. This simpler *liaison* consists of having N turn away from M as he first glimpses M outside the shop, with the camera accompanying his eye movements and coming to rest on a poster advertising an erotic spectacle with naked dancers, while the sound track blends into the rhythms of the belly dance. The next shot takes us to the cabaret, with the dancer beginning the erotic dance that L herself will perform in pantomime, kneeling on a cushion in N's flat, ready to yield to his advances (Scenes 65–66). The thematic articulation is made tighter, the side issue of M's erotic interests is suppressed, the touristic aspect of the cabarets at night (in the style of *Hiroshima mon amour*) is eliminated, and the tempo of the film is accelerated just at the appropriate moment, when the first sexual relations between N and L are suggested.

In the process of converting the presumptive reality of the plot into the interior reality of the narrator's mind, structured or stylized by his perceptions and emotions, Robbe-Grillet invents new filmic means of undermining tradi-

tional realism, even in many scenes not especially charged
with emotion or subjected to the deformations of motivated memory. Some of these have since become clichés
of movie structure: for example, in the scene of N's first encounter with L, the couple gets into the young woman's car as
they talk, in realistic synchronism with their lips as we see
them on the screen. But when the car starts up and drives
away, we continue to listen to this conversation at the same
sound level and thus the same auditory "distance" as before,
in spite of the fact the car has almost disappeared from the
screen. As soon as we no longer see L's lips (and this effect
is repeated later when L comments at length on the falsity of
the Turkish décor of Istanbul), her words become more
poetic, more lyrical, more suggestive of erotic images (cf.
Scenes 24, 43–47). It is as if such scenes, when we no longer
see L speaking, occur only in N's imagination; we never *see*
L as she poeticizes ("And there is a ship like those of your
dreams," Scenes 254–256, for example). At a later stage of
the film, these baroque monologues of L take on the aspect
of X's monologues in *Marienbad;* her voice remains "off"
when she describes the cemeteries of Istanbul, "all abandoned," "crumbling," the walls of Byzantium in ruins, and
when she (or her phantom in N's mind) speaks of this "dream-
world Turkey," with its "false prisons, false ramparts, false
stories" (Scenes 336–343), before she sends N on the wild
drive that will end in his death.

Of special interest in Robbe-Grillet's system of scene linking in *L'Immortelle* are the techniques employed to relate certain principal scenes which unfold twice, as it were: the first
time at the realistic level (yet already modified, presumably,
by the vision of a narrator in love, or jealously suspicious),
and the second time at the intensified subjective level of N's
delirious obsessions either during his long search for L, or in
the period following L's death. There are a number of paired
sequences in this series, including the visit to the antique shop,

the excursion to the beach, the episode of the canoe hangar, and the trip on the Bosporus ferry. A good example is the sequence of the fort under reconstruction, with its high walls, and which forms the background of the scene where the young boy delivers to L the ambiguous message that leads to her disappearance.

As early as the fifth shot of the film's thematic prelude, we see L leaning on the battlements of an old fort, looking into the distance. This almost subliminal, "planted" image slips into the spectator's memory, where other key elements charged with emotion and psychological significance will be stored for future use. Following a sequence related to another shot from the prelude (Scene 7, associated with the cemetery and its iron grillwork, preparing Scenes 100–101), and ending with L's flight from N, we witness the first great development of the picture of L at the fort (Scenes 102–108): N appears alongside L at the top of a tower. The two lovers walk on the battlement wall. While L speaks ambiguously about the work of the stonemasons (are they reconstructing, merely pretending to reconstruct, or even tearing down the walls?), the boy suddenly appears before L and says in Greek that "he" is back. L thanks the boy, then gives N a false translation of the boy's message (according to L, he merely proposed to guide them on a tour of the subterranean passageways below the fort), before leaving in great haste, after making the appointment that she will not keep with N in the cemetery. The only "unrealistic" touch in the sequence, betraying the fact that the whole scene is viewed subjectively by N, occurs (Scene 106) when the workmen, viewed hitherto only at a considerable (and plausible) distance, are suddenly seen close up, as they watch L's flight. Here, as elsewhere, the camera makes a projective zoom, visually amplifying the growing concern of N, and, with him, the spectator.

The implicit meaning of this sequence to N is not wholly revealed until its return at the second level of memory and imagination (Scenes 232–236), following a second meeting between N and the boy. Frustrated by the boy's evasive answers to his questions, N looks away, fixing his attention on an opening at the top of a tower, through which a number of large, frightened birds make a sudden escape (theme of fearful flight, as with L). N succumbs then to one of his many hallucinations: motivated (unconsciously, perhaps) by a mixture of desire to enchain L himself (to keep her prisoner) and fear that she may be held prisoner by M or someone else, N (and the camera as well) *sees* L leaning against the wall in such a posture that her hands seem bound by an iron chain. It is this shot which, as pointed out, leads to a montage of images of castles that could be prisons or harems, iron cages standing in the cemetery, and the like.

These articulations are so numerous and so ramified one is tempted to link them, as elsewhere in Robbe-Grillet, with the principle of interlacing that critics of medieval literature, like Eugene Vinaver, have pointed out in the works of the novelist Chrétien de Troyes, which led to the author's substituting, for the Aristotelian structure of a beginning, a middle, and an end, constructions based on serial arrangements, echoes, modified repetitions and other more complex perturbations of form. The analogy, however, must remain only partial, for there may be found in most of Robbe-Grillet's works a sort of teleological progression toward an emotional crisis, followed by a "resolution" (a return to calm in *Jealousy*, the departure in *Marienbad*, death in *L'Immortelle*).

In addition to the organizing principles of chronological and dechronological sequences of events in *L'Immortelle* which appear to evolve directly from the earlier practices of *Jealousy* and *Marienbad*, we find in the new film some interesting new techniques of handling cinematic (and psychological) time. Pointed out earlier were certain elliptical camera pannings, as well as the use of sound dissolves that carry over into a succeeding shot the sounds or dialogue of the preceding one. At certain highly charged moments of N's emotions, Robbe-Grillet makes use of a new type of rapid-fire flashback to actions accomplished only seconds, or fractions of a second, earlier. A good example is found (Scenes 126–130) when N returns to the spot where L had thrown away the piece of paper from his pocket agenda on which she said she would write her address, before her disappearance (Scene 87). Here are the stages in the sequence that illustrate the new technique:

We see N [. . .] searching for the torn-out page. Finding it, he straightens up; [. . .] he unfolds the paper wad and stares at the page [. . .]. Then he crumples it again [. . .] and throws it into the bushes [. . .]. The shot is cut at the end of this movement. [Scene 126]

Close up of the unfolded page just as N saw it a few instants earlier [. . .]. It is obviously a page torn from a notebook, but there is nothing written on it. [Scene 127]

Continuation of this scene: repetition of N's gesture as he crumples the page and throws it into the bushes. But N is seen from a much closer position, from the hips up; and he is not precisely at the same spot. [Scene 128]

Once again, the unfolded page, held in N's fingers. But N appears still larger on the screen. [Scene 129]

New repetition of N's gesture crumpling the page and throwing it away; he is seen from even closer than in Scene 128, now only from the chest up. [Scene 130]

Conventional cutting or montage would have used a single close-up shot of the torn page, shown just after N picked it up. Then, with the camera again at normal distance, we would see N throw the paper away. This is typical analytical *découpage*. Rejecting the analytical approach, with its strictly linear chronology, mixed with arbitrary changes of camera distance (as in the normal close-up of the page), Robbe-Grillet greatly intensifies the hero's reactions, as well as those of the spectator. The close-up of the blank page is delayed until *after* it is thrown away, as if N felt the full significance of its blankness only a moment after his gesture. The effect is heightened by the repetition of the scene, with N seen in tighter and tighter shots, visually amplifying his emotion. This tightening camera movement, like that of a musical stretto, prepares for later reprises of similar gestures of crumpling and throwing away, first during the search for L after her disappearance (Scene 147), and later, after L's death, when N, with his hand bandaged (thus, in the "present"), again finds the page, looks at it, and throws it down, in a gesture that serves to link two different places—garden and apartment (Scenes 270–271). A gesture of frustration thus becomes the objective correlative of a psychic state evoked in a number of variations throughout the film.

This interlacing or interpenetration of structural elements, so widely used in *L'Immortelle*, acquires even greater density as a result of other recalls, analogous motifs, and interior correspondences. Such are the multiple elements forming throughout the film a network of *doubles* for various characters, each raising the possibility of disguise or mistaken identity in the uneasy ambiguity of this "exotic" Istanbul (true or false), and each, without straining our credibility in the domain of human typology, serving to augment N's suspicious fears, his curiosity, his jealousy, his frustration in the fruitless pursuit of clues to the undiscoverable identity or background of L.

Both M and L have doubles, whose presence increases N's confusion, and who point, as one function of interior duplications, to the idea of other possibilities of plot development, of parallel stories. A man dressed like M and also wearing dark glasses comes out of the mosque as N waits there for L (Scene 57). The same man stares intently at L in the cabaret (Scene 71); it is to him that Catherine sends N during his first search for L (Scene 169); and, finally, we see him sitting next to a woman who closely resembles L (and who is doubtless in the same relationship to M's double as L is to M). In this scene (296), the whole story of N seems for a moment ready to begin again (meeting at the water's edge, conversation between N with the young woman, and so on).

L's double has an even more important role. N sees this woman first in the street during his long search for L (Scene 134). Later, he witnesses an encounter that the woman has with Catherine; the position of the two women is identical to the posture of Catherine and L during their conversation at N's flat (Scene 156). L's double suddenly appears inside the house of M's double, to which N has gone to seek information (Scenes 171–172); she stares fixedly at N. After her appearance at the near duplication of N's first meeting with L, in the scene mentioned above, we see her for the last time in a subjective camera sequence (we do not see N, and the woman speaks directly to the camera) in which she relates to N a distorted version of his own story, while showing signs of fear in a manner reminiscent of several scenes with L (Scene 316). There is even a second double of L, the Turkish woman (of Scenes 188–190) that N sees at the top of a stairway.

Identical characters become, through a change of roles, their own doubles. The fisherman-spy on the wharf in front of N's apartment building (Scenes 13 ff.) becomes, later, an ambulatory pastry seller (Scene 49), then a fishmonger (Scene 62), while the old man selling pastries earlier (Scene 16) becomes the fairly important postcard and trinket seller stationed in front of the mosque. The waiter in the café above the port becomes a steward on the ferryboat (Scenes 42–43). At least once, N and L appear in two different places during a panoramic shot, producing in the spectator an effect of doubling the couple: a canoe is seen from a height and at a distance, emerging into the Bosporus, with N paddling and L sitting at the other end; the camera swings continuously around and up until we see the deck of a steamer, then advances upon N and L standing at the railing (Scene 96). The implicit temporal ellipse is contradicted by the explicit impossibility of the two events in real time. The effect is again to plunge reality into subjectivity, to transform the real into the imaginary.

In another typical example of this transformation of reality by associative emotional deformation is a scene in which N's hand is seen searching a bureau drawer during L's disappearance, as if to seek a clue to her identity. Suddenly, N's hand encounters a black lace garter. The film virtually reels into an agonized series of erotic shots of L, drawn from earlier episodes, and now flashing past with the rapidity of thought. The open drawer again appears on the screen, but instead of the ordinary objects previously seen there—Turkish bank notes, postcards, letters, and other innocent odds and ends—we now find a murderous-looking curved knife, an ugly iron ring resembling part of a pair of handcuffs, and many gum erasers (always an erotic fetish in Robbe-Grillet). Since all this is filmed objectively, without soft-focus blurring or other clues to a subjective vision, the effect is tremendous. As N's hand clenches, in a strangling gesture, the spectator takes upon himself, without the intervention of words and in intensively cinematic fashion, the full force of the sado-erotic jealousy that tortures and obsesses N.

With *L'Immortelle*, Robbe-Grillet moves further toward new realms of film subjectivity. But instead of exploiting the traditional cinematic vocabulary of interiority, the literary apparatus of the confessional or the narrative voice, the "clued-in" flashback, soft focus, and other traditional techniques, Robbe-Grillet prefers to remain almost entirely at the level of objective surfaces, even when they occur in a subjective vision. Nothing is *objectively* deformed (as was, in *Last Year at Marienbad*, the heroine's bedroom in its more "baroque" versions). Working with surfaces of realism, Robbe-Grillet plunges us into psychic depths. Without unusual camera angles or lighting, without photographic manipulation, without recourse to the fantastic décor of the expressionist or surrealist film, he is able to make us feel a more intense subjectivity than that of *The Cabinet of Doctor Caligari* or *Un Chien andalou*. Robbe-Grillet's "new cinema" is a cinema of new forms and structures designed to create new psychic experiences, probing further and further in the search for a new reality to which man can accede only through works of art.

8 Masks and Metamorphoses of the Narrator: *La Maison de rendez-vous* (1965)

> In the evolution of each genre, there comes a time when the genre, characterized up to that point by entirely serious or "noble" aims, degenerates and takes on a comic or parodic aspect. . . . Serious intentions give way to irony, to playfulness, to pastiche . . . and the author himself comes to the foreground. . . . Often he destroys the illusion of authenticity and seriousness; the construction of the subject matter becomes a game. . . . Thus is produced the regeneration of the genre: it discovers new possibilities and new forms.
>
> B. EIKHENBAUM, *Sur la théorie de la prose,* 1925

After the films *Last Year at Marienbad* and *L'Immortelle,* Robbe-Grillet's return to the novel form with *La Maison de rendez-vous* (1965) provoked, as could be foreseen, a new series of debates over the interrelationships between his films and his prose fiction, especially in the light of the influences detected by some critics of the two films upon the novel that followed them.[1] It was natural, in view of the fact that Robbe-Grillet's films had shown close structural and thematic ties to his earlier novels, to seek in the new fictional work traces of the author's cinematic innovations. Yet *La Maison de rendez-vous,* despite a continuous use of what are now termed close-ups, "*travellings*" (dolly shots), dissolves, and cuts, seems

1. Cf. Jean Alter, *La Vision du monde d'Alain Robbe-Grillet* (Geneva: Droz, 1966), ch. 7, pp. 65–88.

no more "cinematographic" than the earlier novels. Instead, this quite "advanced" work appears to point *forward* to eventual cinematic practices as yet unexplored.[2] It is as if composing a novel represented for Robbe-Grillet a more fundamental kind of research in fictional structure than making a film. He has stated that film images have little to do with the use of words in writing novels; without fully accepting this view, we can admit that literary expression remains more open, freer, more creative (by the very nature of the resources of language) than cinematic "writing"—at least, up to this point in history.[3] At any rate, the novel, in 1965, was still the privileged laboratory of Robbe-Grillet's fictional alchemy.

Among the most useful categories of formal structure that may be employed to analyze *La Maison de rendez-vous* are those of scene linking, chronology and dechronology, and modulations of viewpoint. The analogies to cinematic procedures can be considered merely as specific techniques, like tropes in traditional rhetorical practice. The most basic feature of the novel is its combination of many types of viewpoints, not in an effort to arrive at the multiplicity of points of view commonly found in the modern novel (relating events as they are seen by a number of characters, for example), but in order to create a new type of viewpoint that is *unified, but variable.* Transitions from the third to the first person (an "I" who may be visible or not) are accomplished by subtle modulations which, unlike those used by Flaubert to move from one character's viewpoint to another's by means of the *glance* directed by Emma at Rodolphe, for example, have their localisation in the reader himself, a reader who acquires the powers formerly

2. Cf. Robbe-Grillet's films *Trans-Europ-Express* (1967), *The Man Who Lies* (1968), *Eden and After* (1970), and *Glissements progressifs du plaisir* (1974).

3. Cf. Robbe-Grillet's article, "Brèves Réflexions sur le fait de décrire une scène de cinéma," *Revue d'Esthétique*, Nos. 2–3, 1967, pp. 131–138.

attributed to an omniscient author capable of assuming any point of view, of being in any place, at any time. Instead of becoming omniscient, however, the reader is simply *there*, in a role similar to the author's, but, as it were, on the other side of the text.

Since the changes in viewpoint must be modulated, the linking of scenes takes on great importance. While in the earlier *Jealousy* most of the linkings depended on the implicit psychology of the husband-narrator, in *La Maison de rendez-vous* these transitions become chiefly formal in nature, as they had been to a great extent in the *Labyrinth*.

As for chronology, it is by the very nature of the "subject matter" (in Eikhenbaum's sense of the term) a time system of bizarre circumvolutions running the entire gamut of deformations already found in Robbe-Grillet: repetitions, variants, phantasms, contradictions, and impossibilities, along with several new types of temporal distortion, arising from changes in point of view, or bringing about such changes.

Just what is the "subject" of *La Maison de rendez-vous?* The question is certain to raise theoretical controversies over form and content, the intentionality of the author, obsessional thematics, and other issues hotly argued in current literary criticism. The same novel can be seen by one critic in almost empty abstract terms ("a novel of nonmeaning," for example), by another in terms of a succinct résumé ("a sado-masochist kills a girl and invents alibis"), and so on. If the "subject" of a novel must always engender its own form—the only principle on which most modern critics of fiction agree —it should be possible to extract from a given work a kind of résumé that would at the same time take into account the specific content as well as the morphology of the form. In the case of *La Maison de rendez-vous* such a definition might be: a group of developments in various narrational modes, based on materials of popular fiction and taking place in a Hong Kong seen in the light of cheap exotic films and novels, unified by internal linkings and relationships which transform its variants, contradictions, repetitions, and passages from one narrator to another into a harmonious formal coherence. To this might be added an extreme simplification of the materials of the story: the events before, during, and after an evening spectacle in Lady Ava's Blue Villa during which the British police break in to arrest a certain Johnson for the murder of a man named Edouard Manneret.

What, one may also ask, would be the meaning of such a novel? For this question our critical vocabulary is again faulty, and everything depends on the level of abstraction used in our answer. If, for example, the meaning of *Jealousy* is, as might be said, the setting up of an aesthetically satisfying correspondence between the problems of a jealous husband and the novelistic form of his narration, does *La Maison de rendez-vous* have an analagous meaning? The deliberately conventional typology of the novel's characters would seem effectively to rule out (at last!) all psychological "depth," even if the reader attempts to inject such depth; similarly, the "pop" nature of the action and the setting (deluxe bordello, drug traffic, espionage, Chinese quarters, Eurasian girls leading large black dogs on a leash) interpose for the sophisticated reader an ironic distance that effectively prevents him from taking the narrative seriously. Since the pastiche aspect of the novel is so obvious, some critics have not hesitated to see in the book an open invitation to accept it as a pure game: a James Bond *divertissement* for intellectuals, an amusement for the élite, properly spiced with violence and eroticism. The "meaning" of the work appears to be nonexistent, or at least well hidden. It might seem as if the only approach would be to limit one's analysis to the structural principles that unite the various elements. But such a method would fail completely to explain the psychological involvement that the reader experiences in spite of the manifest superficiality of the materials. The reader may not "believe" what he reads, but he finds himself constantly reacting, feeling, even identifying himself with the experiences related. The nonrealism, or even the impossibility of the novel's content permits an emotionalized reading which is not, however, projected upon outside reality, fictional or otherwise. The criteria of the novel derive from this main principle; the work forms a fictional universe in which time, space, causality, and all other coordinates obey internal rules entirely unrelated to classic plausibility ("Could this happen in real life?"). The genre represented by *La Maison de rendez-vous* is not unlike that described by Tzvetan Todorov in his *Introduction to Fantastic Literature*, or that kind of fiction seen as "primordial" by B. Eikhenbaum, in which the "subject" is merely a pretext for "other factors," such as "the technique used to slow down the action, to combine and join heterogeneous elements [. . .], to develop and link episodes, to create different centers of interest, to conduct parallel story lines," and the like.[4] *La Maison de rendez-vous* is Henry James's "house of fiction": the coming together at a narrative center— the reader himself—of all the threads of the figure in the carpet, of all the lines of force that bind the structure of the work.

To extract from *La Maison de rendez-vous* a schematic of the plot, as was done for the preceding novels, raises a number of new practical and theoretical difficulties. First of all, the text is a continuum of 215 uninterrupted pages, without spacing between paragraphs (as we find in *Jealousy* or the *Labyrinth*, for example), without chapters or other divisions. Even a division according to change of narrator encounters obstacles, since certain passages would be attributable either to an "I" who begins one part, or to the third-person narrator who continues it. To complicate matters, the text itself often

4. The text of Eikhenbaum's study "On Prose Theory" appears in French in Tzvetan Todorov's *Théorie de la littérature* (Paris: Seuil, 1965), pp. 197–211. See also Todorov's *Introduction à la littérature fantastique* (Paris: Seuil, 1970).

calls attention to transitions between scenes or sequences ("Suddenly, the setting changes"). To recapitulate all this "*découpage*" would amount to recreating a tautological imitation of the novel itself. So, without attempting an exhaustive résumé, we can try to follow the main aspects of action, setting, and characters as they function within the interlocking, reciprocal internal structural relationships of the work.

Two introductory statements by the author, on two separate pages, announce at the outset the theme of *contradiction:* the first disclaimer that the novel must *not* be regarded as a realistic document on Hong King, designed to achieve verisimilitude in its background and so forth, is immediately negated by the second statement insisting that the places described conform exactly to reality. One phrase in the second passage hints already, however, at the presence of a *narrator* like the one soon to appear in the novel itself (in the first and third person), for the *author* of the second text claims to have spent "the largest part of his life" in Hong Kong. If the first notice corresponds closest to the later comments, in the press and elsewhere, of Robbe-Grillet as "real" author, the second belongs already to the formal framework of the novel, and prepares, outside the "text" (in the strict sense), the double, ambiguous construction and the constant oscillation between narrative poles that characterize the work as a whole.

A narrative voice in the first person, at the start of *La Maison de rendez-vous*, engages in a monologue (or in half a dialogue, the other half of which—the replies of an interlocutor—is suppressed, somewhat as in *The Fall* of Camus) containing a rich repertory of sado-erotic features, many of which recall previous novels and films of Robbe-Grillet: the nape of a girl's neck, a poster advertising a spectacle, two iron rings fixed in a stone wall, garters, an iron bracelet, a length of cord, images of female sexual organs discerned in the bilateral symmetry of Byzantine sculptures. This interplay of self-quotations, which proliferates even further in novels and films to follow, occurs at various levels of the novel's construction, underlining the ambiguity of the relations between the narrator and Robbe-Grillet himself and tightening the links that hold together the separate parts of the work.

From this swarm of initial images, one in particular materializes by means of a passage from the generalized present tense of habitual action to the present tense of immediate action; we arrive "on the scene," and at the same time the first-person mode is modulated to the third person, and removed from the initial "voice." The sentence begins: "Often, I linger to watch some young woman dancing, at a ball"; the frequentative *often* disappears in a series of verb forms in an ambiguous present ("she turns around," "her smooth flesh glistens"), until at last an unmistakable specific present instant is described ("she has now left"), and the first person fades out as two characters move into view, one ostensibly the pseudo narrator of the initial passage, and the other the future protagonist of the novel, "Sir Ralph" Johnson, called "the American." Unless the allusion to a "stout man with a red face who is talking of his travels" is a deliberately false link with what ensues, it is Johnson's account, resuming with "Everybody knows Hong Kong" that introduces (according to the same device of a generalization followed by a specific present action) a Eurasian girl leading a large black dog on a leash, standing in front of a store window in Kowloon—in which a similarly clothed dummy, also leading a dog, forms a mirror image. At this point one of the principal structural devices of the novel makes its first appearance: the transition from a fixed image, or pose (a frozen theatrical scene, an illustration, a store dummy, a painting) to its animation and incorporation into the action of the work. This procedure goes far beyond the author's previous use of such things as interior duplications (the movie poster in *The Voyeur*, for example), and carries forward the animation of the engraving in the *Labyrinth* to make of it a process that not only binds various elements together but brings about the generation of other features.

The dummy in the window not only begins to writhe, in an attempt to throw off the leather thongs that are now described as binding both wrists and ankles (note the "augmented" or heightened animation), but also changes, in the middle of a sentence, into a dancer, referring back to the one detailed some pages earlier and forward to the one who will shortly make her appearance—Lauren or Loraine, the young protégée of Lady Ava and the object of Johnson's impassioned pursuit.

The exposition of the basic elements continues in a constant shifting between supposedly "impersonal" narration, with abrupt jumps between scenes (Lady Ava's salon, streets and shop windows in Kowloon, the interior of a rickshaw with torn cushions), and "attributed" narration ("The man is still speaking. He relates a classic story of the sale of young girls"). The text never remains stabilized in the impersonal or attributed mode, however, since the apparently "off-text" narrator suddenly intrudes into the field of action with such a remark as "(two or three inaudible words)," bringing him forcibly on scene. It is in one of these pseudo-indirect narrations that we are given the first textual résumé of the action, establishing the basis of all the contradictory developments to come: "a classic story [. . .], easy to reconstruct [. . .]: an American, [. . .] who [. . .] naturally frequented the Blue Villa, where Lady Ava put on special performances for a few intimate friends. Once, the police burst in, in the middle of a gathering [. . .]" (p. 19).[5]

Instead of following the sequence of pages, as was done for the preceding novels, a different analytical procedure seems indicated for *La Maison de rendez-vous*, namely, isolating in-

5. Page references are to the 1963 printing of *La Maison de rendez-vous* (Paris: Minuit).

dividual narrative sectors that form a more or less cohesive unit. These units form, so to speak, coexistent plots, often contradictory with respect to each other, but coming together ultimately, through the narrative techniques used, to create a whole. It is not a question of choosing among interpretative possibilities (as critics had sought to do with *Last Year at Marienbad*), but of learning to accept the nonlinear merging of events that would be completely "impossible" in ordinary plot structure. Robbe-Grillet, pursuing his contestation of traditional novelistic forms and techniques, is here explicitly building into the text, in a way that blocks their eventual "recuperation" into some synthetic and plausible unity (based on the psychology of the characters, for example), various alternative plots, P^1, P^2, P^3 . . . P^n.

Here, in résumé, are the main narratives:

1. *The "basic" story: "Sir Ralph" Johnson.* Johnson, a Protean figure, wearing all the conventional masks of the exotic spy novel, both English and American, or a Portuguese from Macao, where he engages in dubious traffic (especially the cultivation of hemp and poppy), is now living in a luxury hotel in Kowloon. He often attends "functions" at the Blue Villa, where the enigmatic Lady Ava offers him a young woman, apparently European, Lauren. The latter, engaged to one Georges Marchat (a young employee of Johnson), reluctantly accepts the (apparent) necessity of becoming a prostitute, and agrees to yield to Johnson on payment of a large sum. Johnson goes to obtain the money from the mysterious Edouard Manneret, millionaire organizer of most of the illegal operations at Hong Kong. On the way, Johnson kills (?) Marchat. When he reaches Manneret's office, he is refused the money. He returns once more to Manneret's and kills him with five shots from a revolver. Going back to Lady Ava's to get Lauren, he finds Lady Ava dying. On an upper floor, the policemen who have come to arrest him are waiting in Lauren's room. The young woman, lying on her bed, ap-

pears dead, perhaps from an overdose of drugs. Like *L'Immortelle, La Maison de rendez-vous* ends with the image of an engimatic woman's face: "And, in her eyes, there is nothing."

2. *Lady Ava's story.* Lady Ava is at the center of many "nodes" of the narration, if not of the entire novel: she is the agent who arranges the sketches and performances that constitute "doubles" for all the subplots. She is the archetype of the deluxe bordello owner in the Far East; she engages in drug traffic (getting her supplies from Manneret); she furnishes her clients with any type of girl they wish. The narrative is continually bent back to her presence, through metamorphoses, curves in the novel's "space," and achronological transitions: the picture on the cover of an illustrated magazine swept into the gutter by a coolie comes alive as her drawing room; various episodes that begin elsewhere are changed into theatrical spectacles performed before her clients; scenes that begin as "*saynètes*" or sketches on her stage unfold in "real" streets and buildings; the Tiger Balm Garden style "statues" in her gardens depict scenes of the various plots. The very titles of certain sketches (such as "The Assassination of Edouard Manneret") suggest that, in a sense, the entire novel takes place in her drawing room through a process of theatrical duplication like that found in *Last Year at Marienbad*. But the scenes on stage never develop without being metamorphosed into some aspect of Lady Ava's "real" life, while at the same time this reality is put into serious doubt by such declarations as: "She has never been in China; the de-luxe bordello at Hong Kong is only a story she has been told" (p. 186). The only reality we can assign to her story, as to the others, is the reality of a *narration.*

3. *The story of Edouard Manneret.* The fragmentary nature of Manneret's story is due to its existence, in large part, only in relation to the others: as part of a theatrical performance, for example, or as the story of a kind of *author* who is at once within and without the framework of the novel

(somewhat like the narrator of *In the Labyrinth*). The textual order in which the appearances of Manneret occur can be listed, with brief indications of the situations in which he figures. This procedure will at the same time reveal the complexity of the chronology and plotting involving Manneret, whose role forms a multiform, twisted thread running throughout the carpet of the text.

Manneret is mentioned first by the "fat man with the red face" who as initial narrator offers various direct and indirect accounts of events in the novel: "Thereupon, with no apparent connection with the preceding remarks, he begins to relate Edouard Manneret's death. 'Now, he was a character!', he adds, in conclusion" (p. 46). Manneret, then, this "character," is already dead at the beginning of his story. What it is that the fat man "told," is not given. The narrative mode at this juncture has already been distorted by an "I" narration of the events of the same evening (p. 23), by a first-person speaker who sees Johnson at a distance (p. 53), while at the same time using the identical phrases that Johnson himself will utter later (cf. "I arrived at the Blue Villa around ten after nine, in a taxi," as told by the first "I" [p. 23], and the passage: "Johnson [. . .] immediately starts to recount the events of the evening: 'I arrived at the Blue Villa around ten after nine, in a taxi' " [p. 96]). It is impossible to identify the character to whom Lady Ava says that Manneret is dead, and who adds, "I know this already, of course, but I let nothing show" (p. 59). Soon an actor takes the part of Manneret in the play about his assassination; he is engaged in *writing that* such and such actions are occurring, in a passage which gradually changes from the indirect narrational form, with "that," to a direct style which puts the events on the nominal level of the "real" story. The text devoted to the play about Manneret mixes possible and impossible scenes (a character goes up an inside stairway, for example, as the décor changes in a way feasible only in the cinema), shifts abruptly from one scene to another, shows Manneret apparently attempting some drug experiment on the young Eurasian girl Kim, and ends with Manneret in a deathlike pose, following which "the spectators [. . .] begin to applaud" (p. 74). At this point the fat man, in a manner reminiscent of the narrator of Raymond Roussel's *La Vue*, looks closely at the stone set in a Chinese ring, carved to represent a young woman stretched out on a sofa. The girl suddenly begins to writhe, coming to life in the office where Manneret sits, still writing, with Kim again standing before him. Taking from him a package (of drugs?), Kim leaves the room, passing the street sweeper who had previously swept into the gutter the illustrated Chinese magazine whose cover had been materialized into Lady Ava's drawing room (p. 35). The coolie is now examining three drawings in the magazine—all scenes of erotic violence in the style of Gustave Moreau (recalling "The Secret Room" in Robbe-Grillet's *Snapshots*). One of these scenes brings us back to the Blue Villa, where the fat man is still peering at his jade ring.

The link between Johnson and Manneret is tightened after the incident when a policeman questions "Sir Ralph" about the death of the "Old Man," of which Johnson pretends to know nothing (p. 94). At this point the textual reprise mentioned earlier occurs ("I arrived at the Blue Villa [. . .] in a taxi"); repeating previous events, Johnson's account brings about a new recital of Lady Ava's soirée, with new theatrical performances, including one that takes place in Lady Ava's room (all four walls, including what could only be the imaginary fourth wall where the spectators sit, are described), where she hides a "real" package, no doubt containing drugs. "During this time" (p. 107), Johnson returns to Kowloon, gives the slip to the policemen who are watching his movements because they suspect him of having killed Manneret, sets out to *look for* Manneret (in order to borrow the money he has promised Lauren), and launches the series of events that will culminate, toward the end of the book, in the murder (the definitive murder, this time?) of Manneret. Thus Johnson at last commits the crime for which the police have suspected him from the outset. Before the completion of this "impossible structure"—the main one of the novel—we encounter various reprises of scenes involving Manneret: Johnson at Manneret's office, where the latter confuses Johnson with his own son (note the Oedipus theme, recalling *The Erasers*), and refuses to lend him money (pp. 133 ff.), before resuming his "writing"; Kim's visit to the Old Man, who attempts some sort of drug or other experiment on her (pp. 124 ff.); Lady Ava's account "once more," of Manneret's death (p. 140); a scene in which Kim's dog breaks Manneret's neck (p. 159); a newspaper item announcing Manneret's death (p. 165); a long scene between Manneret and a "false" policeman, who tries to blackmail him over the disappearance of a young Japanese girl, Kito, who had died from Manneret's peculiar "experiments," a scene ending in another "murder" of Manneret by the false policeman, who poisons him (pp. 167 ff.—this whole episode, which starts out as a quotation from the newspaper clipping, changes into a narration by Lady Ava made to an unnamed "I" [p. 171]); Lady Ava's announcement that Manneret has been assassinated by the Communists (p. 202); and finally, Manneret's murder by Johnson himself, the basic action of the novel, which, announced at the outset, anticipated and contradicted throughout the work, at last materializes as a dénouement that starts the accelerated finale of the various stories (pp. 209 ff).

4. *The subordinate or "lateral" stories.* Other stories are already implied, through the procedure of reciprocity between plots and variations subjected to chronological distortions and more or less systematic contradictions: the story of Lauren, who, like the heroine of *L'Immortelle*, has several names, all starting with L; of her fiancé Georges Marchat; of Kim and her large black dog, which always creates a problem

when Kim needs a place to leave him as she starts up the stairs toward ever more vague rendezvous; of the fat man with the red face, who appears to narrate large segments of the text; of "mad King Boris," who knocks with his cane on an upper floor from time to time, like some *deus ex machina* or extra-textual authority; and, above all, the story of the floating "I," who replaces at will any or all of the other narrators (John-son, the fat man), who rides in a closed rickshaw, who seems possessed of all the powers of the traditional omniscient nar-rator, and who becomes, in the end, no more or less than the spectator, the reader himself, the wearer of all the novel's masks, the magician of all its metamorphoses.

5. *Allusions to previous works.*   Allusions to elements from other Robbe-Grillet fiction are numerous. Most unmistakable are the following: from *The Erasers*, the floating debris, the decaying fish, the Oedipus theme, the name Marchat; from *The Voyeur*, the iron rings, the lengths of cord, the victims with their legs spread apart,[6] the name Jacqueline, the sculp-ture of a hunter riding a bicycle; from *Jealousy*, the dense vegetation, the insect noises, the erasure of a written text; from *In the Labyrinth*, the mysterious package, variations on a

6. The sado-erotic elements of *La Maison de rendez-vous* are often reminiscent of the "decadent" novel that delighted another generation of readers, like Octave Mirbeau's *Torture Garden*. Compare, for ex-ample, this typical passage, which appears in the original edition of *Le Jardin des supplices*, published by Fasquelle in 1899, on pages 285–286: "Clara drew near a tree in whose branches a young woman was uttering a death rattle. She was suspended, by her wrists, from an iron hook, and her wrists were joined between two pieces of wood, drawn tightly together. [. . .] Another woman, in a further niche, with her legs spread, or rather forced apart, had her neck and arms held by iron bands." Many such scenes in *Torture Garden* prefigure the series of more or less parodied tortures that will play an increas-ingly greater role in Robbe-Grillet's novels and films, especially *Eden and After* (1970). While it is true that most of the victims in Mir-beau's novel are men, the resemblances are striking, as shown by the passage quoted.

single name, the stairs and corridors, the velvet curtains (a theme going back to the short piece "Scene" in *Snapshots*), the number 1234567, and especially the animation of a picture; from *Last Year at Marienbad*, the theatrical sketches duplicating or merging with the action of the novel, the statues or other sculptures, the broken glasses; from *Snapshots*, the atmosphere of "The Secret Room," the repeated theme of erotic violence; from *L'Immortelle*, the women's costumes and undergarments (garters, girdles), the women in chains, the "L" of Lauren-Loraine-Laureen, the black sunglasses and large dogs, the repeating of scenes that unfold differently the second or third time, and so on. This technique of veiled autocitation plays an increasing role in Robbe-Grillet's work, and is evident not only in his novels but in his films, from *L'Immortelle* to *Trans-Europ-Express*, *The Man Who Lies*, and *Eden and After*. Self-citation and reuse of earlier techniques of construction are so mingled that it is difficult to distinguish one from the other.

Structurally, the arrangement of sequences in *La Maison de rendez-vous* suggests a highly evolved cinematic order, going beyond the practices of current films. At one level, the familiar division of a film between long narrative sections and groups of short shots, the two types of sequences linked by specific devices (visual analogies, associations of objects, similar gestures, even apparently unlinked "cuts"), may be readily discerned. Superimposed thereon, a number of more "literary" procedures (the "I" monologues, the narrative asides, and the like) complicate the structure further, and serve to create a new model of fictional form.

Let us consider several examples of how the scenes and sequences of *La Maison de rendez-vous* are articulated. The *liaisons* run the gamut from the apparently arbitrary, unmotivated cut to almost imperceptible transitions which the reader grasps only afterward, and which, like the "dissolves" analyzed in *Jealousy*, for instance, contain elements shared by more than one scene, or more than one moment of time, thus functioning as ambiguous links that fade into the continuity of the text.

We have outlined how Robbe-Grillet, in general, establishes the narrative parameters of *La Maison de rendez-vous*, such as interior monologues, ostensibly objective presentation, first-person narration, and authorial commentaries which seem to come from outside the text. Examination of specific passages will allow us to identify the means used to join scenes and longer developments, to bring about metamorphoses, to bend time, thus creating the special structure, progressive and regressive—impossible at the level of plausibility and plausible at the level of fiction—which will in the course of the novel constantly solicit the reader's connivance.

That the novel is consciously made up of *scenes* is made clear in the text, not only for the theatrical "scenes" (which are so often indistinguishable from the "real" scenes of the novel)—of the grouped sculptures in the garden of the Blue Villa, or of the scenes on the cover of the Chinese magazine —but also in terms of the narrative vocabulary. The text reads, quite explicitly, for example, "This scene [. . .] occurs in any case somewhat earlier" (p. 30); "Doubtless, this is the scene in question" (p. 41); "this fragmentary scene" (p. 41); "in the following scene" (p. 47); "this episode" (p. 67). Such overt references to "scenes" occur chiefly near the beginning of the novel, as the reader is shown rapidly the principal events whose variations will come later. Another verbal reinforcement of the effect of a series of scenes is found in the rich use of adverbs of time, usually with ambiguous effect (as with the "now" of *Jealousy*, which nearly always causes a change of time and place): "then," "at this moment," "suddenly," "soon," "meanwhile," "next," "immediately," and "once again" (with echoes of *Last Year at Marienbad*). In addition, motionless or frozen scenes (a procedure found in

Robbe-Grillet's earliest novel, *The Erasers*) add to the impression of theatrical or cinematic divisions.

At times, the continuity of the text is subjected to abrupt cuts, not only in the form of seemingly unlinked scene changes, but also by the appearance of rapid "flashes" in the midst of passages under development. For instance, the scene of the anonymous occupant of the rickshaw with torn cushions (p. 17) is followed immediately by a paragraph in which "The character with the flushed face [. . .] goes over to the buffet" in Lady Ava's salon. The reader may attempt to supply the missing *liaison* by supposing that the scene in the rickshaw forms part of the fat man's narration; but this hypothesis runs into difficulty, since the preceding page contains another abrupt transition that appears to contradict such an explanation. A window dummy (*perhaps* described by the fat man) suddenly comes alive ("The supple body writhes") and it metamorphosed into a dancer whom we may situate at Lady Ava's (p. 15). The text goes on:

And now the same fat man with the red face again intervenes, still speaking loudly of life in Hong Kong and of the elegant shops of Kowloon, where the finest silks in the world are found. But he has paused in the middle of his account, his red eyes looking about, as if concerned about the attention being paid to him. In front of the shop window, the young woman in the black fur coat meets the glance reflected in the glass of the window; she turns slowly to the right. [P. 16]

The phrase "he has paused" gives to the following sentence starting with the words "In front of the shop window" the effect of an independent scene, perhaps taking place at the same time, but elsewhere, and not forming part of the "account" referred to in the preceding line.

The extreme mode of textual "rupture" is that involving the figure of Boris, the "mad old king" whose steps are heard three or four times in the course of the novel, coming from some upper "story" that seems to lie entirely outside the field of the work:

The man playing the part of the hunter has no bicycle, this time, but he holds in his hand a heavy leash of woven leather; and he is wearing black sunglasses. It is useless to insist further on this scenic arrangement that everyone is familiar with. The night is far advanced, once again, already. I hear the mad old king striding along the long corridor, on the floor above. He is searching for something, in his memories, something solid, he does not know what. So the bicycle has disappeared. [P. 32]

This vaguely allegorical personnage functions not only as an image of the author *outside* the text (while Manneret appears to play the part of the author *within* the text), but also as an endistancing figure, a sort of guarantee of fictional unreality. In this sense, the mad king may be associated with the references to a locale that is *not* Hong Kong, but somewhere else (the fat man who *relates* Hong Kong events, Lady Ava for whom Hong Kong is only a *story* told to her), forming a distorting framework that isolates the fiction even from its virtual reality.

Although the ruptures between scenes and other elements seem to work against the novel's continuity, they are constantly contradicted or erased by numerous procedures tending to make the reader accept all sorts of transitions from scene to scene. These later modulations so dominate the seemingly abrupt breaks that a presumption of continuity prevails everywhere in the text, allowing the reader to pass from episode to episode without seeking to impose the usual criteria of causality, chronology, or fictional logic. Once the reader is, so to speak, liberated from such criteria, he finds himself able to appreciate in a new way the manifestly popular or banal materials that the author uses to construct *La Maison de rendez-vous*. Without resorting to parody—another method of finding artistic pleasure in works that one is supposed to disdain—the novel puts together in a different way subject matter considered naive, ridiculous, or worthless, "redeeming" it in an original form. The same modern reader who rejects popular novels of espionage, erotic exoticism, and the like, finds in the subtle manipulation of these same materials by Robbe-Grillet an intellectual and aesthetic pleasure, reinforced, no doubt, by a certain amount of unconscious self-projection. Pop art painters make use of a similar aesthetic stance, but with the important difference that whereas pop painters treat their materials more or less in the same pictorial *style* as do the comic strips or advertisement media that they imitate, Robbe-Grillet writes *La Maison de rendez-vous* in the same pure, almost classical French style that characterizes his work, with no concessions to the phraseology found in the novels that exploit these same materials at the level of popular taste.

Let us examine three ways in which more or less complicated sequences are articulated: the method used for theatrical sketches or sculpture groups, the means used in bringing a picture to life, and the way that a single character moves from episode to episode—not that these three types of structure are always independent, since they may be joined in specific plot developments. Certain techniques give rise to transitions between stage scenes or sculptured groups and either related or presented actions, for example, the device of total immobility (often only temporary, awaiting the animation of the scene). Recalling Robbe-Grillet's earlier use of immobile scenes in *The Erasers, The Voyeur,* and the films *Marienbad* and *L'Immortelle,* we note that until the use of the generative engraving of "The Defeat of Reichenfels" in the *Labyrinth,* all the frozen action was stopped in the midst of its unfolding in the narrative; only the picture of the *Labyrinth* served as a point of departure for new developments. In *La Maison de rendez-vous,* action in process is also brought to a halt (the fat man stops short, his hand lifted), but the majority of frozen scenes are, at their origin, initiative of new action: the store window dummy, the figure carved on a jade ring, an illustration in a Chinese maganize, a group of statues in Lady Ava's garden, a theatrical number, and so forth.

Such is the constant infolding or mixing of techniques that it becomes difficult, if not impossible, to extract from the narrative continuum a single sequence. If, for instance, we try to limit our analysis to the sketch "The Assassination of Manneret" performed on Lady Ava's stage, we find that its beginning is already the reprise of a scene described earlier, occurring at a time when Manneret had not yet been mentioned. Here is a résumé of the development, composed of quotations and a certain number of paraphrased bridges between them; the reader may study the integral text by means of the page references:

Next comes the scene of the fashion display in the window [. . .] at Kowloon. And yet, this scene must not occur just at this place, where it would hardly be comprehensible, despite the presence of the same Kim who is also present on the stage of the small theatre where the performance, continuing its course, now reaches the time of a few minutes preceding the assassination. The actor who plays the part of Manneret is sitting in his armchair, at his desk. He is writing. He writes that the Eurasian servant girl [walks, in the "real" drawing room, towards Lauren, to say to her,] "Come. He is waiting for you." [P. 66]

Round about, the dance continues normally[. . .]. However, accidents begin to happen all around: a crystal glass that breaks [. . .], a small vial of morphine that falls [. . .], a long cry of pain [. . .], and Lady Ava who [. . .] takes the object [a thick brown paper envelope that looks as if it were full of sand] with a quick gesture, weighs it, and hides it at once. [P. 67]

It was exactly at this moment that the English police broke their way into the great salon of the Blue Villa, but this episode has already been described in detail. [The dancers stand immobile as names are taken down. Kim's "double" crosses the room] toward the baroque surrounding decorations, toward the guests [. . .], toward the staring passers-by, toward the small shops

[. . .]. And, when she reaches, at the end of her errand, the *maison de rendez-vous*, the house of assignment, in front of this narrow, steep stairs [she] climbs blindly to the third floor [. . .]. She knocks at a door . . . [goes in without waiting for an answer, and finds herself standing before the "Old Man"], the one who gives his name as Edouard Manneret. He is alone. [. . .] He is sitting in his armchair, at his desk. He is writing. [At this point, a series of movements made by Manneret, standing, sitting, writing.] [Pp. 67–72]

The third scene shows him standing again; but Kim [no longer "the girl whose name is not Kim"], this time, is half stretched out near him on the edge of a sofa [. . .]. [Here, a scene in which Manneret apparently injects Kim with a drug.]

In a final tableau, we see Edouard Manneret lying on the floor [. . .]. On the desk, the page he had begun remains unfinished. [. . .] The complete halt in the action lasts for a considerable time, until the moment when [. . .] the bell ringing [awakens] the spectators, who recognize this ending [. . .] and then begin to applaud. [Pp. 72–74]

So it is at this point that, once again, the dialogue takes place between the fat man with the red face and his tall companion [. . .]. His hand [. . .] remains there, in the void [. . .] with only the index finger outstretched [. . .]. On this finger [. . .] he wears a heavy Chinese ring, in a hard stone, whose surface, artistically and minutely carved, represents a young woman held stretched out on the edge of a sofa [. . .]. [Here, an almost identical scene to that of Kim undergoing Manneret's "experiments."] [P. 73]

Manneret, who has not budged from his desk during the entire scene, contenting himself with turning his head to glance towards the sofa [. . .], then looks down at the written page [. . .]. Kim, standing before him [. . .], straightens up, holding [in one hand] the thick brown paper envelope [. . .]. And without a word [. . .] she leaves the room [. . .], goes down the narrow, dark stairway, difficult to negotiate, that takes her straight back to the swarming, overheated street, with its odor of rotten eggs and fermenting fruit. [Pp. 74–77]

The reader-spectator, held in suspense by the multiple perspectives of this narrative framework, in all probability awaits some sort of return to equilibrium, even temporary, which could be, in the above series, a new, relatively stable episode in Lady Ava's drawing room, in front of the stage. The author no doubt counts on these expectations, on attitudes depending for some persons on their conditioning from the reading of novels, and for others (those who believe in innate structures, for example) on the the inherent norms of narrative genre. Indeed, such a return will occur, but only after many detours linked to preceding developments but progressing through new variations: suddenly, in the passage following the one cited, Kim comes upon the street sweeper who had uncovered the Chinese illustrated magazine that had come to life (p. 35) to become the more or less "normal" field of the novel. This time, the coolie uncovers three new pictures. The first resembles the baroque bedroom of the heroine of *Marienbad;* the second depicts a young girl tied to an iron bed, suggesting the binding of Jacqueline in *The Voyeur* and anticipating the chained heroine of *The Man Who Lies,* soon to be filmed by Robbe-Grillet; the third is a composite of the scene in "The Secret Room" and that of Kim when she has been drugged. All at once, this whole network is again folded back into the narrative spoken by the fat man, *in turn* commented upon by a "higher" narrator, who might, perhaps, be Manneret (except for the fact that he, *in turn,* is described from the "outside" by yet another narrative voice). Here is the passage, with some paraphrasing introduced for condensation:

And, a bit further on, stands the same street sweeper [. . .], holding in both hands as he peers at it the section of illustrated newspaper [. . .]. The largest area of the legible surface is taken up by three stylized drawings.

The first of these drawings [. . .] shows [a young woman] half stretched out [as if drugged] on the edge of a bed with disordered sheets [. . .]. In the second drawing [. . .] only the nar-

row iron bed remains, on which the girl is now chained by her
four limbs [. . .]. The third drawing is doubtless symbolic: the
girl is no longer in chains, but her inanimate body, entirely nude,
is lying across the bed on its side.

Each picture is accompanied by a short title [. . .]. Unfortunately, the street sweeper does not know how to read. As
for the little bald fat man, with the red face, who is telling the
story, he does not understand Chinese; at the bottom of the last
drawing, he has been able to decipher only a few occidental letters and numbers, in small print :"S.L.S. Tel.: 1–234–567." As a
not very scrupulous narrator, who seems ignorant of the meaning
of the three initials ["Société pour la Lutte contre les Stupéfiants"
or Society for the Fight against Drugs] and who emphasizes, to
the contrary, the attraction that these illustrations could have for
the amateur, he states positively to his listener—who does not believe him—that the whole thing is an advertisement for a clandes-
tine brothel [. . .]. The fat man turns his head and considers for
a moment his own hand held up in a fixed position, the too tight
jade ring forming a lump around his middle finger [. . .]. He
takes [a glass of champagne offered to him by a servant, and
which he clumsily lets fall to the floor]. The glass [. . .] strikes
the marble tiles, breaking into a thousand pieces. This development has already been related; it can therefore be dispensed with
quickly.

Not far away, Lauren is at that moment buckling the strap of
her shoe[. . .]. The fat man with the red face lost the thread of
his story when the champagne glass broke on the floor, and now
he raises his glace [. . .] toward the tall American who looks
down upon him with his silent face, no longer trying to hide the
fact, for some time now, he has been thinking of something quite
different. Edouard Manneret, at his desk, carefully erases the
word "secret," so as to leave no trace of it [. . .]. Lady Ava,
sitting alone on her sofa [. . .], has suddenly begun to look tired
[. . .], knowing in advance, all too well, what is going to happen: the brutal breaking off of Lauren's marriage, the suicide of
her fiancé [. . .], the degraded, passionate liaison between Sir
Ralph and Lauren. [Pp. 78–84]

It would be difficult to ignore the radical quality of these narrative modes, with their innovative techniques of liaison between different places and times. Even quite modern critical criteria of narrative identification "with" and "behind" characters (as developed, for example, by Pouillon), as well as recent concepts of objective presentation, appear outmoded by comparison with these unprecedented fictional structures. The reader, tossed about on the waves of this new type of narration, with its constantly changing perspectives, is kept in a perpetual state of uncertainty, waiting for a resolution that in one sense will never come, and in another has already taken place at the outset of the novel.

Does such a work run the risk of becoming futile, or incoherent? Here a number of factors come into play to create a sort of secret unity at the core of the novel: the linkings and modulations between sequences (as we have seen them in the quoted examples), as well as certain psychological principles which operate to a greater or lesser extent for any reader—such as the conditioning or mental set of a reader of fiction (the contemporary reader for whom the novel is written) and the perhaps innate tendency to project onto any experience, even a purely mental one (the act of reading), a unifying *Gestalt*, a more or less continuous or coherent form. As soon as the motivation or justification of narrative viewpoint is abandoned, or fragmented beyond recognition, the universe of the novel is allowed to proliferate almost at will, in any direction. It should be noted, however, that the process of fragmentation which is found in as early a work as *Jealousy* (especially for its chronology), is still applied in *La Maison de rendez-vous* to a sort of "virtual" plot which moves, in a general way, and in spite of the anticipations, recapitulations, repetitions, contractions, variations, and so on, from a beginning (Sir Ralph in love with Lauren) toward a climax (the death of Manneret) and an end (the arrest of Sir Ralph and the death of Lauren). At least one of these basic elements—the death of Lauren—is "saved" for the end of the book, and does not appear, like the other episodes, in the scenes and résumés repeated so often during the body of the text. Aware at last of this final detail, the reader is in a way invited to reconstruct the novel, to perceive in the depths of the complicated, de-chronological structure of the plot the primal subject, the basis and nucleus of this highly evolved piece of fiction. *La Maison de rendez-vous* qualifies fully, in the terms used by Eikhenbaum, as a work capable of producing a "regeneration of the genre" of the novel, leading to new possibilities and new forms.

9 The Narrator and His Doubles: *Project for a Revolution in New York* (1970)

> Let us restate the only meaning that *commitment* can have for us. Instead of being political in nature, commitment is for the writer the full consciousness of present problems of his own language . . . and the will to resolve these problems from the inside. This, for him, is his only chance of remaining an artist, and no doubt also, in a distant and as yet unclear way, of serving some day a real purpose: perhaps even that of revolution.
>
> ROBBE-GRILLET, *For a New Novel*

Since the very title, *Project for a Revolution in New York*, of Robbe-Grillet's latest novel (1970), his first in five years (*La Maison de rendez-vous* appeared in 1965), cannot fail to arouse in the public mind a myriad of contemporary scenes, it seems appropriate to begin with a rapid assessment of the growing role played in Robbe-Grillet's novels and films by themes drawn from present-day society. That these elements are nearly always used in an exaggerated, parodied, or even "pop" style does not necessarily mean that the author takes a disdainful view of them; indeed, the comic and the serious coexist more and more in his works, operating in a very delicate dialectical balance whose ambiguous import has troubled readers and critics. If it is still true that language, narrative structure, and other interior problems of the novel (and film) remain essential to his work, one must at the same time admit that some recent themes and preoccupations, reinforcing and extending

262

the effect of the sado-erotic motifs which until lately constituted the chief links between external reality and Robbe-
Grillet's novelistic universe, seem to suggest a new attitude on
his part toward the social and political situation of the world
today.

This apparent reversal of earlier ideas and practices, noticeable not only in his creative work but also in his essays, appears to offer a sort of reconciliation between Robbe-Grillet's
former opposition to Sartrian *engagement* or commitment in
the political field and the counterproposal that he has made
repeatedly since 1955, namely, that the writer can only
recognize an *engagement* or commitment to art. Henceforth,
Robbe-Grillet seems to suggest, artistic commitment instead of
working against sociopolitical commitment may even contribute to it.

One must at the same time guard against the error of looking upon Robbe-Grillet's latest work in the cinema and novel
as constituting, even remotely, a direct or indirect form of
social or political propaganda. If characters in his latest films
or in *Project* discourse in contemporary ideological fashion,
it must be remembered first that these characters are not
Robbe-Grillet's spokesmen. To take them seriously would be
to fall into an obvious trap. On the other hand, real life seems
so intent upon following in the wake of fictional invention
that the most outrageous situations in a novel like *Project* may
well be echoed in newspaper accounts, and "pop" imagination,
contrived in an atmosphere of artistic commitment alone, may
find itself transformed into brute fact.

Looking back over Robbe-Grillet's novels, we see a gradual
emergence of materials taken from contemporary reality. In
The Erasers (1953), a pseudomythical plot based on the
Oedipus legend unfolded in a stylized Nordic city; in *The
Voyeur* (1958), on a vaguely French island (like Ouessant),
at an undetermined time, Mathias fulfills his role as archetypical sacrificer of a maiden offered up to the passing stranger;

Jealousy (1957) takes place in a distant French colony and involves a classical triangle of husband, wife, and lover. (Despite this "distanciation," Sartre called *Jealousy* an outstanding commentary on "the situation of woman in the French colonies.") The War of 1939–45 forms the background of *In the Labyrinth* (1959), constituting the first overt use of quasi-historical support for imaginary events occurring in a city stylized, like that of *The Erasers*, almost to the point of abstraction. The baroque Central European château of the film *Marienbad* (1961), along with the "false" Istanbul with its bookish exoticism, described in speeches of deliberately inflated rhetoric in its successor *L'Immortelle* (1963), make of these first cinematic ventures a distinct retreat from contemporary sociopolitical reality.

Nonetheless, this very exoticism leads to the introduction of real-life elements according to the special inventive processes which permit Robbe-Grillet to mix imagination and reality in a new mode. In *La Maison de rendez-vous*, a Hong Kong reminiscent of a hundred adventure novels and detective films—though rectified, controlled, and again distorted from the author's personal experience there—becomes the focus of many vectors of literary imagination on one hand and vectors of contemporary reality on the other: drug traffic, sequestration of young Eurasian girls, Communist infiltration, and so forth. Exoticism in a sense begins to replace myth as a structuring device, or to become itself a myth.

Similarly, popular myths of intrigue and violence, against a background of present-day technology, form the basis of *Trans-Europ-Express* (1967), a film interwoven with shuttling journeys of the luxury train of that name, carrying both the author (inner author, that is) and his main character (a drug smuggler) through a melodramatic plot involving police spies, traitors, gang members, and prostitutes. In *The Man Who Lies* (1968), World War II and the resistance movement in Central Europe serve as background for a film whose presumed

historical reality is gradually destroyed by reciprocal contradictions and structured impossibilities. Robbe-Grillet's next
film, *L'Eden at après* (1970), presents for the first time what
may properly be termed a thematic use of sociopolitical
reality. Student alienation and revolt against the establishment
appear clearly and find expression in numerous dialogues.
Nevertheless, an air of parody and aesthetic distance intervenes continually, and this atmosphere, which might at first
suggest the influence of Godard's *La Chinoise*, for example,
turns out to be just as *superficial*—in the sense that Robbe-
Grillet himself uses this term—as the detective story and the
erotic, or even exotic, elements of the same film. The youth of
L'Eden, so "modern" in their clothes, make-up, sexual conduct, literary allusions, and disillusionment with the system
of a consumer society, behave entirely differently from the
revolutionary students of the universities of Nanterre or Vin-
cennes, escaping into a fictional world (first, an undefined
"paradisiacal" student café, L'Eden, then a Tunisia as "false,"
in its way, as the "false Istanbul" of *L'Immortelle*) where the
imitations of group rape and the imaginary assassinations that
they commit appear more as sardonic psychodramas than true
revolutionary actions designed to change the world. If present-day reality has indeed intruded into the author's imaginary
universe, it has been "Robbe-Grilletized" according to the
principles of a fictional architecture that has no apparent concern for social message or political propaganda.

In *Project for a Revolution in New York*, Robbe-Grillet
combines an ensemble of New York scenes and locales (doubtless observed by the author on his frequent trips to the city),
together with various quite contemporary themes (revolutionary cells, suspicious activities in Greenwich Village town
houses, crimes and deliberately set fires in large, anonymous
apartment houses, rape in the subway) in an extremely dense
fictional construction, put together according to a multiplicity
of principles, both structural (relating to narrative mode,

chronology, and the linking of sequences) and metaphorical or ideological. Among the structuring metaphors of the novel is the idea or image of the perfect revolutionary crime, as set forth in an exposé and dramatic sketch at a meeting of revolutionaries. Three actor-activists explain and demonstrate the theoretical basis of this crime: opposing forces of *white* and *black* (an obvious reference to the American racial situation) are to find their synthesis in *red*, the revolutionary color *par excellence*. The color red must then figure in its own tripartite hierarchy: first rape (with a flowing of blood), then bloody murder (by slitting the throat or stomach), then finally a fiery engulfment of the victim's body, crowned by the red of flames. This burlesque Hegelian trinity shows how, far from working against the sado-erotic preoccupations that have so often marked Robbe-Grillet's recent novels and films, the theme of "revolution" can become a parody of social upheaval and furnish the pretext for scenes of torture and eroticism whose like has perhaps not been seen since Octave Mirbeau's *Torture Garden* of the nineties.

In sum, *Project*, like all Robbe-Grillet's novels and films, is a fictional structure wherein all externally derived elements, whether objects, scenes and locales, characters, actions, or themes, are important only as parts of the architecture of the work, the most emotionally charged content—revolution, rape, torture, for example—is justified only by its integration into a system of internal relationships. This is the implicit, as well as the expressed, doctrine of Robbe-Grillet's artistic production. How does this doctrine work out specifically in *Project for a Revolution in New York?*

It is manifestly impossible to convey, in a brief résumé of the novel, the full range of its development of incidents, abrupt cuts, scene linkings, flashbacks and "flashforwards," modulations of viewpoint, and successive metamorphoses of the narrator or narrative voice that tells this singular tale and imposes upon an incredible profusion of apparently discontinuous sequences a secret continuity. The following account is designed chiefly to show, through selective sampling, the main articulations of the work, and to suggest something of its atmosphere and tone.

Project for a Revolution in New York starts with a totally abstract passage: a "scene," already "repeated several times," is described as taking place rigorously like a piece of "machinery," followed by "a blank space, a piece of dead time." Aside from the terms "words" and "gestures," there is absolutely no "content" in this scene. The reader gets the impression that the creator of the text, conscious at first only of his artistic method or procedural intentions (to bring back the various scenes, to integrate them into a perfect mechanism), is tentatively contemplating a sort of Mallarméan empty page, before beginning his work.

Then a question, "But what scene?" introduces the second paragraph, where the text begins to suggest future developments. A first-person narrator speaks, or writes. Closing behind him the outside door to his Greenwich Village town house, he observes the design made by the veins in the wood frame around the glass observation panel: its geometric forms are those of a young woman stretched out on the floor, bound and gagged. Immediately, the first sequence of the novel takes place: a "monstrous" medical experiment (possibly artificial insemination forcibly executed) made upon a mulatto girl by a white-jacketed doctor, whose actions are cut short by the arrival of a character in a comic-strip vampire mask, followed by a fourth person in working clothes, like those of a "plumber, or electrician, or locksmith." The light "fades," and the scene is reabsorbed into a textual repetition of the first paragraph of the novel. Henceforth implanted in the reader's memory, this torture sequence, first presented as a sort of fantasy of the narrator, announces and prepares not only its own *reprise*, but also the development of a series of analagous scenes throughout the text (pp. 7–11).[1]

Another of the narrator's "thoughts" leads inside the house: he fears he may have left his key on "the chest" in the entryway. The mere *naming* of the object is sufficient: "Then there is a chest in the entryway," he states, proceeding to describe it. In the mirror that hangs above it an image suddenly appears: it is Laura, a sixteen-year-old girl who lives (held prisoner, we deduce later) with the narrator. This preparatory *flash* is quickly erased; the narrator, no longer concerned with his key, descends the short flight of steps leading to the sidewalk, noting the presence, across the street, of a character dressed like a movie spy. The fact that the house opposite does *not* have the familiar Z-shaped fire escape of older buildings in the neighborhood leads to a train of thoughts and images concerning a possible assassin, who could climb such a structure, break a pane of glass, and penetrate inside a bedroom. "At least, this is what Laura thinks," states the narrator; and at once a proto-sequence (which, like the preceding, will proliferate later), treated in part from the point of view of Laura, occurs, materializing the arrival of the window-breaking assassin from the fire escape in Laura's room. But the scene blends into the arrival therein of the narrator himself, who explains his lateness to Laura by references to a prolonged "meeting" (the first hint of revolutionary activities).

Again the light fades (this motif is even associated with the very French device of the *minuterie* in the narrator's house!). The ensuing scene of Laura's rape by an "aggressor" is transformed by one of the textual metamorphoses characteristic of *Project* into the first of the many interrogation sequences of the novel. The narrator seems to be explaining to some un-

---

1. Page references are to the 1970 printing of *Projet pour une révolution à New York* (Paris: Minuit).

named person, who combines the qualities of revolutionary leader, judge, and even sometimes literary critic, his actions and their reasons. Suddenly, the narrator reveals that he himself is the recent "aggressor." Various apparent inconsistencies in the use of introductory dashes and quotation marks in the interrogation sequences will later make of these curious passages a favored area of the text for the transfer of narration between one character and another, with shifts from questioner to the one questioned, with logically "impossible" exchanges that distort the fictional field and create new narrative topologies. The first interrogation, for example, causes the text to bend back upon itself as the narrator again relates leaving the house, noting the spy across the street (who is now joined by two policemen), and finding his way to a subway entrance (pp. 12–23).

Descent into the subway, like the fading of light, always leads to a shift of scenes. Laura again appears, watching from her window the actions of the men across the street, inadvertently breaking the windowpane with a sudden gesture of fright, which causes her ring to crack the glass. As her thoughts turn to the narrator, he materializes in the text, ascending the stairs menacingly. Shifting to the first person, the narrator recounts his journey through subway corridors, into a fantastic labyrinth of halls and galleries where an enormous crowd circulates among sexually suggestive slot machines, curio shops selling miniatures (including replicas of the Villa Bleue at Hong Kong, scene of much of Robbe-Grillet's *La Maison de rendez-vous*), pornographic bookstores, and false store fronts. After giving the password at the office of "Dr. Morgan, psychotherapist," the narrator attends the revolutionary meeting. Here the metaphoric synthesis of black and white by the color red is acted out in a *saynète*, culminating in the burning of a body sprinkled with gasoline—a great fire that engulfs "the whole house" (pp. 24–41).

Hinging upon this image and phrase, the text veers into a

passage in which the narrator, having waited too long after setting fire to the building, must descend an outside fire escape, through a broken windowpane. This often-repeated image, in turn, leads back to Laura terrified by noises in the house despite the reassurances of the narrator that they can only be made by mice. Offering to go upstairs to investigate, he goes downstairs instead, continuing his detailed description of the largely uninhabited house. Suddenly a question intrudes into the text: "Why?" uttered by the interrogative voice that will play an increasingly prominent part in the novel. The narrator furnishes further details concerning the fire he had set, and, when the question period ends, goes out to the subway station to "return home," where, ostensibly, he was when the interrogation began (pp. 42–48).

"During this time," the narrator (in the third-person mode) again "breaks into" Laura's house, perhaps at the order of a certain Frank, mention of whose name gives rise to a flashback (with verbs in the past tense) to the "Old Joe's" café where Frank and an agent named Ben Saïd (there will be a "true" and a "false" Ben Saïd) warn the narrator that he is being followed by a double. The narrator stops in front of a store window displaying masks, false breasts, "amputated" hands (designed, of course, to model gloves), and "decapitated" heads adorned with various wigs, among which appear the heads of Ben Saïd and Dr. Morgan's nurse. The narrator returns home by subway, goes upstairs, and calms the frightened Laura "by the usual methods," telling her of the fire on 123rd Street, but *not* of "JR's disappearance and the inquiry concerning her" which have occupied most of his time.

This "gap" in the narrator's report is filled in by a résumé of the story of the sumptuous JR, whom the Organization has sent among the "rich and powerful" as a deluxe call girl, to fill the coffers of the Revolution. In reply to a personal notice in *The New York Times* ("Bachelor father seeks young woman of attractive physique and docile nature for night-time care of difficult young girl"), JR is sent to a Park Avenue apartment, where the "young girl" turns out to be another Laura, this one described as thirteen years old (are there *two* Lauras?), and extremely precocious, as reflected in the ambiguous answers she gives to JR's questions concerning her absent "father." In the middle of their conversation, JR suddenly becomes the first-person narrator—the agreement of genders in French leaves no doubt of this (see p. 58)—describing the sounds of struggle and pleading coming from another room. This "I" (ostensibly, now JR) then looks out the window and notes with astonishment that "the room where we were" is above Central Park and that in the park two men and a woman are gesticulating as they search the bushes. The "I" becomes masculine again (as shown by the French genders); and, in a later development of the same scene, the three figures in the park will become Ben Saïd, JR herself, and the narrator! Passing again before the window display of masks and heads, the narrator once more takes the subway home (pp. 49–63).

On the way, he "thinks again" of JR, who "is still, during this time, at little Laura's." The sounds heard from the next room are revealed as coming from a tape recorder, reproducing the noise of an intruder climbing a fire escape, a windowpane breaking, a young girl screaming. JR leaves Laura's apartment, but the machine continues to play, allowing us to hear a second, then a third visit by JR. The third visit becomes an apparent reality (no longer taped); JR subjects Laura to a curious interrogation, complicated by intrusions from the recorder now playing in the next room. The presence of the three persons in the park is referred to; the modulations of narrative voice become extremely complicated, with JR and then the narrator "seeing" themselves in the park, as finally "the narrator—let us say 'I,' for simplicity's sake" reports the conversation of the three as they search the ground for marijuana cigarettes hidden nearby. To his interlocutor, the narrator states that "from that evening on, we lost all contact" with JR. But in the course of the dialogue, the "chief" detects inconsistencies in the narrator's account, and himself takes over the narration as his conjectures on JR's actions become the "main level" of the text, until his own version is subjected to questioning (by the "chief" himself!) some five pages later (see pp. 78–83).

There follows a sequence involving the rape of JR, divided into several scenes: first, a description of her apartment (with its folding ironing board, a television set showing a program identical to the play performed by the revolutionaries, and other curious furnishings); then, the arrival of the false police-man (revealed later to be the narrator); finally, the flight down the fire escape, the arrival of the firemen, the explosion of the building and the narrator's "taking the subway to re-turn home" (now a familiar refrain). Here, the interrogation resumes with the narrator taking over the account the inter-rogater had begun, only to be questioned closely by the latter concerning Laura (the Laura who lives with the narrator) (pp. 64–84).

Laura, it develops, is reading a detective novel (she reads many, and confuses their plots), whose story, as well as the lurid picture on its cover (a girl bound and tortured), is an obvious *mise en abyme* or interior duplication of *Project* it-self. Moreover, the text of the inner detective novel (which the narrator is also reading) merges indistinguishably with the text of the outer. Its very presence in the house, since it does not belong to the narrator's "collection," proves there was a break-in, perhaps by a locksmith summoned by someone claim-ing to have left his key inside the house: this conjecture causes the locksmith to materialize (he was foreshadowed as early as p. 11), standing on the stoop and looking through the keyhole at the torture scene described at the beginning of *Project*, which is now revealed as the cover of the detective novel, held up behind the keyhole by Laura. Like *Project*, this novel contains a young victim, held a virtual prisoner, threatened by Dr. Morgan with a hypodermic needle, lying bound on the floor while an enormous spider, or a rat, crawls toward her, all of this calculated to force her to reveal her secrets, "one of which is known to the reader, the second to the narrator, and the third only to the author of the book." The superimposed texts become inseparable; the narrator could belong to either. "During this time," he writes, "the narrative that I began proceeds to unfold up in Harlem, in the overheated studio apartment on 123rd Street where the false policeman, wearing his uniform, informs Joan [JR] that she has been condemned to death" (pp. 85–96).

Once more, we witness the rape of JR, prior to the burning of her flat. It is a scene of black humor, cruelty, cold eroticism, and burlesque parody of popular pornography. In the middle of JR's forced revelations of sundry details concerning the Organization, the narrative shifts to an account of Ben Saïd threatened in the subway by three juveniles, two boys with M and W on their jackets, and a girl with her name, Laura, emblazoned on her jacket. Ambiguous phrases abound, applying equally well to the subway episode or the scene of the abused JR, who pursues her narration in the most ignoble postures. As the subway train enters a tunnel, the loud metallic noise it causes is transformed into the noise of the narrator descending the fire escape, after setting fire to JR's apartment, as has previously been described.

"Then," declares the narrator, "I close the book." But the "book" (the paperback that the narrator had begun to read many pages earlier, and which had merged with the "book" of *Project* itself) will continue to figure in the principal action. Laura relates how she had held up its cover behind the keyhole to trick the locksmith; the scene develops once more as if now occurring for the first time, and the locksmith flees, observed from across the street by the "false" Ben Saïd, who writes down this action in a notebook which forms, along with the "dossiers" of the Organization, another of the parallel texts of the novel.

Laura, after the departure of the locksmith, looks at her image in the mirror and murmurs several phrases identical to those spoken earlier by her double, the *other* Laura of the Park Avenue apartment. This is the first synthesis of the two Lauras. Glancing out the window, Laura sees the man in the black raincoat ("whom she has named Ben Saïd after a minor character in the paperback") continuing to maintain surveillance of the house, accompanied now by two policemen with submachine guns (pp. 97–123).

Laura explores the many bedrooms in the house, which seem to multiply. Frightened by the sight of a trickle of blood emerging beneath one of the doors, she starts to turn the porcelain doorknob. On the street opposite the house, the false Ben Saïd points out to the two policemen the subway entrance taken by the narrator, while the true Ben Saïd continues his trip in the subway train, as in the narration begun earlier by JR. The story line becomes extremely complicated at this point, involving the pursuit of Laura by an imaginary, then real, "Vampire of the Subway"—a Famtômas-Judex creature who is a member of the Organization, supplies false reports to the police, and gives courses in "criminal sexology" at the revolutionary school. The narrative again becomes an interrogation; the subway scene is heard on magnetic tape, then seen "live" as a surgeon boards the train, identified by the narrator as Doctor Morgan (pp. 124–138).

A singularly appropriate word, to be used with increased frequency, appears in the text: "Reprise," with its implications of repetition and also of the cinematic "retake." Laura, with blood on her hand, stops on the platform between two subway cars; then she reaches out to turn the porcelain doorknob of a door in her *house* (as in the scene begun earlier). Opening the door, she sees before her the subway car just mentioned. The train comes to a halt in a tunnel. As Laura descends to the tracks to escape, she sees a gray rat approaching. She again seizes the "porcelain" knob (the subway knobs are "copper"), opens the door, and now "the rat is there, trotting about on the white floor tiles" of a bedroom, near the bloody body of a young girl victim of torture. It is Claudia, one of the girls executed by the Organization, "as it has been said." Another "reprise" returns the text to the subway train stalled in the tunnel. Laura is seized and carried off into an opening in the side of the tunnel by the Vampire and Doctor Morgan, while the "true" Ben Saïd, still in the subway car, takes careful notes on the little pad that will also become part of the dossiers of the "chief" (pp. 139–148).

Thus Ben Saïd is identified as the narrator of the succeeding text, which relates Laura's abduction and questioning by Doctor Morgan. In its cage, the rat awaits, ready to eat her alive if she refuses to answer, or lies. "M the Vampire" sits in a corner, watching. The interrogation leads back over most of the episodes previously treated, which Morgan seems to attribute to Laura's own composition, since he asks *her* to explain the use of "reprise," which she defines in terms that apply to *Project* as a whole. One new element of capital importance appears: a vacant lot, enclosed by a fence of used doors, on which is glued an immense photo-mural of the narrator's Greenwich Village town house. Laura's "narration" (with its feminine past participles) is gradually effaced, remaining out of the fictional field until it suddenly comes into play for the last time, some fifty pages later (pp. 149–163).

A young, middle-class couple enters the vacant lot. Four killers, armed with pistols equipped with silencers, shoot down the young man and tie up the girl, whom they abduct. The police will find in the victim's hand a printed card announcing that all young brides will be snatched, while still virgins, from their husbands.

Ben Saïd, at "Old Joe's" café, now narrates the story, but it soon shifts back to the original "I" narrator, who takes his usual route home via the subway. In the train, he sees a girl resembling Laura; but Laura is still at home when he arrives, inspecting the "bizarre fixtures" found there: heavy-duty electric sockets, for example, as if to accommodate "apparatus" of some sort. In a scene of cold cruelty, the narrator forces himself on Laura, then falls asleep, fully clothed, at her side, forgetting the presence in his pocket of a box of matches, which Laura quietly steals (pp. 164–172).

"Unconscious concern over these matches" provokes in the narrator a long dream sequence, beginning in the dark with the striking of matches that illuminate various posters pasted on the outside of the fence around the vacant lot. Detailed descriptions of the scenes on the posters follow, as they are suddenly illuminated by strong stage lights: a movie star, her eyes bound, threatened by an immense phallus; an enormous electric iron (like that in the scene of rape at JR's); the inside of a café; a young couple in marriage costume; and, finally, a life-sized photo-mural of "the front of my own house." The narrator enters the door, using his key, and finds himself inside the vacant lot, where the various objects described in an earlier section of the text are set up like chessmen. On a copper bed is a nude female model, in plastic; the narrator recognizes her as JR. Her "execution" unfolds three times in succession. Each time, the operation involves stuffing the body orifices with material from the mattress, soaking this with gasoline, and setting the body on fire. Each time, it comes to life, writhing in pain, and the narrator repeats an apocalyptic sequence of tortures carried out in obedience to certain obscure "rules of the game," which dictate his movements on the granite flagstones that form the squares of the chessboard.

When the rite finally ends, the narrator finds himself again in front of the photo-mural of his house. The locksmith is there, peering through the keyhole at another torture spectacle, that with which the book began. The scene is no longer the vacant lot, but the "real" house, and again the locksmith flees, but this time, he encounters a new personage, N. G. Brown, whom he persuades to accompany him back to the house. Brown, who is returning, he says, from a masked ball, is wearing the dinner jacket and head mask of the character seen through the keyhole by the locksmith on his first appearance in the text (p. 11). Both men join Doctor Morgan, who is subjecting his young victim to a "cruel operation" (pp. 173–187).

At this point in the text occurs a new type of interrogatory sequence, in which the narrator replies to objections made by someone who seems to combine the (analagous?) qualities of chief of an Organization and literary critic. The narrator defends the eroticism of his descriptions, his exaggerations, the unidiomatic distortions of some New York place names, the ambiguity of the characters, and even the use of the term "cut" to punctuate his text (despite the fact that "cut" will so appear only later). The narrator insists that he must reach the torture scene with Morgan, Brown, the locksmith, and the bound girl threatened by a black widow spider, or "we will never finish up." The surgeon suddenly flees from the scene, pursued by N. G. Brown (pp. 187–193).

Standing across the street, Ban Saïd notes this flight in his little book. Inside the house, the locksmith witnesses (with "spectators"!) the death of the bound victim as a result of multiple spider bites on her "tender portions," following which the spider takes refuge among the books on the library shelves (returning, no doubt, to the paperback novel). The locksmith violates the still warm body of the victim, then takes off his mask: he is the "real" Ben Saïd. As he leaves the house, he remembers leaving the key on the hall stand. The false Ben Saïd, watching from across the street, sees him depart. Laura hears the door close, then finds the body of Sarah (or Clara, or Claudia), abandoned by Morgan, who, as if recalled by this textual reference, reappears and begins again his "operation" on the girl whom he takes to be Laura. He flees once more, pursued now by the narrator, who blends thus with N. G.

Brown. The term "cut" now makes its appearance in the narrative text, starting a coda consisting of an accumulation of quick scenes and accelerated actions which seem to form tentative answers to questions concerning the outcome of the plot, in a final, desperate haste to reach an ending. This montage of "flashes" shows us "Old Joe's" café, Laura at the sill of the door to the torture room, the tape recorder playing its sound track of various scenes, the window being broken, the pursuit of the surgeon, a storefront window displaying the martyrdom of twelve young girls, and, finally, Laura's emergence into the street, her capture in the subway by Morgan and M the Vampire, her interrogation and rape, a view of the city of New York in ruins (except for the narrator's house, miraculously still standing), the torture of the young bride, and a "reprise" of JR's story, whose last act is now described: she is exhibited on an altar in a Harlem underground church, surrounded by twelve girl communicants suspended on crosses in the form of T, X, Y, and Y upside down (pp. 194–213).

In the midst of all this, the narrator speculates on the meaning of his characters and incidents. Confusion increases. Laura is again interrogated by Dr. Morgan and a masked personnage, who, having already been identified as Brown and/or M the Vampire, now rips off his mask to appear—as the narrator! Immediately, like some super-Fantômas, the narrator abducts Laura (leaving in her place the skeleton of another girl), flees down the outside fire escape (while the building goes up in flames), returns to his town house, and closes behind him the door, whose small windowpane "is surrounded by. . . . Cut." This beginning of a cyclical ending, hinting at the design which engendered the first elements of the novel, now blends with events that have already occurred: a suspicious noise is heard from the upper floors of the house, and Laura immediately gives a start, listening intently, "as it has been said." Is the "project" about to repeat itself, or has it found its realization? (pp. 213–214).

A hasty reading of this complex novel, with its ironic, parodylike, mocking, and *ludique* surface, might lead to the tempting but erroneous conclusion that the text of *Project* is designed to be read without conscious reflection, without pause or astonishment at the abrupt changes in narrator, sequences of the plot, locales, or identity of the characters. The reader might, like the rider on a Coney Island roller coaster, let himself be borne dizzily along over the up-and-down switches so cannily arranged by the author-engineer, enjoying the ride without second thoughts. But in a sense such a reader, while apparently following certain recommendations of Robbe-Grillet himself that his novels be read "superficially," would fall into the trap of taking too seriously the pop exaggerations of the work. It must again be emphasized that what really counts in *Project,* even more perhaps than in the author's previous works, is the novelistic structuring, the architectural and stylistic procedures which give value to these themes and archetypes taken from the popular literature of violence and eroticism or from the mythic world of the comic strip.

Readers familiar with the author's earlier novels and films will be interested to note in *Project* both direct and indirect borrowings of materials and structures. In *The Erasers* we find the doctor-criminal of *Project,* the series of identical posters, the photo-mural of the main scene, an organization devoted to political assassination, "frozen" scenes, and other parallels. The design on the doors of the houses of *The Voyeur* evokes in the protagonist images corresponding to his preoccupations, and the famous figure of eight in that novel recurs in the twisting cigarette smoke described elliptically in *Project* (p. 144). The enormous spider recalls the thousand-legs of *Jealousy,* the first of Robbe-Grillet's novels to display the radical reordering of events that prepared the way for *Project. In the Labyrinth* (as well as the short piece in *Snapshots* called "In the Corridors of the Métro") evokes the atmosphere of endless corridors, and anticipates in its construction and rejection of scenes and locales through verbal devices (a "No!" which intervenes, for example, to destroy a preceding passage) a number of developments in *Project*. Some elements appear in so many works that they may well be called Robbe-Grillet's "stock": an interplay of the same names (Frank, Müller, Boris); scenes in which glass is broken (*La Maison de rendez-vous*, *Last Year at Marienbad*, *The Man Who Lies*, *L'Eden et après*); games like blindman's buff; sadistic "simulacres" or psychodramas half-serious, half-jesting; pairs of characters and their doubles; and, above all, scenes of erotic violence, here pushed to their furthest limit.

Some intertextual references to earlier works are obvious: we recognize Elias of *Trans-Europ-Express* in the man furtively scanning pornographic magazines (p. 35); the white Buick convertible of *L'Immortelle* is abandoned in the vacant lot (p. 161), which is itself, like its counterpart in *La Maison de rendez-vous*, a dumping ground for objects associated with Robbe-Grillet's other novels and films. This procedure will not end with *Project*; in the film *L'Eden et après* that follows, common elements recur, including the broken glass, an adolescent gang involved in threatening "games," blindman's buff, bloody scenes with cages and a plough. (Cf. *Project*, pp. 107, 110, 118, 119, 149, 177).

Even apparently new elements are often extensions of previously used materials. The shop window of Kowloon in *La Maison de rendez-vous*, with its plastic dummies or doubles (which, coming alive, enter into the plot) anticipates the display of masks, wigs, and severed hands in *Project*, as well as the plastic-dummy scene of JR's execution. The magazine-cover picture that turns into several "real" scenes of *La Maison de rendez-vous* has its counterpart not only in the paperback-novel cover of *Project*, but also in a new parallel device, the television program that duplicates part of the story. Even the feverish visions of the soldier of *In the Labyrinth* evoke the long dream sequence of *Project.*

If intertextual allusions are used in this fashion to furnish particular materials, they are perhaps less important than certain generative principles or techniques not linked to specific references. One such principle is generation by *nomination,* by the presence of a word (cf. Mallarmé's famous statement, "Je dis, une fleur!"). Robbe-Grillet had used nomination to some extent in the *Labyrinth;* in *Project,* it becomes a regularized procedure, recognized textually by the narrator.

For example, as soon as the narrator thinks or imagines that he has left his key on the marble top of the hall stand, this stand comes into existence: "So there *is* a stand in that dark vestibule" (p. 12). It is as if each phrase of a dynamic, growing text has the power to generate the text that follows; the slightest allusion or comparison, apparently made at random, becomes a prophecy, if not a guarantee, of its future realization in "real" terms. When the narrator wonders why Laura climbed up to a high shelf in the library to take down the detective novel whose cover shows a girl frightened by a spider, he speculates that she may herself have been frightened by a spider, "or a rat" (p. 93). Henceforth, the attentive reader waits suspensefully for the rat that he knows must now appear (even a less attentive reader might well have an unconscious, subliminal, expectation of the event). The rat does materialize, and plays an important part in the subway sequence (p. 140). So self-conscious does the procedure become that it is used as a pretext for reflexive, inner comment. The phrase, "as she would have done faced by a deaf man, or a cat" (p. 207) causes some uneasiness in the narrator, aware of his intention to include nothing gratuitous, to relate everything to the text. He is able to find a deaf man in the trumpet player of "Old Joe's" café, but is obliged to look for an excuse for the absence of a cat: "Since the cat has not played any part in this, as far as I know, it can only be an error" (p. 208). One

282 The Narrator and His Doubles

of the most important characters, the locksmith (who turns out to be Ben Saïd, perhaps the narrator himself), comes into being by nomination, among the random possibilities of a comparison: "a little bald man [. . .] who must be something like a plumber, an electrician, or a locksmith" (p. 11).

The use of doubles, so characteristic of Robbe-Grillet's works since the start of his career, has been repeatedly pointed out: Wallas has a double in *The Erasers*, Mathias has a double in the little Julien of *The Voyeur*, the soldier of the *Labyrinth* sees his own double in the street, doubles are everywhere in *La Maison de rendez-vous*, *L'Immortelle*, and in Robbe-Grillet's recent films. In *Project for a Revolution in New York*, however, doubling becomes a basic narrative structure, permitting extremely complicated modulations of point of view, leading from a character to his double (or triple, or ?) in a network of exchanges of viewpoint. Most of these transitions have been pointed out: the "nominal" narrator, using either the first- or third-person pronoun, merges at one time or another, in passages of varying length, with the beautiful JR, Ben Saïd, Laura, M the Vampire, N. G. Brown, and even the "interrogator." In this series there figure, in addition, the couples and doubles: the true and the false Ben Saïd (who is also, of course, the locksmith and/or the narrator), and, especially, the "two" Lauras who, when first encountered, are of different ages and live in different places, only to blend into a single character toward the end of the novel. Any character in *Project* may, it seems, be, in fact or secretly, the narrator, who, placed at the aesthetic center of the work, orders and controls everything, including the critical commentaries made in the text on the novel itself. The ironic tone of these passages underlines the author's self-consciousness. In the interrogation to which the unidentified critical voice subjects Laura, she tries to justify the use of the word "reprise," which the voice accuses her of using in *her* narration (though it had not occurred in any passages that could plausibly be attributed to Laura): "You cannot tell everything at once [. . .] and there is always a time when a story goes off in two directions, goes backward, or jumps forward, or begins to proliferate; then you say, Reprise" (p. 157).

Interrogation itself is a new technique with Robbe-Grillet, and he gives it, as may be supposed, unforeseen twists. The basis or precedent for these passages is perhaps less literary than one would at first think. We are reminded less of the question-and-answer chapter of Joyce's *Ulysses*, or of Robert Pinget's *L'Inquisitoire* (despite undeniable resemblances), than of the form taken by the innumerable interviews that Robbe-Grillet himself has given to reporters and reviewers, a large number of which are printed in the format of an interrogation. It is obvious that such passages in *Project* are a semiserious anticipation of future critical commentary, a kind of advance reply to objections, folded into the materials of the text itself.[2] Toward the end of the novel, the "interrogator" blends

2. I may be permitted to point out here the source of one exchange between the narrator and his interrogator. On page 189, the latter makes this objection: "Something else: you talk about the 'Greenwich quarter,' or the 'Madison subway station'; an American would say 'the Village' and the 'Madison Avenue station.'" This refers to observations that I had myself made to Robbe-Grillet in May of 1970, after reading a portion of the manuscript of *Project*. The narrator's reply ("no one ever claimed that the narration was made by an American") will surely satisfy French readers, without exactly solving the problem of a correct translation. All the more so since there does not exist, in reality, any "Madison Avenue Station" on the New York subway lines! Other items that I mentioned to Robbe-Grillet (the implausibility of a keyhole in New York through which the locksmith could peer, instead of the normal type of Yale lock; the unreality of the electric sockets with their circular openings, in the French style; the uncharacteristic, European two-tone wail attributed to New York fire trucks; the *minuterie* system) have turned up for comment in his interviews with critics in France and elsewhere.

increasingly into the narrative consciousness of the work. Even the reader becomes involved; for example, at one point he is addressed thus: "You have asked me what the abductors did with the young bride" (p. 207). The melding of narrator, critic, and author leads to a series of first-person reflections: "I have been wondering, for some time, about Laura" (p. 203); "I have also lost track of young Marc-Antoine" (p. 204); "one question that bothers me" (p. 205); "have I pointed out that" (p. 207); "I still needed [. . .] to describe" (p. 208); "it is possible that" (p. 210); and various exclamations, such as "faster!," or, "this time, I have not a minute to lose" (p. 213), as if the author-narrator were in a great hurry to end his task, even if the end of the text is destined only to lead to its "reprise" from the beginning. Interrogation and autocommentary function as a device of narrative structure, a mirror of the author's consciousness, as he makes the melodramatic "revelations" of the coda, binding together, and at the same time untying, all the threads of the plot.

One element of *Project* that seems to sit uneasily upon the narrative conscience of the text is the aforementioned sado-erotic violence of many scenes. The trend toward violence, which has always been present in Robbe-Grillet, seems to have intensified in the later works, reaching a comic-serious climax in *Project*. The torture scenes of *La Maison de rendez-vous*, the sadistic images of the heroine in chains of *Trans-Europ-Express*, the caged women and the victims lying in bathtubs full of blood in *L'Eden et après*, all these "popular" materials (as Robbe-Grillet calls them), are outdone in *Project*. At the same time, the style of the violent descriptions, the minute precision of the language used, the neutrality of tone, give to these scenes a coldness that endistances them, rendering impossible (in theory, at least) any pornographic provocation. The narrator's uneasiness on this subject appears in this exchange with the interrogator:

"Is this really necessary? Don't you have a tendency to insist too strongly, as I have already said, on the erotic aspects of the scenes related?"

"It all depends on what you mean by 'too strongly.' My own opinion, on the contrary, is that—things being as they are—I have remained quite correct." [P. 188]

This "defense" is obviously ambiguous: is "things being as they are" meant to refer to sadistic and erotic occurrences in real life, to popular imaginings and daydreams, or to the purely textual existence of the fiction?

One line of defense that Robbe-Grillet appears to take more seriously than might be thought is the argument that scenes of eroticism, violence, and torture produce a catharsis in the reader (and in the author as well). A number of references in the text of *Project* to the catharsis of contemporary man's un-avowed desires, apparently stated ironically, may suggest that Robbe-Grillet considers his erotic-sadistic inventions somehow therapeutic in nature. He did, in fact, propose such a view in one of the first interviews given to the press upon the publication of the novel.[3]

Robbe-Grillet certainly does not intend to rewrite the novels of the Marquis de Sade, or to subscribe to de Sade's philosophy of using erotic tortures to express an ideological revolt against the idea of a benign God concerned with man's happiness. On the contrary, sadistic eroticism, a "natural" and even "innocent" manifestation in Robbe-Grillet's view, finds in its artistic, mythical, and popular forms (the naïve pornography of paperback covers, comic books, hard-core pornographic fiction) a "healthy" means of expression which may

3. See *Le Monde* of Oct. 30, 1970, p. 19, where Robbe-Grillet replies to a lady who asks "whether he is entirely sane": "I would answer this lady with this reassurance: bringing out into the daylight one's phantasms, as I do, is the best way not to allow one's self to be destroyed by them. If everyone will try this, our whole society will be healthier."

even be socially useful. It is quite apparent that the last word has not been said on this question, and that critics will continue to compare Robbe-Grillet's eroticism, with its possibly ironic paraliterary or therapeutic claims, to that of recognized "erotic" authors of the contemporary scene, such as Georges Bataille or the author of *Story of O*. I have myself, in discussing *La Maison de rendez-vous*, referred to Octave Mirbeau's decadent novel of the nineties, *Torture Garden*; the same work contains even more striking parallels to *Project for a Revolution in New York*. In both cases the descriptions, treated in minute detail, insist at length on cruel and protracted tortures. Laura's torture by rat bites (p. 142, 145 ff.) may be less detailed than the analogous scene of the rat in *Torture Garden*, but the spider episode in *Project* surpasses anything in Mirbeau's novel, and other scenes in *Torture Garden*, such as that of the seven bronze phalluses and that of the victim who dies in the midst of sexual spasms, inevitably recall similar scenes in *Project*.[4]

Robbe-Grillet's novel is related to outside reality, then, despite all its *distanciation* or aesthetic endistancing, by at least two important aspects: the question—fundamentally a moral issue—of its erotic, sadistic implications; and the question of its "realistic" content, or references to current events, "revolutionary" or otherwise. There can be no doubt that many of the "materials" of the work (gangs of juvenile delinquents, arson squads, cells of subversive agents) recall closely the atmosphere of New York in 1970. Even as the novel made its appearance, a "true" news item recounted an incident in the New York subway that would seem almost taken from *Project* itself: a masked gunman had threatened a subway ticket seller

4. See Octave Mirbeau, *Le Jardin des supplices* (Paris: Fasquelle, 1899), pp. 232 ff., pp. 318 ff., and p. 165. In general, Mirbeau's victims are males, Robbe-Grillet's females. Without going so far as to say that Mirbeau's work served as a direct source, it is impossible to deny these curious resemblances.

with a revolver, when a policeman hidden behind her disarmed the robber and tore off his mask, to discover that the masked robber was another policeman belonging to the squad assigned to protect the ticket booths. An anthology of similar incidents (the Manson-Tate and Ota murders, the episode in Atlanta of the engraved invitations to a party at which the guests were assaulted and robbed) could easily rival Roland Barthes' *Mythologies* or the scenes in Godard's films in which characters mockingly read aloud from newspaper accounts of this kind. But Robbe-Grillet is not indulging in deliberate satire, and his inventions, even when "reality" seems to insist on confirming them, remain wholly ironic.

It is, in the last analysis, the artistic process of transforming the idea of social revolution into the metaphor of a perfect, three-part crime, of employing revolution as a metaphor that *generates* settings, characters, and actions, all cunningly arranged on the chessboard of the novel's structure, that reveals the *real* role of "revolution" in this astonishing, dense, apparently chaotic but secretly coherent *Project for a Revolution in New York*.

10 Modes and Levels of the Cinematic Novel: *Glissements progressifs du plaisir* (1974)

> We believe that the true extensions of Robbe-Grillet's work will be found only in the film: arising in literature, these procedures run the risk of monotony. . . . Whereas in the cinema they can resonate throughout a gamut of materials, at all levels.
>
> NOEL BURCH, *Praxis du cinéma*

A number of considerations caused Robbe-Grillet to abandon the publication in *ciné-roman* form of the three films he produced after *Marienbad* (1961) and *L'Immortelle* (1963). With these later films, *Trans-Europ-Express* (1967), *L'Homme qui ment* (*The Man Who Lies*, 1968), and *L'Eden et après* (1970), his main concern was the lack of a suitable format or organization of materials related to sound and picture. Working more and more from fragmentary preliminary texts, notes, and projects, depending increasingly on improvisations made during the shooting of scenes and sequences, Robbe-Grillet found himself, once these three films were "montaged" and completed, with an excess of refactory materials at hand; only a painstaking rewriting or description of the film as viewed on a moviola could assure a written version in accord with the work as shown on the screen. The script for *Marienbad* had been written out beforehand with such minute attention to details that the only task that remained to create the printed text was to select the passages related to picture and sound and splice them together; for *L'Immortelle,* the author was able to use a series of numbered shots, based on voluminous shooting-script materials, with results that were generally less satisfactory than the text of *Marienbad.* The enormous effort that would have been involved in arriving at a novelized version of the next three films seemed to Robbe-Grillet to represent an expense of time and effort that could be better spent on writing a new work. He has discussed this problem in an article on the description of scenes from films.[1] Such practical concerns were in turn reinforced by theoretical views on the basic incompatibility of film and novel, of visual image and literary expression.[2]

The appearance therefore in early 1974 of the *ciné-roman Glissements progressifs du plaisir* (roughly, *Accelerative Slippages of Pleasure*), some six months after the first showing of the film of that title, marked an important step in Robbe-Grillet's evolution. Once again, the author's acceptance of the desirability of providing printed expression of a filmic work seemed to support the view of critics who view his novelistic and cinematic creative processes as essentially related and as both belonging to a unified field of fictional structure. In addition, the unusual format chosen for the printed version of *Glissements* showed the continuing struggle of Robbe-Grillet to create a method of dealing with printed film works that would, while employing the fictional and descriptive style of the author, nevertheless insist throughout on the existence

1. Alain Robbe-Grillet, "Brèves Réflexions sur le fait de décrire une scène de cinéma," *Revue d'Esthétique,* Nos. 2–3, 1967, pp. 131–138 ("To describe the film shot by shot, as it is found in its final form, is neither exciting for the author nor in harmony with the spirit of his creation. I would rather be tempted to write something else entirely.")

2. Cf. my article, "Problèmes du roman cinématographique," in *Cahiers de l'Association Internationale des Etudes Françaises,* May 1968.

"elsewhere" of the actual shots and scenes of the movie, along with the coordinated sound track essential to their effect.

The Introduction to *Glissements* presents the volume not as a literary work but as a document on the film, designed to permit the reader to examine its composition in greater detail and to study its "generative evolution," by learning of the "successive and contradictory stages of its elaboration" (p. 9).[3]

This procedure involves three independent parts: a three-page synopsis; about 130 pages of "continuity with dialogues," divided into some 45 sequences and forming the main portion of the book; and a 65-page "montage record" with brief descriptions of the 626 individual shots that make up the 45 sequences. A large number of black and white photographs, distributed throughout the main section at appropriate places, taken by the author's wife, Catherine Robbe-Grillet, from the vantage point of the camera, reproduce the point of view, framing, and lighting—though not the color—of the shots.

Both the continuity and montage-record sections have special features of interest. The continuity, or shooting script, has been interspersed with many passages, printed in italics, representing, in the author's words, "notes which, absent from the original script, give an *a posteriori* account of details, thoughts, modifications, hypotheses or alternatives, developed in the course of the shooting." The laconic montage record has revealing headings for the sequences (which bear only numbers in the continuity). Both sections employ a systematic vocabulary of special terms applied to film structure: resolution, punctuation (sometimes "interior" punctuation), metaphor, metonymy, "flash," and "fringe," terms not mentioned for obvious reasons in the film itself, as well as overt references to parallels, such as Jesus or Lady Macbeth.

3. Page references are to *Glissements progressifs du plaisir,* by Alain Robbe-Grillet (Paris: Minuit, 1974). As yet, no English translation has appeared.

Robbe-Grillet's attitude toward his own synopsis of the film shows the basic ambiguity of the role in his works of the story line, intrigue, or plot, so often considered by critics as having been deliberately falsified, distorted, and even removed or "pulled off" in Marshall McLuhan's phrase.[4] The synopsis, we are told, exists primarily to sell to some producer the project of making the film; it then may be used to inform reviewers and the general public about what to expect. It is full of *"sens,"* or meaning, but gives little account of the structural organization of the film; in fact, the function of the film is to contest and destroy the story line. The continuity with dialogue continues this process: at the same time that elements of the synopsis are given expanded or intensified meaning, the structures of the film cause the meaning to be dispersed, degraded, and lost. The problem presented by the continuity is that in describing these procedures the author must call attention to them, by his use of terms such as "rupture," and show them at work when repetitions, visual analogies, subjective viewpoints, and other procedures are mentioned in the text. What is merely "given" in the film is described in the text; the revolutionary or "scandalous" nature of the film's subversive structures is thus identified and recuperated into a logical coherence by the act of conscious recognition. It is only in the final portion of the book, the montage record, writes Robbe-Grillet, that the original meaning of the synopsis is "entirely dissolved" in structures that refuse all definition. (Robbe-Grillet's view of the absence of structural clues in the montage record is difficult to reconcile with the bold-faced headings used for the sequences, most of which depend on and at times

4. Quoted, with interesting comments on what he terms "puzzling movies," including *Last Year at Marienbad*, by Norman H. Holland, *The Dynamics of Literary Response* (New York: Oxford University Press, 1968), pp. 163–166. McLuhan's remarks appeared in *The New York Times*, March 19, 1967, Section 2, p. 1.

make more explicit the structural information given in the continuity.)

Conscious of the vogue of structuralism as a general semantic doctrine in our time, Robbe-Grillet takes pains to distinguish his own use of the term structure from that of Claude Lévi-Strauss. For Lévi-Strauss, structure is meaning, the ultimate meaning, "the word of God." But, Robbe-Grillet states:

For us, on the contrary, any structure would consist rather of nonmeaning, the meaning (anecdotal or deep, it does not matter) being capable only of destroying, by digesting it, its own structural organization. For us, structure—effraction in the continuity of meaning, infraction, refraction, diffraction, rupture, serial or combinatory organization in defiance of any global significance that would seek to bring about its reintegration—can only become for a brief instant the locus of a precarious, slipping meaning, always about to collapse. [P. 13]

The great danger, adds Robbe-Grillet, is that a spectator or reader, finding in a film like *Glissements* such popular thematic elements as gory scenes of torture, rape, vampires, and eroticized mayhem, will conclude that the culture that furnishes these themes is expressing itself in the work. Not so, writes Robbe-Grillet, using another reference to current semantics to clarify his point: de Saussure's classic distinction between *langue*, or general language reservoir, and *parole*, or individual act of linguistic utterance, leads to the opposite conclusion. The popular thematics from which the elements of the work may be taken, Robbe-Grillet states, "do not represent the *parole* of the film, but only its *langue*." He continues:

The formalized utterances or statements [*parole*] of a society have been cut up into pieces to reduce them to the state of language components [*langue*]. And it is this second language which will serve as a reservoir of materials for the production of a new act of speech [*parole*], an unreconciled structure, my own "word." [P. 14]

The Introduction to *Glissements* thus appears as a theoretical exposé of considerable importance. On careful analysis, however, many of its declarations and claims appear to be less than exact, and the fundamental division between anecdotal (and thus derisory) meaning and structuration or ("subversive") reconstitution is constantly blurred: not only does the synopsis itself contain highly intellectualized references to formal structures, "the mobile architecture which links through successive slippages the various objects used as evidence of the crime" (p. 19), but the continuity in turn abounds in explanatory comments related to the story line and to the "psychology" of the characters.

With some excisions, the account of the plot given in Robbe-Grillet's own synopsis runs as follows:

In a prison for adolescent girls operated by nuns, a very young girl is being held accused of a murder which she denies: Nora, her friend and roommate, was found dead, tied to her bed, with a dressmaker's scissors plunged into her left breast, piercing her heart.

The accused girl, apprehended in the apartment of the crime by a police inspector who discovers the beautiful but bloody body, has remained mute to his many questions, some of which seem, moreover, rather exaggerated. She has only murmured a few distant words, speaking of a deserted beach [. . .] and of the sea rolling in at her feet.

She is seen again in her prison cell, a white cubic room which recalls by its lighting the two girls' apartment (all white also and almost devoid of furniture [. . .]). The prisoner, now more smiling and loquacious, but still as unconcerned as before with causal logic as with morality or simple modesty, gives an investigative magistrate the version of events to which she holds fast: the murderer is a man she does not know, a madman no doubt, who suddenly broke in upon them.

Her lack of proofs, her reticence on essential points, her silences and contradictions, and her noticeable taste for provocation and mockery seem to militate against her innocence, as does her game of inventing her own more or less absurd hypotheses, under the pretext of furthering the discovery of a truth which seems to concern her very little.

What does appear from scene to scene is that, guilty or innocent, the girl is fascinated by the idea of shed blood—the blood of the crime, the blood of the menstrual cycle, the blood of defloration—perhaps, even, by the idea of drinking the blood of others, or making them drink her own blood.

The first to succumb to these fantasies is the magistrate: abandoning first his arguments and then his anger, he finally allows himself, as if in a dream, to lick a little wound that the prisoner has inflicted (accidentally?) on her foot. Then comes the turn of a too trusting nun, then of an overexcited pastor, less possessed by his God than by grotesque demons from hell. One after the other, they forget their religious duties, succumb to sickness or delirium, and vanish.

Meanwhile, throughout the varying accounts given by the prisoner of her life with Nora (in the white apartment, on a vast empty beach, in an old country cemetery, etc.), of experiences with subversion and degradation—involving episodes in turn violent and tender, hierarchial, disturbing, childish, or cruel, as well as old memories filled with feminine passions and mortal accidents —the mobile architecture which links through successive slippages the various objects used as evidence of the crime is revealed (although previously these objects seemed devoid of meaning): a summer shoe, a praying stool, a broken bottle, a gravedigger's shovel, a glass of bright red grenadine, three eggs in a bowl.

A young woman lawyer now enters the cell. Her features, as well as her behavior, her speech, and her costume, are curiously reminiscent of those of Nora. More persevering, more methodical, more perspicacious than the others, the woman lawyer quickly becomes the most challenging of the girl's preys. Caught up in the web of past events, excited also by the stories told by the prisoner of actions taking place in the prison itself [. . .], drawn finally into a world of chains, fire, kisses, knives, and bites, the young woman lawyer gradually identifies herself with the seductive victim, in a series of changes, abandonments, and charms that lead her to the fatal accident, in which the last pieces of evidence of the case fall into their proper place. [Pp. 17–19]

This résumé is, in fact, a striking example of Robbe-Grillet's use of implicit fictional form lying beneath an apparently anecdotal account. The *prières d'insérer* of *The Erasers* and of *Jealousy* show this to some degree, as does the publicity release of the unpublished film *L'Eden et après*. The principal structural divisions of the film *Glissements* appear clearly in the summary: a beginning by way of flashback, as the titles appear (with Alice already imprisoned in her cell), and the main cycles of narrative sequences, the crime, the inspector's interrogation (interrupted by various scenes from the sea and beach episodes), the judge's enquiry in the cell, the problematical stories related by Alice and projected on the screen as "real," the complicated events involving the nun and the pastor, and finally the blending of Nora's double, the young lawyer, played by the same actress, into the person of Nora herself, slain accidentally this time in the final re-enactment of the crime. Among the most obvious structural echoes of Robbe-Grillet's other works to be detected in the over-all form of *Glissements* we may list: ironic circularity, as in *The Erasers* (in the case of *Glissements*, a second crime duplicating the first); massive sequences throwing successive doubts on previously narrated events, as in *L'Immortelle;* serialization of objects chosen from Robbe-Grillet's pseudopsychiatric "stock" (shoes, broken bottles, eggs), as in *The Voyeur, Marienbad, L'Eden et après*, and elsewhere; subjective narration transformed into objective visual presentation, with realistic sounds; and, obsessively, the panoply of sado-erotic trappings (chains, torture instruments, mannequins) which, making their first grandiose appearance in *La Maison de rendez-vous*, now constitute a hallmark of Robbe-Grillet's "thematic" reservoir, both in films (*Trans-Europ-Express, L'Eden*) and in novels (*Project for a Revolution in New York*).

Aside from the "immediate" (that is, innocently narrative) values of the continuity, which range from grand-guignolesque terrors to sudden humor and ridiculous parody, the chief interest for the critic or student of Robbe-Grillet is undoubtedly the incorporation into the text of a multitude of clarifying structural and thematic commentaries that serve as a guide to the intentions and designs of the author. The important difference between this *ciné-roman* and that of a non-cinematic Robbe-Grillet novel is that in the latter, principles of scene linking or cross reference are almost always implicit; it is up to the reader to recognize analogies, formal counterpoint, reinforcements, and allusions. Here, on the contrary, the author makes these explicit:

The two visual references to the end of Sequence 29 found inside Sequence 30 [. . .] showing Alice hiding her face in the hollow of the woman lawyer's neck, do not serve as punctuations. Their function, as one understands [sic!], *is to cause to slide toward the cell a certain number of signs belonging to the scenes in the caves, thus imputing this scene entirely to Alice's and the lawyer's accounts. In particular, the vampire bite will appear in Sequence 31 on the lawyer's neck. Likewise, the decapitation and the crucifixion on a wheel slide in both directions to give rise to Sequences 29a and 36a.* [P. 109]

If, indeed, Robbe-Grillet seriously believes (as he suggests in the Introduction) that the naming of structural manipulations robs them of their subversive role in the creation of his new *parole* ("rupture ceases to be [. . .] subversive, as soon as I call it rupture"), why did he make his text so openly descriptive of integrative details, implicit symmetries, and hidden intentions? As fascinating as all this may be to the critic or student, how does it affect the work as a text to be read? One solution to the apparent dilemma would be to conclude that *Glissements* is a work in two major parts, generically separate but aesthetically interdependent: the film and the *ciné-roman*. What the latter permits is to reconstruct the structural message hidden beneath the interplay of sound and picture in the film; it is, in fact, a sort of critical exegesis which says of the film all that it is possible for criticism, as the author himself would have it, can say. Robbe-Grillet, as he states, has cut into pieces the material cultural elements which serve in the creation of his own creative language, and from these composed his film. The text as presented, with all its complications, reiterations, numbering system, cross references, and identifications of analogies and serial linkings, is an elaborate manifesto and statement of the syntax, methods, rules, and generative operations involved in this individual act of creation or *parole*. In a sense the text of *Glissements* is designed to serve as a barrier against, if not to render useless, all other critical interpretations or explanations.

Viewed thus, *Glissements* fits into a general pattern of author-explained works familiar to readers of the *nouveau roman*. But while Jean Ricardou, Claude Ollier, or Claude Simon use separate essays as texts to reveal structural designs, Robbe-Grillet has always preferred to incorporate such revelations into the work itself (as in his latest novel, *Project for a Revolution in New York*), making of them subject matter at a second remove. This aesthetic incorporation of overt structuration allows the critic to continue to operate *vis-à-vis* the printed text; he now analyzes and evaluates both the filmic or novelistic fiction and its avowed constructive principles as forming a multileveled fictional mode in which structures exist as components along with narrative elements such as characters, events, motives, and objects. Even the traditional novel had anticipated such developments (*Tristram Shandy* is a classic example, but many novels have overtly called attention to flashbacks, analogies, parallel montage, and other procedures). Future works may extend the process in surprising new ways. A long theoretical description of types of image-sound relationships in *Glissements* will illustrate the extent to which the printed text constitutes its own analytical commentary:

A musical composition develops as Alice paints her body. Then, during her conversation with the nun, a scene of washing, with running water, shower, etc. is heard off screen. Let us point out, for inattentive amateurs, that the sound materials heard in the cell are either without connection with the action [. . .], or in direct realistic relationship (a scaffold is erected in the prison courtyard during Nos. 23 and 29), or else in metaphorical relationship (the flames of hell in No. 33). In the present instance, since Alice should wash her body and doubtless will do so shortly, what would be involved is a metonymic linking! Of course, either type of liaison *can undergo slippages toward other categories: the port of No. 7 is perhaps a metaphor of escape, or the anticipation of future scenes by the sea; and, similarly, a metaphoric sound can become a metonymy in the light of a following sequence (the sea breaking over Alice's face and the end of No. 21), or the opposite: here, for example, the sounds of faucets running are also only an ironic metaphor of the purification of the soul. It has surely been observed that these same categories and slippages were already found in the work with the appearances of various objects used as signs of punctuation.* [Pp. 126–127]

It becomes obvious, in such passages, that the structural strategies of the work are themselves transformed into fictional material; the *ciné-roman* (as well as the film when reviewed in the light of the printed text) is not only the conversion into a personal style (*parole*) of thematic stereotypes and attitudes (e.g., sado-eroticism), but also an aesthetic construct "about" filmic metaphor, metonymy, image punctuation —"about," in other words, accelerative slippages of structures that form a sort of gigantic over-all sexual metaphor. The constant use of the word "*glissements*," at times accompanied by the adjective "*progressifs*," in Robbe-Grillet's own analyses of sequential montage and inner punctuations, makes a connection with the highly suggestive title (which adds to slippage and acceleration the unmistakable adjunct "of pleasure") that leaves no doubt as to the intended analogies. The idea of slippage, in fact, extends into the story line (before the woman teacher falls from the cliff by the sea, Alice says, "Now love will slip"), into the implied psychology of the characters (the woman lawyer is said to "slip" gradually into the role of Nora), into the objective correlatives of the crime (the bottle that "slips" to the floor, p. 61 and elsewhere), and even into the mock-serious poem recited in prison by Alice, which in turn forms a lyrical *mise en abyme* or inner duplication of the story and themes of the film ("fish slipping through the overly dense sea weeds"). In Robbe-Grillet's earliest novel, *The Erasers*, the key structural word was *décalage*, or displacement; in *Glissements* it is slippage; displacement is still involved, but now its dynamics predominate: process takes precedence over result.

The essentially metaphoric texture of *Glissements* appears not only in the "slipping" relationships and transitions between scenes but at times within a single sequence. The arrival of the police inspector early in the film is thus treated in metaphoric terms that necessitate distortions of nominal reality: the inspector is, by definition, in search of an elusive truth, the identity of the murderer. His actions reflect doubt and the exploration of multiple possibilities; to reinforce this metaphorically, the apartment is suddenly seen to contain a multitude of doors (even some in the ceiling), through which the inspector tries to pass, as if, in Robbe-Grillet's words, "in search of some hidden center" (p. 34). In the scene of the photographer (p. 52), the clicks of a camera cause the scene to "slip" from one décor to another, each typifying a "set" in an album of stereotyped images of "archetypal signs of popular novelistic convention."

Archetypes, in fact, play an important role here, as elsewhere in Robbe-Grillet. In *The Erasers*, the Oedipus of

Sophocles (and Freud) served as a more or less hidden model, never mentioned openly in the text. In the film *The Man Who Lies*, Robbe-Grillet in a number of interviews pointed out the deliberate analogies with the legends of Don Juan and Boris Godunov. These "noble" parallels are present in *Glissements* in the form of open textual references to Lady Macbeth and Jesus, and thinly veiled allusions to martyred saints like Joan of Arc, burned at the stake (Sequence No. 42, Alice's "imaginary" immolation). But more and more, Robbe-Grillet uses the term "archetype" to describe popular, even paraliterary models, which, from *La Maison de rendez-vous* to *Glissements*, form in large measure his thematic and visual repertory. In the most general sense, these archetypes relate to violence and sexuality, and are "structured" into scenes related literally or metaphorically to physical torture (especially cutting, with broken glass or scissors, but often using outright depictions of torture instruments, such as the rack or wheel, as in the "Epinal pictures" of Sequence No. 30), to maiming (the dismembered dummy), and to rape. A variety of correlatives occur also to blood (red paint, red liquid in a bottle) and to sperm (especially the gluey contents of freshly broken eggs). Specific character stereotypes include the overzealous inspector and magistrate, the erotically naive but susceptible nuns, the severe but corruptible pastor and woman lawyer, and the lesbian inmates of this "nunnery-prison." Sometimes an archetype is so designated in the dialogue itself, enlarging the notion of popular model to that of model conscious-of-itself (as many Freudian models are today): Alice, questioned about the blue shoe (the first appearance of a shoe theme in Robbe-Grillet was in *Marienbad*), replies, "It is a foot fetish" (p. 67).

Fundamental to many fictional structures in Robbe-Grillet is the theme or construct of the *sosie* or double, which emerged fully first in *L'Immortelle*, to be followed by a long series of doubles in *The Man Who Lies*, *L'Eden et après*, and *Project for a Revolution in New York*. In these three works, one of the main characters blends with his double (figured visually in the film *L'Eden* when Violette meets and embraces her double). In *Glissements*, the mode of the double again varies, in that a literally identical character (i.e., actress) plays a "different" role, physically and psychologically, only to be gradually metamorphosed into the role of the original character, duplicating her appearance and conduct, and suffering an analogous fate which sets the circular plot spinning in a new cycle ("Now," says the inspector, "everything must begin again"). Plot is not only open-ended, in baroque style, but becomes a *perpetuum mobile*, in an infinite vista of future "slippages."

In earlier works, especially *Marienbad*, Robbe-Grillet employed a sort of subliminal "planting" of future plot developments in fragments of overheard conversations among accessory characters, in enigmatic exchanges which, deprived of their eventual connection with the story, would seem reminiscent of the dialogue of characters in a Harold Pinter play. Abandoning the pretext of an implied source for such preparatory elements (in the situations of secondary personages), Robbe-Grillet in *Glissements* allows his inspector, for example, to ask of Alice on his first appearance a series of "ridiculous" questions, all of which to some extent prepare for future developments ("Where did you spend your last vacation?" "Do you like eggs?" "How many pairs of shoes do you own?" "When did you make your first communion?" pp. 36–37). The "omniscient-author" commentary which Robbe-Grillet makes on these questions brings out once more the gap between the film and its printed text, which reads: "In fact, many of his questions are more or less directly related to episodes shown in the rest of the film; but, at this juncture, the spectator cannot guess this and the policeman appears insane" (p. 37).

Thus a vestige of "justification" for the seemingly random questions is offered by the hypothesis of madness on the part of the inspector. But when it is the turn of the image montage itself to provide and coordinate elements related to future developments or to thematic ensembles, the idea of psychological justification disappears entirely, and only the visual sequences "exist," in a phenomenological field. At best, the term "punctuation" used in the commentary imputes the structuration to the author of the film; it is not thrust into the *diégèse*, or fictional universe, in which the presumed plot occurs (cf. the punctuational sequence No. 14a, where the vacation seascape, the shoe, the bottle, and the praying stool appear without apparent connection). Whereas in an early work like *Marienbad* all such real or imaginary image clusters could, if necessary, be explained as associative memories or imaginings in a given character's mind (A or X), in *Glissements* no attempt is made to justify many of them as subjective sequences. (A possible trace of the previous technique of justification of all scenes as subjective may be found in the lawyer's remark to Alice, "But nothing exists except in your little head," p. 133.) The scenes follow one another according to principles ranging from traditional cinematic practices ("a brief scene [. . .] linked to the preceding one by a final movement of Alice's head," p. 93) to the most complicated type of associative, dechronological constructs: *"The description of the martyrdom of Saint Agatha is heard off screen against a shot (27a bis) constituting an anticipated return to the beginning of 27a; it is, in fact, an interference of 27a with 27"* (p. 94).

Threading throughout the innumerable "punctuation" image clusters, flashbacks and "flashforwards," contrapuntal sequences, free interchanges between the "real" (often placed between quotation marks in the textual commentaries) and the imagined, there may be discerned a basic linear chronology corresponding to the story line of the synopsis. Robbe-Grillet takes great pains to explain the details of this "diegetic" time scheme. It is as if, in order to exercise their full aesthetic effect, the nonchronological, "free" structures need to work against conventional temporal linearity, without which, having nothing to contest, the author's *parole* would function in a sort of uncoordinated void. As early as the initial account of the *générique* or title sequence, references occur to shots relating to "the story that begins"; the parallel actions of the police car with its wailing siren tearing through the streets and the ambiguous murder scene in Alice's apartment are analyzed in such a way as to emphasize the mystery of the inspector's arrival immediately upon the death of Nora. In Sequence No. 7, the reappearance of an identical shot of Alice in prison—identical to the one which opened the film—marks the point of departure, in "real" time, of all events, creating automatically for any scenes prior to the murder of Nora (such as the police inspector's search of the flat, as well as later scenes with Alice and Nora) a framing pattern of *retours en arrière* or flashbacks. These often occur with sound-image counterpoint. In Sequence No. 11, Alice relates to the magistrate earlier scenes with Nora, which occur visually against the sound track of her account. This conventional structure is often used to pass "realistically" into the flashback scene, whose natural sounds take over: in the sequence of the teacher's fall from the seaside cliff, "Alice's voice continues as [. . .] we see on the screen the scene described, which shortly continues without commentary," and with, finally, the dialogue of the actual episode (pp. 55–58).

Frequent clues to a linear chronological armature of events are given in such authorial comments as "This is in fact the beginning of the scene whose end we saw in No. 4c" (p. 48), "Alice [. . .] is relating the preceding events to Sister Maria" (p. 85). A striking example of intercalated scenes, whose hypothetical or imaginary nature is emphasized by their forced insertion into what would otherwise constitute an unbroken temporal sequence, is found in the development of the "Epinal pictures" section of the film and the episode of the lawyer's lesbian advances to Claudia that follows. Both of these sequences are undermined, at the diegetic level, by surrounding references to a solid chronology in which no time for either exists. The lengthy scene in which the lawyer questions Alice, itself punctuated with brief flashes of thematic reinforcement (a girl about to be decapitated, a gravedigger at work), leads to an ostensible end when Alice complains, "At our slightest fault, we are led down secret stairs to underground dungeons [. . .] as if we were still in the Middle Ages," and buries her head in the lawyer's neck, sobbing (pp. 98–102). There ensue some eight "*tableaux vivants*" characterized by Robbe-Grillet as drawn frankly from the kind of colored illustrations in "Tortures of the Inquisition" and pictures on similar themes in the well-known Epinal series. From time to time, a brief shot of Alice hiding her face in the lawyer's neck underlines the subjective nature of the torture scenes and implies that they are being "told" by Alice, though her fixed posture next to the lawyer's shoulder seems to offer little opportunity for such a recital, which is furthermore accompanied by no sounds other than dripping water, sobbings, and a final outcry. The linear story line is then resumed in a return to Alice and the lawyer (her neck is now marked by the vampire bite), who leaves the cell on the pastor's arrival, to be followed by the camera in the long sequence that culminates in her seductive caressing of Claudia. However, as the sound track swells with the sound of the sea and of a bottle breaking, we are suddenly once more in the cell with Alice and the pastor, at the moment of the lawyer's exit; the scene just witnessed has not, in "real" time, occurred at all. To leave no doubt, Robbe-Grillet writes: "The scene shifts at this noise, and we see, as if opposite the lawyer's glance, the face of Alice in her cell. She is with the pastor: the scene follows No. 31 immediately, without the hole in time that would be required by the duration of No. 32 [the lawyer and Claudia]" (p. 116).

Elsewhere, a return to an already heard portion of dialogue causes the chronology to bend back upon itself, usually over a very short span (as in No. 39a, with its quick intercalated flash shot of a man listening outside the door, overhearing the final words that we have just seen and heard the lawyer pronounce inside the room, p. 134). In an oversimplification, we may say that a re-edited, reductive montage of the linear anecdotal line of *Glissements* could almost produce a conventional film, with a quite traditional "final switch" in plot: as the inspector arrives to announce that the crime has been solved, that the real murderer has been apprehended, and that Alice is innocent, he finds the dead body of the lawyer, in the role of Nora, and apparently slain as before. (In *The Erasers*, twenty years earlier, Robbe-Grillet had ended with a similar irony: the inspector Laurent telephones Wallas, moments after the latter has—accidentally, or mistakenly—shot Dupont, to say that the case is solved, and that Dupont is alive.)

If the chronology of *Glissements*, despite its ruptures, contradictions, free associative movements back and forth in time, and other dechronological manipulations is nevertheless structured upon a basically linear progression, the levels of diegetic reality and mental images in the characters' minds are similarly reinforced by numerous implications of psychological justification for "unreal" scenes and sequences. In *Last Year at Marienbad*, Robbe-Grillet invited the spectator-reader, in his preface, to view all the visual materials as either observationally realistic (the nominal décor) or as completely subjective: visions in the minds of the two protagonists, A and X. The cinema was, he stated, the ideal vehicle for conveying directly, through images, mental content. Obviously, the use throughout *Glissements* of hundreds of "punctuations," involving image clusters for which the creator of the film alone is responsible, and which cannot be assigned to the psychology of the characters present or absent from the sequences, marks a substantial change in Robbe-Grillet's conception of film as pure mental content. What is worth pointing out, in this connection, is that despite such a radical evolution in re-admitting into the fictional work a type of authorial intervention which had been so often denounced as the fallacy of the omniscient author, Robbe-Grillet in many instances constructs his sequences as if he were adhering to his earlier doctrine, and refers to them in commentaries that leave no doubt that they are to be viewed as subjective projections in the *Marienbad* style.

As previously pointed out, a large number of flashbacks are presented against an initial verbal account which, whether we view the ensuing scenes as belonging to the "real" past or to the (lying?) imagination of, say, Alice, at least marks the sequence as subjectively recalled. A typical comment on such a development is, "The dialogue [. . .] continues off screen against a scene, past or imaginary, representing Alice playing with Nora" (p. 47). What is startling about such a scene is that it can become "contaminated," so to speak, by the imagination of a listener. (In *Marienbad*, such conflicts between two imaginations reached a high point in the bedroom scene of A disobeying, in her own imaginary memories, the commands of X as he "corrects" her vision.) As Alice relates the intrusion of an assassin wearing black gloves, the screen shows the examining magistrate, who is listening to Alice's account, suddenly present at Nora's bedside, wearing the black gloves referred to. A simplistic psychological reading of the scene would suggest that the magistrate's latent sado-erotic obsessions (which he shares with the lawyer, the pastor, the nuns, and everyone else in the film) cause him to "intrude" and to see himself in a role he secretly longs to play; he has, as Robbe-Grillet puts it, "succumbed" to his sexual fantasies.

In *The Man Who Lies*, Robbe-Grillet used a dialectic interplay of narration and contrapuntal, often contradictory, visual presentation of the events narrated; Boris' various lies ran a gamut of possibilities from ostensible sincerity to farcical exaggeration. But each such subjective sequence ends with a return to Boris in the nominal present, from which the action continues. In *Glissements*, the past scenes evoked by Alice's narration are sometimes rejoined to the nominal present in a nonlinear fashion which imposes a new type of distortion on the time line of the film. For example, Alice begins a long verbal account to the magistrate of Nora's activities as a prostitute (p. 67): the images, and then the sound, represent the scene and allow it to continue as a presumedly real flashback. Following an apparently gratuitous punctuation shot of an iron bed awash on the seashore, a false continuation of the flashback occurs, in which Alice plays the prostitute's role, instead of Nora. A more complicated punctuation introduces the scene of the "bloody eggs" and the tortured store dummy, until finally "we find ourselves again in Alice's prison cell, where the girl is relating the preceding events to Sister Maria" (p. 85).

Since it is impossible to determine at what point Alice's first narration to the magistrate has ended, or blended into her account to Sister Maria, the problematical time zone of the flashbacks, although basically subjective and obeying a presumptive order attributable to associative tensions or interest, is carried far beyond the "recuperable" time zone of motivated imagination which Alain Resnais, for one, had discerned in *Marienbad*.

We may see in the metaphorical and thematic objects of *Glissements* the evolutionary outcome of Robbe-Grillet's object serialism, which manifested itself first in significant fashion in *The Voyeur*, with its figure-of-eight images associated with sexual violence (the rolled-up cord binding Jacqueline's wrists) and voyeurism or watching eyes (the design on the doors of the island houses). The shoe fetish appeared in realistic context in *Marienbad*, where it was subsequently "derealized" in the heroine's fantasies, becoming multiplied in her obsessive vision. The still unpublished film *L'Eden et après* contains thematic object groups similar to those of *Glissements* (blood, sperm, sharp cutting objects, images of torture). The correlation between the key objects of *Glissements*, which provide the materials for the punctuation scenes and which figure as well at the level of the plot (realistically or metaphorically), and the subject matter of the film is fundamentally a diegetic one: that is, each object can be related to the story, if only presumptively. We are not dealing with the kind of "nondiegetic" filmic metaphor practiced, for example, by Eisenstein where an emotion such as joy is metaphorically reinforced by a wholly extraneous shot of bursting spring buds and flowing streams. The blue shoe, the broken bottle, the iron bed, the store dummy, the red paint, the praying stool, all fit into the story line. Even the broken eggs are part of Alice's games with Nora. The one persistent nondiegetic theme is that of the gravedigger (and the associated funeral pyre and scaffold), who with his shovel and pick turns up out of the earth a shoe, a bottle; however, even this character may be rationalized as realistically preparing Nora's grave, or that of Alice after her eventual execution.

But if the objects themselves belong to the fictional field of the film, what of their arrangements and recombinations in the various inserts that serve Robbe-Grillet's never defined purposes of "punctuation"? Are we to see the film as taking place at two separate levels, the diegetic and the nondiegetic? Should the punctuation scenes be viewed, at the level of the images and sounds of the film witnessed on the screen, as analogous to the commentaries and analytical observations added to the printed text, a kind of aesthetic superstructure serving a documentary or critical end? Such an explanation would hardly be in accord with the dynamics of a film viewer: to him, everything seen or heard is inevitably included in the diegesis or world of the film. The cinematic field thus expands to engulf its own thematic abstracts, its metaphors, its nonanecdotal structures, its punctuations. Instead of seeking to reduce all its images and sounds to a "justified" subjectivity, a work like *Glissements* converts even its justified scenes, such as those analyzed above, into elements of more or less "pure" structure. The process is not fundamentally different from that followed in Robbe-Grillet's most evolved novel, *Project for a Revolution in New York*. *Glissements* becomes a film not "about" an ambiguous death, an inquiry, a sensuous heroine who corrupts her magistrate and lawyer, and an ironic outcome based on a rather conventional surprise, but "about" the metaphoric structuration of sexuality and violence. Process becomes plot, in a new fictional mode whose future in film and novel remains to be determined. The art of Robbe-Grillet continues to evolve, pushing constantly against the previous limits of fictional structure.

Selected Bibliography

For the convenience of readers who wish to read Robbe-Grillet's works in English, the following translations are available. The French titles and publication dates are given in brackets; all were published by Editions de Minuit, Paris.

The Erasers [*Les Gommes*, 1953], translated by Richard Howard. New York: Grove Press, 1964.

The Voyeur [*Le Voyeur*, 1955], translated by Richard Howard. New York: Grove Press, 1958.

Jealousy [*La Jalousie*, 1957], translated by Richard Howard. New York: Grove Press, 1959.

In the Labyrinth [*Dans le labyrinthe*, 1959], translated by Richard Howard. New York: Grove Press, 1960.

Last Year at Marienbad [*L'Année dernière à Marienbad*, 1961], translated by Richard Howard. New York: Grove Press, 1962.

Snapshots [*Instantanés*, 1962], translated by Bruce Morrissette. New York: Grove Press, 1968.

L'Immortelle, 1963. Remains untranslated.

For a New Novel [*Pour un nouveau roman*, 1963], translated by Richard Howard. New York: Grove Press, 1965. Contains the following essays referred to in Chapter 1: "A Future for the Novel," pp. 15–24; "Nature, Humanism, Tragedy," pp. 49–75; "Joë Bosquet the Dreamer," pp. 95–109; "Samuel Beckett, or Presence on the Stage," pp. 111–125; and "New Novel, New Man," pp. 133–142.

La Maison de rendez-vous [*La Maison de rendez-vous*, 1965], translated by Richard Howard. New York: Grove Press, 1966.

Project for a Revolution in New York [*Projet pour une révolution à New York*, 1970], translated by Richard Howard. New York: Grove Press, 1972.

Glissements progressifs du plaisir, 1974. Remains untranslated.

The following books and articles, listed in chronological order, will be found especially useful in understanding the evolution of Robbe-Grillet criticism. Most of these, with many others, are described and analyzed in *Alain Robbe-Grillet: An Annotated Bibliography of Critical Studies*, by Dale Watson FRAIZER (Metuchin, N.J.: Scarecrow Press, 1973).

Bernard DORT. "Le Temps des choses," *Cahiers du Sud*, Jan. 1954 (No. 321).

Roland BARTHES. "Littérature objective," *Critique*, July–Aug. 1954.

Roland BARTHES. "Littérature littérale," *Critique*, Sept.–Oct. 1955.

Robert POULET. "Alain Robbe-Grillet et le roman futur," *Rivarol*, Nov. 8, 1956.

Robert CHAMPIGNY. "In Search of the Pure Récit," *American Society Legion of Honor Magazine*, Winter 1956.

Bernard DORT. "Sur les romans de Robbe-Grillet," *Les Temps Modernes*, June 1957.

José-María CASTELLET. "De la objetividad al objeto," *Papeles de Son Armadans*, June 1957.

Gaëtan PICON. "Du roman expérimental," *Mercure de France*, July 1957.

"Le Roman d'aujourd'hui," in *Arguments*, Feb. 1958. Articles by Roland BARTHES, Bernard PINGAUD, Jean DUVIGNAUD.

"Le Nouveau Roman," special number of *Esprit*, July–Aug. 1958. Articles by Olivier DE MAGNY, Bernard PINGAUD, Bernard DORT, Jacques HOWLETT, Luc ESTANG, and others.

"Cinéma et roman," special issue of *Revue des Lettres Modernes*, Summer 1958. Articles by G.-A. ASTRE, Jean DUVIGNAUD, Michel MOURLET, Collette AUDRY, J.-L. BORY, P. DURAND, and others.

Claude MAURIAC. *L'Allitérature contemporaine*. Paris: Albin Michel, 1958.

Renato BARILLI. "La narrativa di Alain Robbe-Grillet," *Il Verri*, Jan. 1959.

"Midnight Novelists," special number of *Yale French Studies*, Summer 1959. Articles by René GIRARD, Bernard PINGAUD, Bernard DORT, W. M. FROHOCK, Germaine BREE, Jacques GUICHARNAUD, and others.

Otto HAHN. "Plan du labyrinthe de Robbe-Grillet," *Les Temps Modernes*, July 1960.

Phillipe SOLLERS. "Sept propositions sur Alain Robbe-Grillet," *Tel Quel*, Summer 1960.

Jean RICARDOU. "Aspects de la description créatice," *Médiations*, Grillet," *Nouvelle Revue Française*, Nov. 1960.

Edouard Lop and André Sauvage. "Essai sur le Nouveau Roman," *La Nouvelle Critique*, March, April, and June, 1961 (Nos. 124, 125, and 126).

Bruce Morrissette. "Roman et cinéma: le cas de Robbe-Grillet," *Symposium*, Summer 1961.

Jean Ricardou. "Aspects de la description créatrice," *Médiations*, Autumn 1961.

Lucien Goldmann. "Les Deux Avant-gardes," *Médiations*, Winter 1961–62.

Hazel Barnes. "The Ins and Outs of Robbe-Grillet," *Chicago Review*, Winter 1961–62.

Gérard Genette. "Sur Robbe-Grillet," *Tel Quel*, Winter 1962.

J. G. Weightman. "Alain Robbe-Grillet," *Encounter*, March 1962. (Reprinted in *The Novelist as Philosopher*. New York: Oxford University Press, 1962.)

Bruce Morrissette. "De Stendhal à Robbe-Grillet: modalités du *point de vue*," *Cahiers de l'Association Internationale des Études Françaises*, June 1962.

Robert Abirached. "Robbe-Grillet No. 2," *Nouvelle Revue Française*, Oct. 1963.

Francisco Yndurain. "Sobre *le nouveau roman*," *Filología Moderna*, Jan. 1964.

"Un Nouveau Roman?," special issue of *Revue des Lettres Modernes*, Minard, 1964. Edited by J. H. Matthews. Articles on Robbe-Grillet by Renato Barilli, Christine Brooke-Rose, Ben F. Stoltzfus.

Ben F. Stoltzfus. *Alain Robbe-Grillet and the New French Novel*. Carbondale: Southern Illinois University Press, 1964.

Jean-Bertrand Barrere. *La Cure d'amaigrissement du roman*. Paris: Albin Michel, 1964.

Olga Bernal. *Alain Robbe-Grillet: le roman de l'absence*. Paris: Gallimard, 1964.

Bruce Morrissette. *Alain Robbe-Grillet*. New York: Columbia University Press, 1965.

Jean Miesch. *Robbe-Grillet*. Paris: Editions Universitaires, 1965.

Jean Alter. *La Vision du monde d'Alain Robbe-Grillet*. Geneva: Droz, 1966.

Jean Ricardou. *Problèmes du Nouveau Roman*. Paris: Seuil, 1967.

Bruce Morrissette. "The Evolution of Narrative Viewpoint in Robbe-Grillet," *Novel*, Autumn 1967.

Gerda Zeltner. *La Grande Aventure du roman française au XXe siècle*. Paris: Gonthier, 1967. First published in German in 1960.

Bruce MORRISSETTE. "Games and Game Structures in Robbe-Grillet," *Yale French Studies*, No. 41. ("Game, Play, Literature"), 1968.

Pierre ASTIER. *La Crise du roman français et le nouveau réalisme.* Paris: Debresse, 1968.

John STURROCK. *The French New Novel.* New York: Oxford University Press, 1969.

Jean RICARDOU. *Pour une théorie du Nouveau Roman.* Noris: Seuil, 1971.

Stephen HEATH. *The Nouveau Roman.* London: Elek, 1972.

Leon ROUDIEZ. *French Fiction Today.* New Brunswick, N.J.: Rutgers University Press, 1972.

Les Critiques de notre temps et le Nouveau Roman. Paris: Garnier, 1972. Anthology of critical articles by a variety of writers.

Nouveau Roman: hier, aujourd'hui, Vols. 1 and 2. Paris: Editions 10/18 [Union Générale d'Editions], 1972. Articles by the principal novelists and critics of the *nouveau roman*, as well as their debates at the Cerisy Colloquium of 1971.

George SZANTO. *Narrative Consciousness: Structures and Perception in the Fiction of Kafka, Beckett, and Robbe-Grillet.* Austin: University of Texas Press, 1972.

Jean RICARDOU. *Le Nouveau Roman.* Paris: Seuil, 1973.

Index

The index includes proper names, principal references to works by Robbe-Grillet, and significant themes or literary techniques discussed. The Bibliography is not included, and should be consulted separately.

315

The Novels of Robbe-Grillet

Designed by R. E. Rosenbaum.
Composed by York Composition Co., Inc.,
in 11 point linotype Janson, 2 points leaded,
with display lines in monotype Deepdene.
Printed letterpress from type by York Composition Co.
on Warren's No. 66 Text, 50 lb. basis
with the Cornell University Press watermark.
Bound by Colonial Press, Inc.